Dance Steps with Alfred Adler

Dance Steps
with
Alfred Adler

An Interpretive Soul Psychology

Randolph Severson

Foreword by Robert Sardello

 GOLDENSTONE PRESS | *Benson, North Carolina*

Published by Goldenstone Press
P.O. Box 7
Benson, North Carolina 27504
www.goldenstonepress.com

ISBN: 978-0-692-38437-4

Cover and book design: Eva Leong Casey / Lee Nichol

Chapter Two was first published as the article "Adler, Agon, and Aggression,"
by Randolph Severson, in *Individual Psychology*, Volume 46, Issue 3, pp. 324-357.
Copyright © 1990 by the University of Texas Press. All rights reserved.

Printed in USA

GOLDENSTONE PRESS

GOLDENSTONE PRESS seeks to make original spiritual thought available as a force
of individual, cultural, and world revitalization. The press is an integral dimension of the work of the School of Spiritual Psychology. The mission of the School
includes restoring the book as a way of inner transformation and awakening to
spirit. We recognize that secondary thought and the reduction of books to sources
of information and entertainment as the dominant meaning of reading places in
jeopardy the unique character of writing as a vessel of the human spirit. We feel
that the continuing emphasis of such a narrowing of what books are intended to be
needs to be balanced by writing, editing, and publishing that emphasizes the act of
reading as entering into a magical, even miraculous spiritual realm that stimulates
the imagination and makes possible discerning reality from illusion in the world.
The editorial board of Goldenstone Press is committed to fostering authors with
the capacity of creative spiritual imagination who write in forms that bring readers into deep engagement with an inner transformative process rather than being
spectators to someone's speculations. A complete catalogue of all our books may
be found at *www.goldenstonepress.com*. The web page for the School of Spiritual
Psychology is *www.spiritualschool.org*.

10 9 8 7 6 5 4 3 2 1

TABLE OF CONTENTS

For my Father and Mother

Adler saw, and saw through, man as a creature of incredible insignificance and incomparable grandeur.

— Manes Sperber

By what sign do we ordinarily recognize the man of action, who leaves his mark on the events into which fate throws him? Isn't it because he embraces a more or less long succession in an instantaneous vision? The greater the share of the past that he includes in the present, the heavier the mass he pushes into the future so as to put pressure on the events in preparation: his action, like an arrow, moves forward with a strength proportional to that with which its representation was bent backward.

— Henri Bergson

As Acknowledgments

We should consider every day lost on which we have not danced at least once.

— Friedrich Nietzsche

Many people assisted in bringing this book to completion. First, I want to remember Dr. Heinz Ansbacher, foremost of Adlerian scholars, who many years ago read an early draft of several chapters and was warm in his encouragement, generous in his praise. To Robert Sardello, Teacher, I owe an incalculable debt. For their consummate skills in the art and craft of bookmaking I extend my thanks to Lee Nichol and Jocelyn Chafouleas, and to Gregory Frisby, a brilliant young psychology student, for his diligence and accuracy in helping prepare the book for publication. To Eva Casey, Lee Nichol, and Robert Sardello for the beauty of the cover. For my friends, family and wife, Sally, who are at the bottom of this list only because they have served as the foundation for everything I have done, words are not enough…

FOREWORD

N	o greater questions haunt the soul than questions of power—
what is it, whence does it arise, how to use it, what to do when it
is abused, how to get it, how to defend ourselves from unjust power,
is it inevitable that power in our time leans only toward violence and
destruction, even world destruction? Does power always corrupt?
Such questions cannot be adequately answered singular, purely log-
ically, conceptually, not even philosophically. Alfred Adler is one of
a very few with real, practical, cultural ways of working toward a full
understanding of power, and does so within the context of what can
rightly be called a psychology of life itself.

Now, at this time on the edge where there seems to be only a
singular meaning of power—power as dominance—we need someone, a genius, to guide us carefully through the many and often too
clever ways we can fool ourselves in relation to power. One of these
deceptive ways is by shirking from it, in effect trying to hide from it,
for power seems to threaten our notions of freedom. Another way is
that of wanting power almost more than life itself.

In this book we have not one, but two geniuses as impeccable
guides through this sticky web. Alfred Adler, the third and perhaps
the most significant of the originators of depth psychology—who
the other two, Freud and Jung, more or less dismissed—is the first
of these guides. The other guide is Randolph Severson, who in this
writing deeply identifies with the very soul of Adler, and thus sees
Adler more comprehensively than Adler himself was able to do.

The method of this writing astounds, and continues to astound
from beginning to end. There is no known name for this method, not

in this time, but it works through a certain kind of love, the capacity to love someone one has never met, a giving oneself over to another so thoroughly and completely and purely that the soul-being one identifies with reveals its location, action, significance, possibilities, and accomplishments, as a revelation of culture. A person is fully understood when seen as a luminous soul presence within the larger world as soul-radiant. Readers will leave this book knowing, intimately, Alfred Adler, and also feel—perhaps for the first time—the radiance of Western culture. Thus, while the depths of a life stand before us, so do the depths of our very existence.

I think this method also has to do with the love of power, which, if we think about it, is almost a complete impossibility. We know, of course, of the love of power as the bottomless desire for power, the desire to wield power. That way to power differs from what I am thinking. Here, in this writing, we find we are taken into the imagination of someone able to give oneself completely to the imagination of power, to allow it to inform, reveal, and speak its own nature, in its fullness, without yielding to the impulses to use the power now felt for one's own aggrandizement. Alfred Adler had this capacity, and in identifying so completely with Adler, this capacity is now held by Randolph Severson.

Power corrupts—that has become the cliché, with its element of truth—and the terrible difficulty is how to approach power and yet remain willing for it to be what it is, avoiding infection or addiction. This is a challenge even in the thought realm, much more so in the world at large. The wonder of this writing is that in finding the way through this dilemma, the writing helps us all through that most basic of all tendencies: the misuse of the will. The accomplishment of this writing can be seen as being gifted by one who has found the holy grail of power that can do no harm.

Alfred Adler brought to the world something incredibly precious that the other two soul psychologies were not able to do—the revelation of how soul acts in the world. The other soul psychologies, even now, engage in seeing the individual through the perspective of soul, of depth, of archetypal patterns, or of deep memories, which

iv

are forms lying behind and governing the individual personality. These psychologies hold that coming to terms with these forms, developing the imaginal capacities to do so, opens the individual to realms larger than the individual, relieving the ego from being the false carrier of powers not our own. This view characterizes Jung. For Freud, it is a matter of setting up the ego as the controller of all one surveys, once the controlling influence of memories as autonomous forces are revealed. For both Freud and Jung, coming to terms with power amounts to containment.

This book explores life without containment, for parceling soul through fostering inwardness—"be present imaginally, but never act out," says the dictum—goes completely counter to the very best of history and culture. Perhaps the problems of life, as understood by psychology, cannot be all put at the doorstep of the ego. Rather, ego becomes problematic only when a sense of belonging to world is lost. It is this loss of heroic ideals that makes ego pathological—the loss of belonging to Earth, to action, to engagement, to virtue, to passionate encounter and most of all, to belonging completely with and for others in love, to be will-filled for the community, for the good. What then is ego? It is what is left when all of the world and others are left out of consideration. Psychology arrived when the world began to be abandoned. It, alas, has not worked to recover the world, but to navigate something like a soulless terrain. A psychology of life proceeds differently.

Randolph Severson delves into each of these intricate themes as tributaries embedded within the psychology of Alfred Adler. And like any flowing river with its tributaries, the way meanders, richly and profoundly. He takes us through the soul of history, myth, stores, urban life, manners, style, war, and courage in search of the soul of life.

The main river of Adler's work, the root metaphor, is most surprising, for it is the metaphor of the City. Soul as City, City as Soul. This is an incredible insight by Severson. Saying it here, in this summary way, risks much, risks that such a notion will not make any sense, not for anyone steeped at all in psychology, which, after all, concerns the individual. Such a grounding sense of the soul, though, is phenomenologically given, rather than propounded as theory. We are not encased beings, isolated entities, nor is soul. We are forever bound up with and are essential aspects of each other. Only one who is not born of the seed of a father and the womb of a mother escapes this fate—and gift. We are given as "held-together," regardless of the perceived separation. City celebrates, in all aspects, this inter-bond-edness of being human. A psychology founded here begins with the given—and stays with it. What an exceptional revelation! Not information, but revelation!

Such a founding revelation does not get very far as long as psychology conceives itself as belonging to the logic of science as a way of knowing. Science begins and lives and breathes by going where ignorance rules. And, in the case of psychology, in order to be counted among the knowledgeable, the immediately given does not count, for the implications are too great. If what we need to know already reveals itself, then it must either be wrong or superficial. Adler was relegated to the background by the accusation of superficiality. However, that is because his contemporaries did not know—and, in truth, even now few know—how to plumb the depths of "the superficial."

Randolph Severson has found the keys to the unending depths of what presents itself as already given, and in total. Not one key but many keys. The main key lies in the style of the writing itself, which bears no pretence of "objectivity," which in the case of psychology trying to join the science party is only pseudo-objectivity anyway. The writing itself can only be characterized as a rhythmic festival of speech heard by the heart, loudly rumbling through every nook and cranny of the body and out the pores. Mind-boggling, we could say, for the mind cannot straighten it all out without destroying what always has and always will be essential to life—rhythm, movement. "Rhetoric" is perhaps the term for what I said above about method-without-a-name. To say this word too soon would confuse, I feel, for the conception of rhetoric remains generally quite narrow in our time. I don't know the rhetorical tradition well, but Randolph Severson steeped himself in it for years. And it is really the only true way of comprehending Adler, for he developed a rhetorical psychology. Which is truer than true, and not to be compared to science and logic; if a comparison is needed, look to poetry.

How else could the passion that is life—the ideals, the good, the delicious, the seamy, the bravado, the chivalry, the style, the *duende*, the courage, the courageous heart-defining life fully engaged, worldly, looking always for the good of the whole—find expression? Psychology as the celebration of being earthly beings. Such an ingenious notion. Therapy then becomes more like learning to orate one's life, daily—the upsurges along with the blues, both, at once, bearing the extremes of bursting joy and being so lost as to give up, grieving and gratitude with equality. This is the psychology of Alfred Adler, yes, a dance, for sure, with Randolph Severson *duende* guitarist, bringing out the very best of the complexity of the haunting, passionate writing and practice of Adler.

Why submit to the gods when they are instead inviting us to play with them? Our playground is their playground, and if we refuse to play, the playground will soon become someone's corporate headquarters of a devious kind of power—the Corporation of World Domination.

Robert Sardello, Ph.D.
March, 2015

PROLOGUE

The soul is the task of man.

— Nicolas Gomez Davila

This is a psychology book, pure and simple. Pure in the way of a First Principle, an essence, a distillate, a lyric. Psyche-Logos: Psyche, Soul, Spirit, Mind, Indwelling Breath. Logos: Word, Speech. It is pure in that it intends to speak exclusively from, to, about, and for the soul. It is simple because its only goal consists of this. Jung may have believed that modern man is in search of soul. Modern psychology is not. The reverse is true. Modern psychology is in abject, headlong flight from the soul, its beseeching, inescapable, vigorous demands. An unsympathetic view might scorn this flight as cowardice.

The method deployed here derives from the goal. It represents an attempt to "be psychological." In another place I have written:

> To be "psychological" means to be intensely intellectual, thoroughly philosophical, impressionistic, intuitive, improvisational, imaginative, ambitious—like Bernanos, like Faulkner, like Lorca, like Yeats—imaginative. It means to be experiential, phenomenological, empathetic, attentive as a poet, or St. Thomas, to particulars and the sensory dimension—"O Taste and See," and the beauty and honor and strength, the essential nobility, that have remained invisible, glimpsed, if glimpsed at all, through a glass darkly, as St. Paul says. It means be-

ing attentive to the vice hidden in every virtue and the virtue hidden in every vice. It means being steeped in the march and magnificence of history and tradition, in thrall to the glory of the arts, in awe and fascinated by those sweeping, ubiquitous patterns that echo hauntingly and reverberate through history, like signs and miracles, like the beating of an angel's wings or the footsteps of the gods. It means to be reverent before ancient ritual and rite and the world's Great Religions; irreverent in the face of cant, intolerance, hypocrisy. It means remembering that what is most important in life is usually immeasurable no matter how sophisticated the methodology or instrument. It means to be rhetorical in speech and prose and poetic in vision, for this is the language and vision of the soul. Psychology, to be *psychological,* to be the logos of the soul, must express the soul. And finally, to be psychological means to reach out to God, in the way of the Psalmist, with fear and trembling, passion and joy, wondering all the while "What is Man that Thou art mindful of him?" for the soul is primordially ordained to God, to the three great Transcendentals: Truth, Goodness, and Beauty. As St. Augustine says, "My soul is restless until it rests in Thee"; as he also says, "O Beauty, too late have I loved Thee." This is psychology: nothing less suffices.[1]

This method originated with commentary on Scripture—the Talmud, the Bible, the Koran and on the sacred texts of Hinduism, Buddhism and Confucianism. Familiar with the Fathers' and the Doctors' of the Catholic Church use of it, and its medieval variations which took on extravagantly poetic form, Jung reclaimed it as amplification. James Hillman describes it best: we "select [symbols] with a view to moving the soul by speaking symbolically with its images. Symbols are not things so much as rhetorical agents, ways of persuading images toward their fuller scope and depth."[2] For Hillman, amplification imparts knowledge; presumes a cosmology by reaching across centuries and geographies; is a therapy; and a ritual.

To bow to the regrettable redundancy, this is a work in Soul Psychology. As such, it is deeply indebted to the epic achievement of the Archetypal Psychology of James Hillman. Although many of the books that purport to build on his work belie it, James Hillman's Archetypal Psychology is a lifelong martial defense of the soul. Hillman was a Warrior. The chief virtue of the warrior is courage; with the soldier, the military man, it is discipline. Hillman laid claim for psychology to those virtues that he found represented in the Warrior Caste in multiple societies. He writes, "In our most elevated works of thought—Hindu and Platonic philosophy—a warrior class is imagined as necessary to the well-being of humankind. The class finds its counterpart within human nature, in the heart, as virtues of courage, nobility, honor, loyalty, steadfastness of principle, comradely love, so that war is given location not only in a class of persons but in a level of human personality organically necessary to the justice of the whole."[3] As a defender of the soul, as a defender of these virtues, of what he sometimes called the "thought of the heart" and imaged as the Lion that roars in the desert, Hillman ennobles the psychology and makes common cause with Alfred Adler, the psychologist of the Will to Power, of the aggressive instinct, of *thymos*, of the striving for superiority, of the great "upward drive." This book is flamenco in prose—flamenco means flame-colored—in an effort to re-claim the Flamenco Spirit in the soul of what Adler at least one times called, his "cultural psychology."

INTRODUCTION

Yet there must be power. Power there must be.
Because, if there is not power there will be force.

— D.H. Lawrence
Movements in European History

In his magisterial *Modern Times*, the historian Paul Johnson re-views the dust and chaos of this century, where after he concludes that the modern temper is governed by the will to power. The old Victorian world, which marched to a saner drum, was extinguished by the trenches. Incumbent rituals, barbered lawns, closed carriages, scarlet waistcoats, silver canes, mystic generals, dynastic thrones, great beauties, gaslight, fog, archdukes that glittered in the street: all these vanished into the mustard air. Pale gallants rushed off to war to return convulsed with horror. Shades chattered about a new decline and fall. The city fell. "Eliot's 'Unreal City…Falling Towers.'"[1]

The western city, whose spires and arches had once stormed heaven, disappeared into a violet cloud of doubt. Under the daily threat of death, which bloomed from the Guns of August, the vigor of our culture faded, so that the only winners were the bloated, bat-tlefield rats whose nightly scrut, scrut, scrut redeemed the time of its uncharity.

From the rat's belly emerged a world that seemed to teem with treasure. During the years just prior to the war, and for a decade thereafter, the modern mind was formed. What Sergei Diaghilev called "a new and unknown culture" was taking shape in the magic abstract colors of the Blue Riders—Marc, Kandinsky—whose first group exhibition occurred in 1911; in the discontinuous music of Schoenberg; in the poetry of Pound, Eliot and H.D., much of which first surfaced in *Poetry*, the "little magazine" founded in 1912; in Vaihinger's *The Philosophy of 'As if'* (1912); Unamuno's *The Tragic Sense of Life* (1912); Jung's *Symbols of Transformation* (1912); Adler's *The Neurotic Constitution* (1912); in Freud's *Totem and Taboo* (1913); Thomas Mann's *Death in Venice* (1913); Husserl's *Phenomenology* (1913); D.H. Lawrence's *Sons and Lovers* (1913); and in the *A la recherché du temps perdu* of Marcel Proust (1913). The year 1913 found Joyce, Tzara and Lenin all holed up in Zurich. Throughout all of Europe, where the lights were slowly going out, the great blaze of a venerable civilization dimming into a murderous dusk, a heightened sensibility nonetheless prevailed and stuttered out new beauty.

But that new life soon withered to reveal an underlying *void* into which swarmed a new kind of creature: brown shirted Calibans: charismatic, bold, each of them convinced that destiny had fingered them to rule. These brooders, these men of power, prevailed in deed and spirit perhaps because the *ennui* of the times favored their ascendancy. Mussolini marched on Rome; Hitler took the stage at Nuremberg; Stalin triumphed over Trotsky; Mao waited in the wings. And even though we may have dispatched the worst of them, toppling the fascist monsters from their bloody roost, their influence has not waned, at least not in the heart where too many of us still ache to wear the crooked title of *der Fuhrer*. Because we dwell in an epoch almost entirely bereft of *gemeinschaftsgefuhl*, we all hunger for the privileges of power which we desire to grab, consolidate and use, quickened still by this wholly terrestrial *ethos*.

Reflecting on the sad tale of our century's events, Johnson considers various theories that purport to explain them. There is Freud, who gazing upon the naked mysteries of sex, located our tragedy in the Great War of instincts against civilization, which later, in a visionary fit, he powerfully divined as a cosmic struggle between Eros and his dark brother, Death. And yet, our century's chief villains seem to have lusted for something more than sex. The hearts of Mussolini, Hitler, Stalin, Mao–do they not house a darker purpose?

Before the grandiose dreams of a totalitarian ruler, the Freudians must fall silent, for they cannot integrate such grotesque excess into the economy of their system. The monster upsets their suave and modulated clarities. Next, there is Marx, who ascribed to economics the central office in human affairs. But Marx was too much the statistician to ever grasp the complex motivations of twentieth century leaders. The Marxist system acquired the persuasive force to sway men's minds only after Marx had been totemized and englobed by a rich mantle of symbols: the red flag, saints and tanks, the hammer and the sickle. Marx as sage and Marx as symbol are two widely different things, in that the first was merely another peddler of abstractions, whereas the second belongs to a pantheon of heroes, which for many retain the powers of inspiration. Marx cannot explain the Calibans, though these things of darkness have often usurped his name. From the British Museum, where Marx read history, his eyes crawling over tables of statistics, to the titanism of Red Square, where his image appeared to sanction and even sanctify the oppressive machinery of a single regime, is a road paved with lies, corpses, dementia and treachery. Were Marx to cast an eye on it, he would surely have seen it for what it was: a frigid, life denying aberration.

No, thinks Johnson, to understand the character of the times requires the tutelage of Friedrich Nietzsche, who understood that all men natively crave power, doing so with voracious, overpowering intensity. What is power? The working definition throughout this book assumes with Nietzsche that 1) the Will to Power is the determining drive in human nature. It is the basic need and the final goal. Power is the ability to affect a goal through the exertion of strength. The increase of power means the increase of strength, might, command, control, suasion or influence. Whether it is Life over Death (survival); Mind over Matter (security); for Love or Money (success); or Good over Evil (*virtu* or significance), all human beings strive to maximize their power.

From where Nietzsche sat, sequestered in his "strange room," power appeared to be a tonic in men's souls from whence it spills out into a gladiatorial reaction to every challenge, transforming every chance event into an unconscious *agon*. Nietzsche knew that dreams of Triumph overshadow dreams of sex and money. Power spans the material with the incorporeal sphere, both of which it dominates, sometimes productively, sometimes as an obsession. Unlike Freud or Marx, Nietzsche grasped that we cannot live without power, that we perish in the absence of its psychological rewards. He saw that where power flourishes, it disciplines the sprawl of human appetites into the compact unity necessary for dramatic deeds, bold actions, passionate engagements. He saw that the will to power climaxes in the Baroque life enacted as a drama—he called it "giving style to character"—for which reason Nietzsche loved the Dionysian mask in whose form the fires of ambition give way to artful flair. Charging fantasy with sparkle, the will to power transforms the mind into a dazzling making-fluid, a fire about the head, which is power's mark in the impressionable air. In Javanese culture, for example, one speaks of power as a kind of radiance, a *wadju* or *tedja* "which [is] thought to emanate softly from the face or person of the man of Power."[2] In his role as skald and anatomist of power Nietzsche also mapped its degradations; for when power is denied, it fans out wordlessly along secret, subterranean paths, disguising itself, for example, as passivity, depression, a thirst for spiritual freedom or liberation, union with a powerful person, submission, devout obedience, scientific detachment or stoic self-control, as dramatic virtue, public decency, perfect objectivity, dedication to a cause, sense of duty, a complacent conscience cleansed of all impurities, all of which, at times, can be safeguards of superiority, the devious ploys by which we circumvent our own inadequacies to attain a false, illusory preeminence. By being pretentiously bad or good or victimized or helpless, we retain our sense of power. Repress the will to power and it will return to distort conduct into something clogged, course, little, mean, a senseless flat amassing of resentments, while inward life corrupts into a pageant of disastrous cruelty, as it did for Alberto Giacometti, before discovering his art, who here remembers a fantastic nightly office:

I could not go to sleep at night without having first imagined that at dusk I had passed through a dense forest and come to a gray castle which stood in the most hidden and unknown part. There I killed two men before they could defend themselves. One was seventeen and always looked pale and frightened. The other wore a suit of armour, upon the left side of which something gleamed like gold. I raped two women, after tearing off their clothes, one of them thirty-two years old, dressed all in black, with a face like alabaster, then a young girl round whom white veils floated. The whole forest echoed with their screams and moans. I killed them also but very slowly (it was night by that time), often beside a pool of stagnant green water in front of the castle. Each time with slight variations. Then I burned the castle and went to sleep, happy.[3]

Giacometti's obsession is not unique or even exceptionally bizarre, though we usually sublime the more perverse *exotica* into less ego-alien forms. Though the proportions vary, some combinations of these four forms of behavior and fantasy are the usual wages of repression of the will to power, so that in consequence we simultaneously become: 1) voyeurs of violence; 2) maintain our self-control and balance through silent vows of retribution and fantasies of revenge; 3) while our dreams and hypnagogic imagery erupt in cruelty; and 4) our interpersonal *personas* of helplessness, dependency, complacency or self-righteousness grow compulsively tyrannical. The deep forest; the pale young man; the torture; the frightened woman screaming; Giacometti's ghastly fantasy merely compels us to remember what Nietzsche always knew: that the will to power cannot be eschewed without extinguishing the stellar fires of the self.

Although this view may shatter a rash of sentimental notions, modern history confirms it, which is precisely Johnson's point. What Johnson marvels at is Nietzsche's clairvoyance in grasping how the "death of God" would affect power. Nietzsche, Johnson notes, intuited that if God has died, then the geography of the human spirit seismically shifts. Something base befalls the will to power, so that it battens, sickens, solidifies in hate until, like chaos come again, it produces a new despotic brood. Nietzsche—

> ...saw God not as an invention but as a casualty, and his demise as in some important sense an historical event, which would have dramatic consequences...the decline and ultimately the collapse of the religious impulse would leave a huge vacuum. The history of modern times is in great part the history of how that vacuum had been filled. Nietzsche rightly perceived that the most likely candidate would be what he called the "Will to Power" which offered a far more comprehensive and in the end more plausible explanation of human behaviour than either Marx or Freud....And, above all, the Will to Power would produce a new kind of messiah, uninhibited by any religious sanctions whatever, and with an unappeasable appetite for controlling mankind.[4]

Regardless of whether or not God actually exists, installed somewhere within the aether, to the soul of western man he has always spoken as a living symbol—a symbol of a transcendent order, the goodness and being of which is indestructible. Further, inasmuch as God created the world in seven days and continues as its eternally creative ground of being—As it was in the beginning / is now and ever shall be—we automatically assume that these perfections are also immanent in the natural world. As the old gospel song has it "He has the whole world in his hands." But now that He has died, cut down by metaphysical polemics, the world itself hovers over a void into which, perhaps, already it has fallen. Having lost our belief in God, we don't believe in the world much either. Theoretically, imaginatively, we've already vaporized it into an epiphenomena. The death of the One has not meant the return of the Many or the re-birth of Pan, broad and rank and beastly, disporting in the foam; it has meant, instead, the death of the All—spirit, matter, nature, God, the City itself, all overcome by the wasteland. Unreal City. From Chaucer's "April with its showers sweet" to Eliot's "April is the cruelest month" is the measure of our ruin.

God and Gaia gone. Insofar as the will to power is concerned, the "death of God" betokens not only its liberation from all transcendent norms and obligation but also its "liberation" from the world itself. In effect, the "death of God" has dispossessed power of its secure foothold in the earth, its necessary anchorage. *With nothing reliable to stand on power has nothing to stand against* and thus turns in upon itself. Without immutable laws to bless it; without the earth to offer it both possibility and resistance, power perforce becomes raw and illegitimate, a lawless, limitless self-devouring beast that eventually cannibalizes its own substance. In the sonorous strength of Shakepearian language:

> Force should be right, or rather, right and wrong,
> Between whose endless jars justice resides,
> Should lose their names, and so should justice too.
> Then everything includes itself in power,
> Power into will, will into appetite;
> And appetite, an universal wolf,
> So doubly seconded with will and power,
> Must make perforce an universal prey,
> And last eat up himself.[5]

When power feeds upon itself like Shakespeare's Wolf, citizens become conformists; celestial spirits become infernal spooks, while nature loses its irreducible autonomy to become so much raw acreage at the service of the strongest spell or arm. Extensions of the Wolf and his bulging appetites, the conformist, the fakir and the strongman dominate our times.

This thesis is a melancholy thought against which something in us rebels, rising up in an indignant chorus of dissent. Surely there is something more to life than mutations of the will to power. And yet the somber, clotted investigation of Michael Foucault into what he terms the "micro-physics" of power are sufficient to throttle this revolution in its tracks; for Foucault has demonstrated that power is a constant, perhaps the only constant in contemporary Western affairs.

> [P]ower in the West is what displays itself the most, and thus what hides itself the best: what we have called "political life" since the 19th century is the manner in which power presents its image (a little like the court in the monarchic era). Power is neither there, nor is that how it functions. The relations of power are perhaps among the best hidden things in the social body.[6]

Even the soul itself, which is the metaphysical substrate underpinning the entire discipline of psychology, may be nothing more than a fiction of power, a powerful fiction, created so as to better subjugate any cell of resistance still existing beyond the body politic. The "...non-corporal soul is not a substance; it is the element in which are articulated the effects of a certain type of power....On this reality-reference the various concepts have been constructed and domains of analysis carved out: psyche, subjectivity, personality, consciousness, etc...."[7] In Foucault's view, the *ethos* of power conditions even the way that we conceive of power so that—

> Perhaps, too, we should abandon a whole tradition that allows us to imagine that knowledge can exist where the power relations are suspended and that knowledge can develop only outside its injunctions, its demands and interests. Perhaps we should abandon the belief that power makes us mad and that, by the same token, the renunciation of power is one of the conditions of knowledge. We should admit rather that power produces knowledge...[8]

Because of our universality of power, it is only through the most rigorous, archaeological reflection, which is nothing more grandiose than "a regulated transformation of what has already been written," can we even identify the psychological dynamics whereby power extends its tenacious control. The work is more a loosening, in the most modest sense, than it is a liberation; that is, at best it opens up a minimalist space of fracture within a complex system of devices, stratagems, ploys and regulated forces. The space can be sustained only through a constant exercise of emendation which reveals the incongruity of human desire with civilization's structures.

If power is a constant in Western history, if power is the equivocal angel with whom we all must grapple in lifelong *auseinandersetzung*, then this vindicates the *Individual Psychology of Alfred Adler*, who was the first and only of the great psychologists to recognize power's preeminence in psychic life. In part this was a debt to Nietzsche, and in part a response to the dramas of the clinic: "Among all great philosophers...in Nietzsche's work, one finds almost on every page observations reminiscent of those we make in therapy."[9] But regardless of the relative weight of inspiration, the outcome was the same: "We wish to point out the absolute primacy of the will to power..."[10] It was not that Adler endorsed the norm of power, but he refused to hide his eyes behind makeshift illusions about *Eros* and *Thanatos*, economic man, the noble savage or the collective unconscious. Instead of romanticizing, he looked upon the present squarely, perceiving the shape of things to come. He saw the superman sharpening an axe. So he gambled his life upon an exploration of the will to power, hoping thereby to exhume gold, hoping to find a desirable expression, an ideal norm that would not spell disaster.

It has been said that all great thinkers think but one great thought which they spend their lives elaborating. The thought is like a daimon, an unearthly force that instills life with a purpose. It appears with sparkle and unedited freshness. In the first chill of the morning, when the torch burns low, the dew sparkles on the grass, or in the brooding dryness of a sleepless night, the daimon grips the vitals of a man, suddenly appearing to transform his life. Occasionally he finds this daimon in the face of another, as Freud did with Fliess and Jung with Freud, and occasionally it stirs within, as it did for Adler. But whatever its genesis, such a man will henceforth be what Kierkegaard calls a *daimonic* man, possessing and possessed by his one great thought. When in the grips of a daimon, life takes on an impersonal design. "My troubles are my own," said Adler. One tries to be clear, struggles to understand, experiments, revises constantly, formulates, reformulates, starts again; but once the daimon has entrenched itself, there is no escape. All that remains is a life of divine bondage, or wrestling with the angel and of being ravished by it, as was Leda by the swan. "Being so caught up / so mastered by the brute blood of the air, / Did she put on his knowledge with his power / Before the indifferent beak could let her drop?"

Adler was such a daimonic man, as Sperber notes when he acknowledges Adler's "Socratic aura."

> Adler's biographers, especially the women among them, often lyrically praise his "aura." Their descriptions may be naïve or exaggerated, but in essence they are perfectly true. Anyone who approached Adler free of distrust or dislike would be received in a genuinely Socratic manner. This manner enabled Adler to make even the most insignificant person feel he would talk with Adler as with an equal. Adler was certainly a highly ambitious man, with a controlled but by no means quiescent will to power, but his manner went beyond a mere technique for quickly establishing contact; it was the outcome of his philosophy of life .[11]

Way, too, loved Adler, perceiving in him the same visionary brilliance.

> "He is like the piping Silenus in the statuaries' shops, which, when you open them, are found to contain images of the Gods."…To those who knew him, the mind of Adler, like that of his great forerunner, was subtle and

delightful to a degree that quite overshadowed the physical heaviness of which in his early years he has been so
sensitive. But the stocky, unimpressive little figure, the
large mouth, the broad, stubborn, combative chin were
heavy always in an attractive way. Distortions though
they were from the Grecian norm of gracefulness, they
possessed a formidable, masculine power, and were
in any case offset by other features, equally strong but
more beautiful, the massive imaginative brow, and the
extraordinary eyes, large, heavy lidded and dreaming
behind the convex lenses of the spectacles. The speculative disposition which Freud had noted in him, appeared above all in his eyes—eyes that a great artist
might have had and which certainly denoted a rich, even
heavy, subjective life. But every now and then a look of
startling directness would pierce through the filmy, visionary look, quickly and comprehensively gather its
impressions, and vanish as suddenly as it had appeared.

...One felt both the amplitude of his imagination and
his quick, bold, almost ruthless penetration of reality.
The power which made his personality radiant sprang
both from the impression made by these inner resourc-
es and from the directness and virility of his whole challenge to life.[12]

And yet, these two verbal cameos of Adler, both of which sil-
houette a gracious profile, and both of which ring lovely due to their
author's natural artistry, clash with other contemporary portraits,
where Adler comes off as a slightly querulous man, unattractively
aggressive. He had, they say, a flammable and expansive ego. A bit
rotund, a bit Rotarian. What might account for the incongruity is
that both Sperber and Way were truly touched by Adler, whereas
others stayed emotionally remote; and in being touched had something in them warmed to life that might have otherwise stayed dor-

mant. This new increment of being, which in Adler's quiet, charismatic presence sprang to life, newly catalyzed, freshly empowered, in turn looked back to Adler, as to its source, and thereby caught the flash of a visionary wing. Because of the awakened presence of this dominant, they divined what others missed.

We can name this dominant by noting how Way commences his eloquent reminiscence, that is, with Alcibiades' famous phrase about the inner radiance concealed within Socrates' outward grossness. Together with Sperber's, Way's perception corresponds to what we might call the *Alcibiades Complex*, by which we indicate a consistent style, attitude, construct, fantasy; a way of standing, seeing, speaking; to which the world co-causally responds, revealing specific beauties which are the counterpart of this beautiful perspective.

By speaking of the Alcibiades Complex, we invoke one of the most famous names in all antiquity, a figure of great enchantment and appeal. Who was Alcibiades? "...the most brilliant political figure of Athens."[13]

Nietzsche numbers him among his heroes.[14] In his famous biography of Bolingbroke, Walter Bagehot notes the recurrence of this type in history.

> There lurks about the fancies of many men and women an imaginary conception of an ideal statesman, resembling the character of which Alcibiades has been the recognized type for centuries. There is a sort of intellectual luxury in the idea which fascinates the human mind. We like to fancy a young man in the first vigor of body and in the first vigor of mind, who is full of bounding enjoyment, who excels all rivals at masculine feats, who gains the love of women by a magic attraction, but who is also a powerful statesman, who regulates great events, who settles great measures, who guides a great nation. We seem to outstep the *moenia mundi,* the recognized limits of human nature, when we conceive a man in the pride of youth to have dominion of the pursuits of age, to rule both the light things of women and

the grave things of men. Human imagination so much loves to surpass human power, that we shall never be able to extirpate the conception.[15]

Socrates loved him, comparing his love to the divine transports of the maeneds, in that just as they draw milk and honey from dried wells, so Socrates hoped he educed nobility from the soul of his friend. In Plato's *Symposium,* Alcibiades steps forth ivy clad, a drunk and exotic creature whose entry spellbinds and then entertains, causing the glittery assemblage to attain new heights of beauty.

Plutarch presents him as a man whose style of fantasy was a fantastic style: all that he did, he did with aura and flourish. As an avid soldier he was steady in battle, valorously holding the line when others fled, as he did when the Athenians were routed at Delian, where it was only the courage of Alcibiades that rescued Socrates. Serenely self-obsessed, he was indifferent to the crowd's opinion, whose swells and sways he worked to his own purpose. He once cut off the tail of a prize dog in order to defy the mob and when his friends remonstrated, he responded that "better they talk about this than vent their malice elsewhere." As even the poets recognize, his tongue was streaked with brilliance, and he had a lisp which he converted into a stylish instrument accompanying his voice. Timing, savvy, this was his *métier.* On all occasions he knew when to bluff, when to fold, when to sit back quietly. Perhaps the true character of the man nowhere shone forth more visibly than near the end of his career when he returned to Athens at the head of a fleet adorned with shields and spoils, lurching forward musically, as the oars kept time with a flutist and while a tragedian, attired in robes of purple and bedecked with ornaments from the theater, conveyed instructions to the crew. In the admiral's ship a purple sail unfurled, at the foot of whose mast sat Alcibiades, in full Asiatic state. Thirsting for glory, coveting beauty in every guise, whether it be in the dark, swift eyes of a Persian courtesan or the craftsmanship of a silver drinking vessel, Alcibiades mesmerized the Greeks, who could never really spurn him, not even in the wake of treachery or complete disaster.

What then is the Alcibiades Complex? Because throughout this work we shall be hammering out a definition, let me tick off only the most stellar features. Since Alcibiades seems to have approached perfection, that inexhaustible ache that impels us to new heights, new summits of achievement; since Alcibiades lives forever, a dazzling monumental presence on the pages of Plato and Plutarch, let us say that he represents our hunger for immortality, for eternal renown, the charismatic name. Since Alcibiades was a brilliant, spirited man, let us say that he represents our spirit, but spirit understood as a *numinosum*, a drifting, forceful midnight wind that addresses our prophetic selves, our kingly natures. Since Alcibiades possessed the pluck to skirmish with whatever challenged him, let us call him by the ancient name of courage, which is the lyrical emotion. And since Alcibiades was gifted, let us say that he represents our gifts, the solar dazzle of our inner spectrum, the purple band, our natural excellence, as well as corresponding to that perspective that focuses on goals and strengths and purposes instead of nosing about obsessively for stinks. And, further since Alcibiades courted glory and counted himself the greatest among the captains and the kings, exercising power as if by divine right, let us say that he represents the will to power in its original form. Perfection, spirit, courage, all is boldness, dazzle, strength of purpose, a creaturely embodiment of the *élan vital*, the *panta rhei*. He is a spirit at once amazing and unattainable. He is power itself, naked, sensual, dauntless, fresh.

Adlerian psychology awakens the Alcibiades Complex, which is in the nature of a Grand Awakening, for to read Adler is to feel this passionate character stirring in the breast. "My heart in hiding / Stirred for a bird,—the achieve of; the mastery of the thing!" said Hopkins. Our hearts in hiding stir for Alcibiades, his eucalypti torsoed masteries. At the beginning of his lectures Adler would sometimes evoke the Alcibiades Complex by subliming its essence into a Pythagorean symbol. A pale, rotund, undistinguished looking man would appear before a blackboard, where from bottom to top he would draw a firm, white line. Under Adler's hand the blackboard would become a kind of cosmos, a powdery blackness where there appeared not an anxious white dot suspended in a void but a trajectory of animated purpose. Geometry is one of the oldest forms of magic and on the strength of this incantation Adler would remark: "You see, that is the life of the psyche. Everything psychic is movement from below to above." This is the Alcibiadian connection, an existential vision where life becomes not an odyssey but an argosy, not a journey towards the stabilities of home but an enchanted episode of daring. And man becomes an optimistic creature, a tremendous upward aspiration continually underway.

Alas, today the tiger's eye seems wholly lost to Individual Psychology. It has gravitated elsewhere. But during the early years, the sap-time of the discipline, the fearless eye of Alcibiades seemed brashly prominent, quickening the work of a diverse collection of spirits who gathered around Adler and whom I do not wish to homogenize, except to say that they were all united by a certain brilliance of conjecture, a speculative *élan*, in which I think it is just possible to detect a flashing prow below a purple sail. It is these men I would emulate: I would recapture here some touch of Brachfeld's genius; Sperber's nerve; Neuer's classical range; the fluid comprehensiveness of Lewis Way; Adler's gift for synthesis; Ansbacher's scholarship; the crash and sweep of Crookshank's prose. These are the sediments I would uncover; the inspirations I would breathe. Each reflects Alcibiades.

And yet, this awakening is undoubtedly a risk, for Alcibiades was a duplex being whose sensational turnabouts finally overshadowed his nobility. If Alcibiades was Athens' most brilliant politician, he was also her destroyer; if he was a soldier who braved the worst of hardships, he was also a mercenary who auctioned off his sword; if upon returning to Athens in the noonday tide of his career, he restored the glories of the gods, he commenced his rise by opportunistically defacing them. Every virtue was shadowed by a fault.

> But with all these words and deeds, and with all this sagacity and eloquence, he intermingled exorbitant luxury and wantonness, in his eating and drinking and disso-

lute living; wore long purple robes like a woman, which dragged after him as he went through the market-place; caused the planks of his galley to be cut away, that so he might lie the softer, his bed not being placed on the boards, but hanging upon girths. His shield, again, which was richly gilded, has not the usual ensigns of the Athenians, but a Cupid, holding a thunderbolt in his hand, was painted upon it. [16]

Alcibiades could be cruel, debauched, sordid, wicked. Above all else he was constant, in creed and deed, loyalty, even gender. And in appearance, where his form was like a magic glass, utterly beguiling, in which others glimpsed their ideal selves. Let an Athenian stand before him and he would at once change colors, manifesting hues of eloquence and grace; or in the presence of a Spartan, Alcibiades would become the anti-type to the Athenian type, appearing as the embodiment of Spartan courage and resolve. When in Rome, Alcibiades outdid the Romans, always. So cruel in victory that he was responsible for the slaughter of innocents at Melos, whose citizenry dared to toss aside the yoke of Athenian enslavement; so traitorous in defeat that he changed sides like changing clothes, Alcibiades gravitated, as if by ancient instinct, to a natural home in Persian courts, where he soon rose to prominence, becoming at one point the chief adviser to a satrap who being full of guile himself prized wickedness in others. His death was grim, being foreshadowed by two dreams, in one of which he found himself attired in the robes of his favorite mistress, who combed and painted him as if he were a girl, while the other presented him with a severed head cut away from his burning corpse; where after Alcibiades awakened to find himself in a burning house, from which he escaped only to be cut down by a sheet of arrows. In terms familiar to any Adlerian, Plutarch sums up his character.

His conduct displayed many great inconsistencies and variations, not unnaturally, in accordance with the many and wonderful vicissitudes of his fortunes; but among the many strong passions of his real character, the one most prevailing of all was his ambition and desire of superiority...[17]

Enfolding into his own strong spirit the best and worst of the human condition, cut from the flamboyant cloth of eros, Alcibiades was the type, and flower, of the striving for superiority.

In Adlerian fashion we may gather up these motifs by adducing an early recollection. Alcibiades' duplex fate and character is marvelously coagulated in his apocryphal first memory, which Plutarch, whose interest in this datum foreshadows Adler, helpfully provides—

> Once being hard pressed in wrestling, and fearing to be thrown, he got the hand of his antagonist to his mouth, and bit it with all his force; and when the other loosed his hold presently, and said, "You bite, Alcibiades, like a woman." "No," replied he, "like a lion." [18]

Here we see the aggressive instinct in full flower, the fantasy of life as conflict, the sublime conceit, the will to triumph, the savvy, the lion roaring in the heart to shield inferiority, the contempt for the defeated, and all this coupled with a sensual gloss of homo *eros*, the vague contours of a contrasexual development.

Alcibiades considered himself a lion. In my mind's eye I see him rather as a flower whose curving brilliance flashes up from some barbaric underground, or as a peacock, perhaps, fire-feathered, whose scream arches cruel and beautiful across the crushed green glitter of a lawn where he struts in sleek, imperial magnificence.

We must be cautious then about toasting Athens' most illustrious name, for not all is splendor here, there is also ample shadow. If we're to make the Alcibiades Complex the foundation stone of our revisioning of Adler, then we must somehow defuse his grandiosity so as to draw his visionary impulse into a more secure connection in *gemeinschaftsgefuhl*. By *gemeinschaftsgefuhl*, which is an Adlerian concept, whose meaning we shall soon elucidate, I mean here nothing more than acceptance of the phenomenological determinants of "situatedness" and "being-for-another." By *gemeinschaftsgefuhl*, I mean awareness of systemic issues, I mean care for the soul of one's *paideuma* (Frobenius, Pound), *culture* (Nietzsche, Spengler, Dawson, Eliot, Jones), *public orthodoxy*, (Kendall, Wilhelmsen), *for the soul of the world* (Hillman, Sardello, Severson). We must enlist his solar brilliance in service of the earth. By heightening virtue; imparting prudence; sponsoring empathy; implanting rhythmical consistency into this inconsistent heart; we may perhaps avoid the savage pitfalls that were the consequence of Alcibiades' alienation from *gemeinschaftsgefuhl*, from tradition, earth and body politic.

Only the subtlest, ablest teachings can achieve this. One way is Plato's. From Plato to Plutarch we know that while Alcibiades was still a boy, Socrates lit a torch for him which he carried even to the day when he calmly downed the hemlock. Marveling with all of Athens at the boy's exalted charms, Socrates burned with ardor, chastely, nobly, selflessly. Psychologically this signifies that the Alcibiades Complex will always constellate the Platonist in us, the part who sups on dreams, who will fly to him, captivated by the inexhaustible beam of splendor. For the Platonist, however, the complex alone is never enough in that it will appear deficient in that inward beauty of the soul to which Platonists attach such supreme importance. Regardless of the outward fairness or charisma, the complex will always appear entrapped within the Cave, too enamored with the sensate and therefore cut off from the divine nourishment of the forms. The Platonist disowns the brashness of the complex; dislikes the preen and pout. Because the Platonist degrades the world conceptually, Alcibiades will always appear flawed *because* he loves the world rather than because he degrades that love by seeking to convert the world into his private garden of delight. And so Socrates undertook to teach the boy, and the man the boy became, by impressing him with a love for truth, which for Socrates, and for Plato after him, necessarily equates with the renunciation of appearances and shadows in order to mount to the realm of forms, the identities that are the archetypal foundations of our material existence. Again, in comparison to the myth-rich sonorities of Platonic rhetoric, it asks Alcibiades to cultivate his soul, to sacrifice through internalization, to contain, reflect, interiorize, to establish a connection with the gods. This will check his restlessness. This will sober his high desire. Go, Go, says the bird, Alcibiades. Take time for the experience, says Socrates. When this ploy fails, as it is bound to do, given Alcibiades' thirst for glory in the tangible here and now, Socrates conscripted Aphrodite; that is to say, he shifted his rhetoric away from exaltation of the beauty of the forms, which was falling on deaf ears anyhow, to praise for the form of beauty, to Aphrodite, smiling, pellucid, lovely. And beauty was something Alcibiades coveted. Where dialectic failed, perhaps Diotima might succeed with her doctrine of the *kalon kagathon*, her wiles, her cult of beauty, her sophisticated values, her *cosmoi* and cosmetics. Where brilliant *techne* failed, perhaps the bewitchments of the comb and mirror would succeed. Perhaps her anima could tame his animus. Perhaps her Aphrodite could seduce his Mars.

But the verdict here is in, is in *historically*, for Socrates did not wean Alcibiades away from his appetite for earthly renown nor did it derail him from his fast track towards destruction. It did not save him from the sheet of arrows, not the burning house nor the final dream which seemed to bring his life full circle to tell him, "No Alcibiades, you are not a lion. You are a woman." Despite all of Plato's myths; despite all of Socrates brilliant dialectic, despite Diotima's bewitching beauties, Alcibiades consumed his life in a holocaust of thrill. If our object is to heal Alcibiades, and to heal the earth and community through him, then Platonism is not the answer. Where Socrates failed could we succeed by employing Socratic methods? Can the pupil surpass the master? What *hubris* to presume! By remembering history, then, perhaps we won't be doomed to repeat it, hung like Ixion on an eternal wheel. Though Plato's pharmacy might have many uses, it lacks the antidote we need. For Alcibiades, and all he sires, the whole Platonic tradition will always seem "all transcendence" as it was for Yeats, who although he admired Plato recoiled from too much other worldliness whenever he found it, even when he discovered it in the sacred texts. "And I declare my faith: / I mock Plotinus' thought / And cry in Plato's teeth…."

For a better example, we turn to Aristotle, successful tutor to a King of Kings. And specifically to one bright star in the Aristotelian firmament, Sir John Fortescue, a medieval chancellor of England, who was faced with his own Prince Harry, his own Alcibiades, to whom he was required to give a lesson in power. Like Alcibiades, Fortescue's young Prince balked at the idea of allegiance, much less submission, to the customs of the community, to ancient norms, privileges, and proverbs. Why should he, God's chosen, obey what Adler called the "iron logic of the community?" Were not his European royal brethren greater, since their power was absolute, unruffled by common limitations? They obeyed no will beyond their own. He would bend the knee to God but not to the community. No, says Fortescue—and his answer echoes down the ages—your cousins are not true kings, not truly powerful, because power sans limitation is not true power at all. In order to demonstrate his teachings Fortescue resorts to his famous image of the community as a body politic.

> Saint Augustine, in the 19th book of the *De Civitate Dei*, chapter 23, said that *A people is a body of men united by consent of law and by community of interest.* But such a people does not deserve to be called a body whilst it is acephalous, i.e. without a head. Because, just as in natural bodies, what is left over after decapitation is not a body, but is what we call a trunk, so in bodies politic a community without a head is not by any means a body. Hence Aristotle in the first book of the *Politics* said that *Whensoever one body is constituted out of many, one will rule, and the others be ruled.* So a people wishing to erect itself into a kingdom or any other body politic must always set up one man for the government of all that body, who, by analogy with a kingdom, is, from "regendo", usually called a king. As in this way the physical body grows out of the embryo, regulated by one head, so the

kingdom issues from the people, and exists as a body mystical, governed by one man as head. And just as in the body natural, as Aristotle said, the heart is the source of life, having in itself the blood which it transmits to all the members thereof, whereby they are quickened and live, so in the body politic the will of the people is the source of life, having in it the blood, namely, political forethought for the interest of the people, which it transmits to the head and all the members of the body, by which the body is maintained and quickened.[19]

Your power recalls your head, says Fortescue, which is the seat of your immortal soul by the glory of which you're brother to the angels. And yet, note well, Fortescue continues, the head cannot fulfill its role nor even live unless it be united to a body. Your power ultimately depends, then, upon a deep and cherished continuity with a *corporate body and blood of traditions, observances, and laws.* You must love these limits and you must cherish them as the veritable life blood of your power. You must love the world, therefore, not so much because it is good and beautiful (the platonic antidote to Alcibiades) but because it is the condition and source of your power. Insofar as your royal nature is constituted by will to power, its perfection requires you to cherish limitation.

Power must treasure limitation or else destroy itself; thus runs Sir John's distinction. Let me digress a moment to point out that a less classical, more conventional way to pose our issue is to say that Adlerian psychology awakens whatever natural gifts we have for leadership. (We're here substituting the conventional *idea of leadership* for the classical image of Alcibiades.) Adlerian psychology trains leaders we might say. But the problem here is that the very gifts that make for leadership—the passion, stamina, the decisiveness, the purpose and resolve, the habit of command—are themselves ethically neutral and can be put to base uses as well as noble ones. The desires can bend infernally, the aboriginal sensation stray. The talents can easily be squandered on the comforts of the self. Indeed, when the complex stirs autonomously, this is usually the case. I encounter Alcibiades daily in the clinic. He comes in the form perhaps of a juvenile delinquent, slouching, sullen, an amalgam of grease and bones, pimples and biceps, the proverbial leader of the pack who has both charm and cunning. Or he comes in the form of an ex-con's on probation, truculent, complaint about the judge's order to seek counseling. Always I find the same natural savvy and authority, the dignity and gifts, but always mixed with incredible entitlement and grandiosity. The rules, the laws, are for wimps and home boys. Perhaps another name for Alcibiades is simply the psychopath, the sociopath, the anti-social personality, the character disorder about which the text books say that the only cure is the emergence of an *esprit de corp*. But are not many of history's greatest "leaders,"—generals, diplomats, the captains and the kings, at least in one part sociopath. Is not sociopathy another name for the morality of kings? Must all grandeur be delusional? And even when the complex is aroused by the rhetoric of therapy, the first emergent impulses are uniformly grandiose. Whether we call it the Alcibiades Complex, or the gift for leadership, the clinical task remains the same: to persuade the Complex into commitment to the city.

On the articulate strength of Fortescue's analogy we aim to psychologically construct our theory. But there are many other paths to follow. The medium of myth might shed some light: the primary document here needs to be Plutarch's *'Life' of Theseus*. Poetically, the cornerstone is Shakespeare's *Henry V*; philosophically, we would summon Bolingbroke away from his conspiracies and amours in order to address his *The Patriot King*, which is the *locus classicus* of our position. Or we might wade back through ancient history to take our lessons from the Scipios, the Grachii, Caesar, or Marc Antony. Closer to home are their modern counterparts, the tory patriots and politicians: Bolingbroke himself, who not only wrote but lived; the Pitts, especially the elder; and Benjamin Disraeli, romantic politician. For additional philosophical material, we might go to school with Voltaire and Diderot and the other French *philosophes*, consulting them for their ideas of an enlightened monarch, the philosopher king. Or we might, with profit and immense appreciation, assiduously study the writings and iconic life of the great modern "Republican Monarch," Charles De Gaulle, together with those of his keenest interpreter, Andre Malraux. For an example of a great failure, a man whose mind was formed in this tradition but who scorned and mocked it, we would study the career of Bismarck. A disordered Europe was this man's legacy. Insofar as the definition of power is concerned, each of these approaches would yield, I think, an identical conception. We would find in them both foreshadowing and fulfillment of Fortescue's idea.

Adler belongs to this tradition. But he not only belongs, he crowns it with a concise and eloquent expression. The Adlerian conception of power rests upon a tripod of assumptions. First, and uppermost, for Adler, power is not so much an extraordinary quality or attribute (through it sometimes features these astonishments) as it is a universal goal of behavior. Power is thus something that we desire rather than something we possess. Second, inasmuch as Adlerian psychology counts itself a social psychology, we must say that power always entails a context. It can neither *exist* nor be *understood* apart from its historical, bodily, social matrix. Third, the force of power requires the presence of a counter-force, and autonomous agent that resists it. Power requires resistance. To push when nobody pushes back is to end up face flat on the floor, or, more poetically, it is to float within the blue depths of the aether. For Adler, the soul of power may be distilled as follows: *power consists of a style of imagination that engages the "world" whose intractable autonomy is the pre-condition of its existence.* Whether thru an effort to transcend, overcome, or cooperate with those limits of resistance, when the imagination is engaged it *feels* powerful. The imagination that does cooperate with those limits in the fashion of an artist who cherishes and respects the materials with which he struggles and in terms of which he must materialize his vision, *is* powerful in the Adlerian sense. Abstract, but accurate in the essence of my thesis.

From the Sophist to Adler our best theorists of power have always known that power is fundamentally suasive. The conventional, popular, Machiavellian notion considers power as an unlimited desire whose nature is to continuously aggrandize itself. Kings extend their influence; states swallow states; the big fish gobbles up the little one. As one stadium troubadour has put it: "The poor man wants to be rich. The rich man wants to be king. The king ain't satisfied till he owns everything." Instead of ripeness, more is all. But in the absence of some internal or external check, power ultimately destroys itself. If power is only an aggrandizing appetite, then the realization of its goal would also signify its annihilation. After all is eaten, what is left? Only itself. The extension of power would then mean self-devouring, self-destruction. So this cannot be power unless power equates with suicide, unless power is another name for the void. Ultimately, according to this conception, to be all powerful would mean to simply not exist, which is a logical and metaphysical absurdity. In fact the opposite is true. For power to flourish, it requires an audience, an Other whose autonomous being is power's own life blood, its nerve and soul, the charter of its very existence.

This book unfolds as an excursion into power, the formative goal of which is the examination and ultimately the re-enactment of Adler's *agon* with the Alcibiades Complex. My purposes are neither scholarly nor, properly speaking, historical. That is to say, I do not presume to either summarize or clarify Adler's system, for that task has already been superbly done by Heinz and Rowena Ansbacher whose concerted efforts are both the preliminary and condition of my project. Nor will I venture to critically map the complex historical development of that system, for this too has been completed, sans cant or superfluities, by Paul Stepansky. I come neither to praise nor bury Adler, but rather, in the ancient and medieval manner, to invoke him as a kind of worthy hero whose vision and example might illuminate our times.

In Chapter One we examine the Adlerian "theme," both in regard to tradition and to theory, so as to create a kind of primer or conceptual framework in terms of which the subsequent work coheres.

In Chapter Two we delve into aggression. As the Ansbachers have shown, during Adler's career he traveled from an instinctivist, deterministic paradigm to a more open ended one, which was perhaps always incipiently present, to something more akin to what we now call phenomenological psychology. In this chapter I'm going to tread a similar path, moving away, on the basis of an Adlerian text, from the classification of aggression as a kind of native, autonomous, physiologically determined impulsion to something more inclusive and more radical, to aggression considered not only as an instinct, but also as a form of thought, a style of fantasy, a manner of behavior, a code of manners and civilization. In short, to the more comprehensive concept of an *agonistic* style of life.

In Chapter Three we exhume Adler's Nietzschean roots to argue that the gaya scienza is a chivalric science. Though Nietzsche is the "subject" of this chapter, I make no pretense to any formal Nietzschean scholarship, certainly not of the kind available in the professional philosophical journals. My venture is more thickly strewn with obstacles for my object is the determination of what Nietzsche might have privately meant to Adler, who, I think more than anyone has realized, built his school upon this titanically exuberant foundation. Success will then depend as much upon our psychological kinship with the Adlerian *habitus* as on our strictly factual knowledge of Nietzsche. Both are preconditions of any magnitude of insight.

In Chapter Four we continue with Adler to review how he himself continued, although in ways not obvious, the classical debate about the nature of power. There is a rumbling of chariots in Adler, a clash of arms, also emperors and saints. We show that Adler reclaimed and rehearsed the two great classical ideas of power, which are power as transcendence and power as control, or to express the dichotomy in images, power as the Sage or Strongman, as Socrates or Caesar, the apparently irreconcilable antithesis of which created an impasse that the classical mind was unable to transcend. But, moving along Augustinian lines, Adler did transcend it, by reconnecting power to the earth in the form a new dialogical and ultimately fraternal conception of power, of power as *gemeinschaftsgefuhl*.

In the final essay we rhetorically sum up with a chapter on the hero whose fiery animus Adler labored to rekindle. *Rhetorically—*

after Freud completed his dream book, he apologetically wrote to Fliess about the style.

> …what I dislike about it is the style. I was quite unable to express myself with noble simplicity, but lapsed into a facetious circumlocutory straining after the picturesque. I know that, but the part of me that knows it and appraises it is unfortunately not the part that is productive.[20]

I do not apologize but rather try to place myself squarely in the great sophistic-rhetorical tradition, to follow the Sophist Gorgias, theoretician of the magic spell of words; to write with passion, musicality and style. Lacan once wrote somewhere that he considered himself to be the Góngora of death psychology. I should be pleased to be its Gorgias. So let the rhetoric now sound to coax Alcibiades into chivalric renown.

CHAPTER ONE

---

*Perhaps these constructs are better imagined as fictions—
if we would be true to Adler. For despite the characteristic
dreariness of his style, he is not as literal, as unimaginative
as he seems. All of his basic constructs can be read as a poetics of life, much as Freud's theory of dreams and Jung's theory
of archetypal images are poetics, imaginative undertakings.*

— James Hillman

Imagine a poet, trim and hazel-eyed, with reddish-golden hair, born atop the steaming horseflesh smells of a stable, orphaned by a father who cracked his skull, packed off to school, returned to nurse an ailing mother, whose sickbed he guarded with a sword, sunk in adolescent gloom, apprenticed to a doctor, opting for the muse instead of medicine—imagine this poet as he now stands bent, one late October evening, his face shining with excitement, pouring over, with a friend, a 1616 folio of Chapman's Homer. Courtesy of the Elizabethan Chapman, a rich, fresh world was opened to our poet, so that his eye could now absorb the bright and grave dimensions of Achilles' rage and shield; Helen's conversation with Priam on the walls of Troy; Diomede's raid; Hector's imponderable nobility as he takes leave of his wife—a noble, mythopoetic world from which he had hitherto been debarred. Our poet and his friend especially thrilled to Chapman's timeless phrase: "The sea had soaked his heart through..." Beguiled by the images, braced by the hard, clean phrasing, his head swimming with the striding rhythms, so different from

Pope's account, with its corseted emotions, our poet went home to pen these words:

> Much have I travell'd in the realms of gold,
>> And many goodly states and kingdoms seen;
>> Round many western isles have I been
> Which bards in fealty to Apollo hold.
> Oft of one wide expanse had I been told
>> That deep-brow'd Homer ruled as his demesne;
>> Yet did I never breathe its pure serene
> Till I heard Chapman speak out loud and bold;
> Then felt I like some watcher of the skies
>> When a new planet swims into his ken;
> Or like stout Cortez when with eagle eyes
>> He star'd at the Pacific—and all his men
> Look'd at each other with a wild surmise—
>> Silent, upon a peak in Darien.[1]

—which were later retouched and gratefully entitled "On the First Looking into Chapman's Homer," the poem by which John Keats, a twenty year old poet, took possession of his maturity.

In this first chapter I want to relate the substance of the similar experience of first looking into Adler, whose work shares this at least with Chapman's Homer: it largely goes unread. Who was Alfred Adler, this obstreperously radiant man, whose life embodied his main motif of inferiority: who started life as a delicate, clumsy, ailing, pampered child overshadowed by an elder brother who continued to the end as the "real" family success, the one who gathered something solid, money instead of marginal wisps of fame; who bore slight and hardship and tragedy and exile that left him scarred and sapped; who was refused time and time again all academic laurels which should have come first in the form of an accepted dissertation—Adler's wasn't—and then the culminating chair, denied twice, first in Vienna, then at Columbia; whose stature and reputation were always dimmed by the greater luminosity of Sigmund Freud; who died on a street in far off Scotland, that grim and dour land a world away from the *gemutlichkeit* of Old Vienna; whose letters and works have never been collected, though they have been continually pilfered as if they were an anonymous public trust;[2] and whose good name has become the dumping ground for other's undigested animus, especially from the left, so that his work has been maligned as everything from dull, reductive, bourgeois, authoritarian to a platitudinous collage of common sense. Because Adler was not a man to easily shrug aside a slight, which is not to say that he cultivated grudges, but rather, that Adler claimed a keen, spirited and chivalrous sense of honor that made it difficult to turn the other cheek, these insults vexed him, prompting inner turmoil, so that in the end his inferiority feeling shaped his character, therefore determining his fate.

And yet, Adler, at the same time, boasted a quiet, enduring courage that compensated for nearly every fault. It was courage that overcame a fragile constitution through a resourceful training that left him unconquerably sturdy; it was courage that nourished the enlightened stoicism that unhesitatingly maintained that all his problems were his own; it was courage that kept advancing hard won knowledge even when those truths were ridiculed as mindless platitudes; it was courage that crossed swords with Freud; courage, whose last thought, while gasping on the street, was not to ask for help but was instead a remembrance of his son; it was the courage deposited in the *élan vital* of his texts which has kept the flame of individual psychology alive, a source of warmth and wonder, during the long century of the psychoanalytical supremacy.

Adler's life reverberates with such symbolic import because almost alone among the great twentieth century psychological thinkers Adler firmly shunned the lure of gnosis. Though we shall touch on gnosis several times throughout this study, let me here define it as that view of life that conceives the restlessness of our natures to be caused by the existence of two possibilities, each of which exerts a tantalizing lure, providing gravity and aspiration to every project, until we either harmonize their frictions or else unravel completely in the task. Failure entails psychological disunion. The oldest confabulations speak of pneuma and psyche. The most modern call it the spirit and the soul. From the clash of these attractions stem our vitality and uniqueness, for which reason their rifts and conjugations have spellbound centuries. Naming gnosis as the Magian world view, Spengler amplifies our theme.

> But still more important than all this is the opposition of Spirit and Soul. (Hebrew *rauch* and *nephesh*, Persian *ahu* and *urvan*, Mandaean *monuhmed* and *gyan*, Greek *pneuma* and *psyche*) which first comes out in the basic feeling of the prophetic religions, then pervades the whole of Apocalyptic and finally forms and guides the world-contemplations of the awaken Culture—Philo, Paul and Plotinus, Gnostics and Mandaeans, Augustine and the Avesta, Islam and the Kabbalah. *Rauch* means originally "wind" and *nephesh* "breath." The *nephesh* is always in one way or another related to the bodily and earthly, to the below, the evil, the darkness. Its effort is the "upward." The *rauch* belongs to the divine, to the above, to the light. Its effects in man when it descends are the heroism of a Samson, the holy wrath of an Elijah, the enlightenment of the judge (the Solomon passing judgment), and all kinds of divination and ecstasy. It is poured out . . . The man *possesses* the soul but he only *participates* in the spirit of the Light and the Good; the divine descends into him, thus binding all the individuals of the Below together with the one is the Above. This primary feeling, which dominates the beliefs and opinions of all Magian men, is something perfectly singular, and not only characterizes their world-view, but marks off the essence and kernel of their religiousness in all its forms from that of every other kind of man.[3]

Adler rejected gnosis in order to assert a generally Western world-view, which Spengler misnamed as Faustian. A better name is the heroic. Or the chivalric. In the Magian world-view the goal of life is containment, reflection, internalization. Its symbol is the cave. But for chivalric man, the soul of life is motion, action, history. Its symbol is the road. Adler both lived and died on the street. He lived and died heroically. Courage was his theme.

As this theme provides the intrigue of Adler's life, which seems so nobly paradigmatic, especially when compared to many of the other early titans, so perhaps it courses through his written legacy. Perhaps engagement with his written work will clarify those conquests that his biography so unconditionally rehearsed.

The first thing we note in reading Adler is that Adler was a reader, a man incandescently aflame with a passion for ideas. His works abound, even bristle with the evidence as he ranges across history and culture to enlist a Greek poet in an explanation of his dream theory:

> Another well-known dream is that of the Greek poet Simonides, who was invited to go to Asia Minor to lecture. He hesitated and continually postponed the trip in spite of the fact that the ship was in the harbor waiting for him. His friends tried to make him go, but to no avail. Then he had a dream. He dreamt that a dead man whom he had once found in a forest appeared to him and said, "Because you were so pious and cared for me in the forest, I now warn you not to go to Asia Minor." Simonides arose and said, "I will not go." But he had already been inclined not to go before he ever had the dream. He had simply created a certain feeling or emotion to back up a conclusion that he had already reached, although he did not understand his own dream.[4]

Or by conscripting Caesar to illuminate how all humans dwell in the world of meanings:

> A classic example of this play of subjective ideas in human actions is furnished by Caesar's landing in Egypt.

As he jumped ashore he stumbled and fell on the ground, and the Roman soldiers took this as an unfavorable omen. Brave as they were, they would nonetheless have turned around and gone back, had not Caesar thrown out his arms and cried out, "I embrace you, Africa!" We can see from this how little the structure of reality is causal, and how its effects can be molded and determined by the self-consistent personality."[5]

Who were Adler's authors? Vaihinger, with whom he maintained a lively correspondence, and Nietzsche, certainly; but also Heraclitus and the Stoics; Bottome claims he read Aristotle assiduously;[6] there is Shakespeare, about whose affinity with Adler a leading scholar writes—

It is not far from the mark to say that the Adlerian can turn almost at random to any page of Shakespeare and find corroborated there many of the basic principles of Individual Psychology. I am suggesting, too, that we attempt to establish contact between the behavioral sciences and the humanities once more, for each has much to teach the other. Throughout his career Adler never lost contact with literature and philosophy, and in fact those two disciplines were often absorbed into his scientific observations and provided reinforcement for those observations. There are numerous references to Shakespeare in his writings: his analysis of phobia, hypochondriasis, and melancholia makes reference to *Hamlet*, as does his discussion of the inferiority complex; his analysis of the plight of the second child and his study of the duality of obedience and defiance refer to *Macbeth*. Had we world enough and time, we could cite numerous other examples of direct use of Shakespeare by Adler and of correspondences in world outlook between the two.[7]

Cervantes, Tolstoy and Dostoevsky also figure; I number also Kant, Carus and Hegel and of course Bergson; an ear for classical allusion might note Plutarch, Simonides, Aeschylus and even Caesar's *Commentaries*. In commenting on Adler's *magnum opus, The Neurotic Constitution*, completed during 1912, Ellenberger enlarges our perception—

> "A great variety of authors are quoted: physicians, pediatricians, and university psychiatrists such as Kraepelin, and Wernicke, and among representatives of newer schools, Janet, Bleuler, Freud and many psychoanalysts. Among philosophers Nietzsche and Vaihinger are the most frequently referred to, and among writers Goethe, Schiller, Shakespeare, Tolstoy, Dostoevsky, Gogol, and Ibsen."[8]

Instead of being reduced to a mere state of surface ornamentation, Adler's authors are worked into the very matrix of the text, where their presences can go easily undetected. But they are there, pulsing with a nourishment that is unrelenting, a vital and expansive force that imparts to Adler's work an indefinable air of dignity and authority that comes from keeping close touch with the allusions to the famous lives of musicians, poets and painters fly thick and fast, to his most mature considerations, Adler's work is securely grounded in the illuminations of history.

Now as Unamuno says, we are all men of flesh and bones, so that our ideas are never wholly pure, unsoiled or diaphanously pristine; but instead reflect the conditions of their conception. Our ideas bespeak the language in which they sound; the history and passions in which they were annealed; the legends that foreshadowed them; the women that inspired them; the familiar things that called them forth. Therefore, by reading his favorite authors Adler set his roots down in several different soils. Symbolic geographies, we might call them, whose climates were then transmitted to his work, where they clashed and fused and finally intermingled to form a uniquely fresh inspiration.

The first geography arrived through Nietzsche. It is the Hyperborean North, the land of Goth, Teuton, of *Northerness*, the green and glacial ethic of ageless times in solemn forests in touch with sky and sea. This is the north of Thames and Dances of Greenland and Green Man, of Vikings and Robin Hood, of Swedish Kings and red beard Barbarossa. D.H. Lawrence sets our scene—

> By Germany, in that time, was meant all the land north of the Rhine....No one knew how far it stretched....In the illimitable shadow the pine-trunks rose up bare, the ground was brown with pine-needles, there was no undergrowth. A great silence pervaded everywhere, not broken by the dense whisper of the wind above. Between the shadowy trunks flitted deer, reindeer with branching horns ran in groups, or the great elk, with his massive antlers, stood darkly alone and pawed the ground, before he trotted away into the deepening shadow of the trunks. In places fir-trees, like enormous Christmas-trees, stood packed close together, their dark green foliage impenetrable. Then the pines would begin again. Or there were beeches in great groves, and elder bushes here and there: or again a stream or pond, where many bushes grew green and flowery, or big, healthy, half-open stretches covered with heather and whortleberries or cranberries. Across these spaces flew the wild swans, and the fierce, wild bull stood up to his knees in the swamp. Then the forest closed round again, the never-ending dark fir-trees, where the tusked wild boar ran rooting and bristling in the semi-darkness under the shadows, ready to fight for his life with the grey, shadowy wolves which would sometimes encircle him.[9]

Auden, with a haiku brevity contrasts it with an over ripened South:

Altogether elsewhere, vast
Herds of reindeer move across
Miles and miles of golden moss,
Silently and very fast.[10]

This is the Northerness that was loved by William Morris and the Inklings. From the long ships it evolved into tall cathedral towers, whose spires and arches stormed heaven. Then, after running riot in the ecstasy of Gothic, this Northerness underwent despotic, sensual enlightenment in the hands of Frederick the Great. Goethe preserved it; the Danes Ibsen and Kierkegaard passed it on; Wagner degraded it; Nietzsche maddened it, crucified by a spirit he could not whole-heartedly embrace. In the Nazis it became a mendacious faith, corrupted, almost, beyond redemption.

The Normans coagulate this spirit. Uncivilized bullies who blossomed with a *wander-lust*, the Normans, at least when they first swaggered onto the stage of history, were little better than a Viking panzer-gang; and yet out of Norman blood sprang Richard Lion-Heart who in addition to hacking flesh and limbs with his broadsword was also a finely cultured gentleman. In his curiously brilliant fantasia on the history of the west, Lawrence evokes him:

Richard was a great leader, a great man: not an Englishman, for he could never speak English: a Frenchman, an Aquitanian, writing and singing his poems in the language of Southern France: a tall, rash man, fair, handsome, brave, a great leader, a terror to the Turks.[11]

In the Normans we glimpse the paradox of Northerness, of the inward blaze that created not only the Vikings who burst out of the sea mists in their sleek, horned, marauding ships to work their bloody mayhem but also the Court of Charlemagne where the lion of the sword lay down with the lamb of learning to create a renaissance. Let Richard come home to Robin and we have the archetype of Northerness.

Let me cast this more conceptually. This North is the land of *homo ludens*, whose phenomenology has been exhaustively distilled by Juan Huizinga. The talent of *homo ludens* lies in his ability to absorb every dimension of human life into the fabric of play. Just as play is characterized, in Huizinga's view by:

> ...an activity which proceeds within certain limits of time and space, in a visible order, according to rules freely accepted, and outside the sphere of necessity or material utility. The play-mood is one of rapture and enthusiasm, and is sacred or festive in accordance with the occasion. A feeling of exaltation and tension accompanies the action, mirth and relaxation follow.[12]

So in the hands of *homo ludens*, every aspect of human life, no matter how sublime or insignificant, unfurls in an atmosphere charged with inter-animating symbols, pageantry, high drama, ritual colors and the sumptuous rapture of untrammeled joy. War becomes a knightly contest where the foes preen and pout before delivering even the knockout blow according to the laws of chivalry; where the trial becomes a rich, solemn, cathartic drama out of which justice is somehow coaxed; where philosophy becomes a riddle match, a test of injudicious wits and memories where foes are publicly bested and then dispatched; and where even poetry becomes a combative, dazzling, bragging match with truth tossed in the scales. *Homo ludens* caters to his own instinctual hunger for delight until such persistent cultivation succeeds in making light of life, each precept an illumination, a redemptive metamorphosis out of which comes fun—*fun*, that lively, brilliant, imponderable element in the absence of which human life is needlessly impoverished.

Northerness, then, in my conception of it, which we have tried to ballast here, betokens something quite specific and far removed from the blonde beast, all grin and swagger, rattling in his cage. And this Northerness is equally distant from even the vaguest whiff of the sanctimonious priggishness which we often associate with the Reformation. No doll house here but there is the sense of destiny. And so in arguing that Nietzsche imparted something of the air of Northerness to Adler, I also imply something quite specific. I mean to say that Adler's vision sparkles with something of the Northern sea and sky, something lyrical, sportive, brilliant that soulfully enriches it. It is the dimension which leaves us wondering at Adler even as the Romans always wondered at the North.

A second wind drifts up from the South, from below the Alps and Pyrenees, from Italy and Moorish Spain. Wallace Stevens imagines his poetic hero baptized by this wind, seized into the ethos of its elemental fate. "He heard A rumbling, west of Mexico..."[13]

If Northerness filtered to Adler's work via the conduit of Nietzsche, from Vaihinger comes the grape and orange blossomed breezes of the South. This is the South of Romeo and Juliet, of daggers and sonnets, of Petrarch on the mountain, Augustine in the garden grass, of Beatrice and the Borgias, poison and banquets, Cordoba and the Escorial, Cardinals' hats and Casanova, hidalgo and condotierre, of priests and soldiers, or soldiers become a priest, as did Ignatius, who upon asking for a tale of chivalry was given the gospels instead, where after, as they say, the rest is history. The South is the home of imaginal man, of Keats' poetical character, whose mind is blown like glassware, sensuous and dreamy, awash with angels, but with every sense alert, to further, sensate pleasure. For such a soul life is but a dream, the world a stage, we are such stuff as dreams are made of. And yet, this imaginal man very much belongs to Caesar. As the existentialists would say, his being is wholly a being in the world. If he is continuously generating fictions, creating reality everyday through fantasy, seeing through and seeing shadows, his imagination is nonetheless a power in the blood, born of the blood, and nose, incensed and incensing, alive on rooftops and in the streets, welcoming the lusty revelations of the senses.

Two figures here are central. The first is Vico, cracked brain Vico, who earned a living writing blurbs, melancholy and irritable, short tempered, man of affairs and recluse, who always urged the primacy of fantasy in history and the constructions of the real. Ernesto

Grassi, the authoritative philosopher of rhetoric, comments and the buttresses through timely quotation.

> Insight into relationships basically is not possible through a process of inference, but rather only through an original in-sight as invention and discovery (*inventio*). From this comes Vico's continual emphasis of *inventio* as primary over that which he calls "critical," i.e. purely rational thought. Once again only insight into "common" or shared characteristics in the above-mentioned sense makes possible the lending of meanings that allow things to appear [*phainesthai*] in a way that is human. Since such a capacity is characteristic of fantasy, it is this, therefore, which lets the human world appear. For this reason it is expressed originally in metaphors, i.e. in the figurative lending of meanings. "Hence poetic wisdom, the first wisdom of the gentile world, must have begun with a metaphysics not rational and abstract like that of learned men now, but felt and imagined as that of these first men must have been, who, without power or ratiocination, were all robust sense and vigorous imagination." In another place Vico states: "The poetic characters of which we speak were certain imaginative genera...to which they reduced all the particulars appertaining to each genus." Along these lines he also says: "Fantasy collects from the senses and connects and enlarges to exaggeration effects of the sensory effects of natural appearances and makes luminous images from them, in order to suddenly blind the mind with lightning bolts and thereby to conjure up human passions in the ringing and thunder of this astonishment."[14]

Vico keeps the imagination allied to *ingenium* or wit, and as Norman O. Brown has noted, is thus the perfect antidote for Yeatsian occultism and Jungian solemnity.[15]

The second is a Spaniard, Balthasar Gracián, courtier, mannerist and Jesuit, a royal favorite both in council and at table, and author of a compendium of worldly wisdom. The book teems with point, sagacity and glitter. A sampling:

> The Truth, but not the whole truth.
> A Grain of Boldness in Everything.
> Do pleasant Things Yourself, unpleasant Things through Others.
> Do not take Payment in Politeness.
> Know how to play the Card of Contempt.
> Never have a Companion who casts you in the Shade.
> Trust your Heart.
> Know how to get your Price for Things.
> The path to Greatness is along with Others.
> Do not wait until you are a Sinking Sun.
> Cultivate those who can teach you.[16]

Gracián reminds us of the worldliness of all true wisdom, all genuine imagination. When the imagination is truly alive, it is *vital*. It blazes in palpable forms and beauty. It is a gaudy, voluptuous, ambitious act that reawakens sleeping essences. Gracián keeps imaginal man bound to the stinks and scuffles of the city.

In his essay "The Theory and Play of the Duende," the murdered poet Federico García Lorca has captured the meaning of this South, doing so in a lush and chiseled prose style that strains toward the condition of a lyric. Duende, according to the poet, is the soul of Spain. It is the nerve, spine, pulse, and gaze. Duende generates Spain's anguish and elation. How do we get duende?

> There is no map nor method to use in seeking the duende. All that is known is that the blood is burned by a river of broken glass that exhausts—and makes one forget all the sweet geometry he once knew; it rips apart style. It makes Goya, that master of silver, rose, and gray in the best English style, paint on his hands and knees

in tones of pitch black. It strips Mosén Cinto Verdaguer
with the cold of the Pyrenees and takes Jorge Manrique
to the Paramo of Ocaña to await death and dresses the
delicate body of Rimbaud in a green jester's suit and
makes the eyes of dead fish appear on the face of Count
Lautreamont at dawn in the boulevard.[17]

Duende irrupts as well in Ortega's two horned bull and the Mi-
notaur of Picasso, bellowing with rage. And if duende is the bull,
duende is also the matador, for whom, as Ordóñez says "each bull is
a world."

Without a doubt, Diego Mazquiarán Fortuna is one of
the best matadors that has been or ever will be recorded
in the history of the bull fight. Possibly the best of his
time, which coincided with the best and most important of them all, in that glorious epoch of the two giants,
Joselito and Belmonte. Fortuna was a stylist, a virtuoso
of the stab of the volapie. He dominated and performed
that skill with the highest perfection. He measured the
tiempos like no one else before him. He measures the
distance demanded by the qualities of the bull and the
kill; he demonstrated his perfect understanding of the
suerte while many matadors who enjoyed a good billing
have the defect of always beginning from the same long
or short distance in the ultimate moment. All of this,
and his figure, gave a beauty and unsurpassable arrogance to his style and motivated the delirious ovations
that were so often lavished upon him.[18]

In the matador, the serene geometer of death, delicate and
poised, plumed and sworded, his inner frenzy tamed into a nerve-
less splendor, as he proudly and murderously eyes the bull, and in
the bull gazing back, beast eloquent, motionless and watchful, his
nerves like tiny flames flickering at the edge of delirious muscles,

snorting, foaming, each breath a taurine zephyr, stomping, pawing, stupendously measuring and being measured, and then the blaze of perfection, the instant when matter is all matter and the soul flames upward, here we meet the indelible essence of Southerness.

If Southerness appears in Adler, then full appreciation of the Adlerian ethos may be beyond the ken of most Americans. We always stumble over Southerness, perhaps because our nation was formed by trampling down its vineyards. Are there other reasons? Yes, because America, as the poet said, is always *North*. To the Northern mind—Protestant, Cartesian, scientific, positivistic—with its groundless assumption of superiority, its airs of divine entitlement, the South, and all the South evokes, appears threatening. And so we promptly move to disarm the threat, which we typically do by splitting the image. Rather than one single overpowering reality, which is both perilous and beautiful, and like one of Rilke's angels, were it to lean too close it would slay us; we dream up a domesticated tandem that placates fear, while propping up our senseless superiority.

On the one hand we create a *sepulchral South*. This is the land of the dead, of graves and moans and endless deserts, where everything is washed in bone white, all vitality bleached away. This land is dry and treasure-less. We imagine Spain, Italy or Mexico as derelict places, stricken by tentacular poverty, afflicted by malfeasance, corrupt officialdom. Since the law and order that is so precious to the North means nothing to the South, we imagine its life to be lawless and anarchic, succumbing to schismatic turmoil. Further we see it as a pagan land, full of voodoo, harems and weeping statues, a scene of exotic rites and rituals practiced by Greek, Roman, Inca, Catholic, Moor. But if in our dreams the South can be sepulchral, it can also be a festive place, a *fiesta South*, a source of animalizing rejuvenation. "O for a beaker of the warm South," cried Keats. This is the Spain of the Germans, the Italy of the Romantics, the Mexico of Lawrence, Artaud, Dahlberg and Olson. If the first South is Hades, the second is Pluto, in that now more than ever it seems rich to die. The fiesta South is not impoverished but is instead rich with natural treasures, cultural wealth, artistic jewels. And although the South knows nothing of the apotheosis of rational and law abiding man, of Kant and the categorical imperative, it swears obedience to a higher law, a law appealed to by Antigone long ago, a law that embodies the old verities of courage and compassion, pride and honor, family and faith. When the beaker touched by the fiesta South is raised to the lips, and the dry and wordless tongue responds to the fermenting juices of the ripening earth, then the old gods, the nameless ones who fed on cakes and honey, seem more real and more true than those who have usurped their places.

The third tributary of Adler's thought leads back through Bergson, the cultured keeper of the *élan vital*, to its source in France. This is the France of *la gloire*. Louis XIV summed up its creed.

> The ardor that we feel for *la gloire* is not one of those feeble passions that cool with possession. Her favors, which can never be obtained except with effort, never cause disgust, and he who can refrain from longing for fresh ones is unworthy of all those he has received.[19]

This is the France of Joan of Arc and Napoleon, D'Artagnan and the Count of Monte Cristo. Here we find the cuirass and the saber, the jangling spurs, the marshal's baton and the *pantaloon rouge*, the paladin, the chevalier, the France of the cavalry charge before Sedan whose splendid gallantry drew forth an astonished hurrah! from the enemy Kaiser. This is also the France where chivalry saw its finest hour, with its progeny of *preux*, that matchless vitality which, in witness to it, drew forth such bittersweet, indescribable emotion:

> "It is a joyous thing, is war...You love your comrade so in war. When you see that your quarrel is just and your blood is fighting well, tears rise to your eye. A great sweet feeling of loyalty and of pity fills your heart on seeing your friend so valiantly exposing his body to execute and accomplish the command of our Creator. And then you prepare to go and die or live with him, and for

love not to abandon him. And out of that there arises such delectation, that he who has not tasted it is not fit to say what a delight it is."[20]

And whose bright candle was ultimately darkened by the fever of the gold bug and mindless bloodletting, to be finally snuffed out at Necropolis where Saracen swords dropped heads like buckets, mowing down the knightly flower of France in vengeful execution.

If the chevalier and the sun king dwell in France, then France accommodates humanity turned hero. And what is the hero? The definition of the hero is that the hero defines himself through deeds, or rather, that definition through deeds is the only criterion that he accepts. Deeds determine being. I act, therefore, I am. Here, if only here, amid the vineyards and salons, what Goethe says is true: In the Beginning was the Deed. Sublime deeds; valorous acts; decisive strokes; the drama of events: these are the quiddities of life; all else is artifice and straw. The general may be loquacious or mute; pray or be an atheist; he may be royalist, Jacobin or Bonapartist; just so he sounds the charge. Perhaps this explains why man as hero has so often relished war, or at least warmed to those civilizations hospitable to Mars; for it is upon the battlefield, amid the roar and mutter; amid the eyes bulging and the muscles straining with the darkest inspirations of the blood, that deeds stand boldest, with uncompromising clarity, immune to the erosions of time and doubt. In battle, my fate, your fate, the fate of nations, children's souls, wholly and inarguably depend on how I act, just now, just here, in the pitiless duration of the moment. In war, the deed becomes the engine of the cosmos, the power that moves the spheres. The hero thus woos war, often with self-destructive ardor. While the bugles may fade, the echoes linger. Napoleon knew that his name would be immortal even if his soul was dust.

It is the French connection then that clarifies Adler's identification of courage as the criterion of mental health.[21]

A further happy consequence of Gallic influx is that it keeps Adlerian thinking *cosmopolitan*, which enabled him to avoid the crippling impasse of the civilization-culture conflict on which so much of German thought has run aground. The disease of this distinction first caught fire in Spengler and then spread to all of Germany. But the French stayed pure in that they have always valued culture in all its rich, destabilizing, vital and sometimes toxic ferment, to which nothing human, neither in the minds or loins, neither in the syllogism or De Sade, is alien; without at the same time opposing culture to what the instinct for culture, with all its feverish hothouse bloom, perceives to be the fossilizing tendencies of civilization. Because the French have always welcomed the dream of civilization, with its ideal of a universal language, law and liberty, while at the same time cherishing culture, they have managed to overcome the German error.

The green and glacial ethic that captivated Nietzsche; the rejuvenating Southerness of Vaihinger; Bergson's spirit: in Adler these elements unite to create something distinctive and meaningful. Though Adler steeped himself in his authorities, he authored something entirely fresh. Adler articulates a cosmopolitan psychology. *Adlerian man is urban man.*

Let us commence at once to a definition: *this Adlerian style of life* to which Adler himself alluded:

> And Individual Psychology? Has it not also its own particular conception of life? Has it not also a specific point of view regarding the behavior of the individual in his and its relation to outside problems? Of course it has. But in the first place we have tried to prove that our conception of life is more capable of objectivity than the conception of other psychologists. And secondly we know that we also are predisposed by our philosophy of life, while others do not know that they always find what they have known before.[22]

—may be defined as a heroic or chivalric form of consciousness that imagines life, in all its aspects, as a contest. As befits its French connection, the heroism is theatrical, even exhibitionist. It is scarlet

18

garbed and armed. It braves life as a gallant. The imagination is of the Italian kind, worldly, witty, more attuned to the social mystery than the celestial one. Adlerian man is courtier rather than crusader. And the contest to which it is incurably addicted, reflect their ludic, metaphorical ground in the imaginations, so that they always stay at least an ace away from lethal. We are speaking here of tilts and tournaments rather than the survival of the fittest. The assumption is that if we're always playing at war, then rarely will we need to suffer its literal enactment. If the metaphor is indestructible, perhaps this vitiates the need for actual blood and guts.

Can we hang some flesh and meat on the skeleton of this definition? Who is this urban man? Who is Adlerian man? What are his characteristic moods and typical sensations? *Urban man is that being whose ideal is a social, convivial existence* rather than profit, power or sexual fulfillment, which is another way of saying that urban man desires a life informed by social interest. He aspires to a life that is luminous and saturated with *gemeinschaftsgefuhl*. Towards the future he casts a sanguine, cheerful eye, convinced that things can't help but get a little better, while towards the past and all inherited things he shows a sincere reverence born of the hard won knowledge, a knowledge carried to the heart, of how beautiful and perilous a thing it is to create and build, and how shamefully easy it is to destroy. With women, he is amorous and courtly, while towards men he shows unfailing courtesy. He enjoys sartorial plumage but tends to be a bit untidy. Like Churchill, he will prefer silk underwear. Like Churchill, he may sleep in them. His wit is sharp and glittering; and he easily takes offense, being very jealous of his honor, which he sometimes defends obsessively, and often heroically. In bearing he is dignified and graceful, though the grace may disappear at times behind a reserved façade that may seem stilted amid unfamiliars. He genuinely respects religion, though this respect may be tinged with a wry and gentle skepticism that may unsettle the orthodox. "What religion are you?" a reporter asked Mr. Disraeli. "All gentlemen are of the same religion," responded Disraeli. "And what religion is that?" inquired the reporter. "Gentlemen never tell." His moods swing widely from ecstasy to sulks. He succumbs sometimes to impromptu euphorias. His rhythms are those of the athlete and poet and the hunger, that is, his inward climate is one of long droughts and sudden rains. He may incline toward melancholy in the absence of pretty, curious distractions. To many he may seem lazy, whereas to others the same relaxed composure will express a genius for leisure. For the basics of existence, for the sensate particulars of food and drink and flesh and conversation, he shows a special fondness, an appetite not unwilling to indulge. Perhaps nothing more delights him that a well turned phrase. His *métier* is language, but he is a learned man rather than a scholar. His library will house the classics, with a shelf crammed thick with novels. Scott and Cicero, Dumas and Castiglione. His main gift will be for sweeping synthesis rather than the depth of the minute attentions of analysis. His most sublime affection will be for friends. He thrills to scenes of chivalry and *cortesia*. He prizes tact, vitality, resourcefulness and boldness and is affronted most by the simple meanness and mean spirits who trivialize all the forms and traditions that chain time and chasten, if but ever so slightly, the tragedies of life. Pettiness dismays him, in response to which he sometimes comes unhinged. Reputation rather than conscience is his guide, whereby he keeps his self-esteem tied to the opinions of others rather than himself. To some he may seem a trifle touchy and disposed towards arrogance and distance. Shyness is the better explanation. If at times his smiles and thank you's seem painted on and false, it is a superficiality that cherishes another's feelings and comfort much more than the paltry claims of truth. His development is always a mysterious procedure. He may succumb to hero worship but these heroes will always seem alive; master spirits whose life blood animates and courageously inspires.

Let us call his chief virtue *urbanity* and risk no more than a dictionary definition.

> **urbanity** (L. *urbanitas*; cf. F. *urbanite*)
> 1. Quality or state of being urbane; courtesy of manner; politeness; suavity; refinement; hence, a civility; or

courtesy
Urbanity—the tone of the city, of the center, the tone
which always aims at a spiritual and intellectual affect,
and, not excluding the use of banter, never disjoins
banter itself from politeness; from felicity (M. Arnold)
2. State of being urbane; also urbane life
3. Urban conversation, especially when witty or factitious
Syn. – affability, courtesy, blandness
Ant. – assertiveness, crudeness, roughness

It's what Nietzsche calls "giving style to character."

One thing is needful—To "give style" to one's character—a great and rare art! It is practiced by those who
survey all the strengths and weaknesses of their nature
and then fit them into an artistic plan until every one
of them appears as art and reason and even weakness
delights the eye. Here a large mass of second nature has
been added; there a piece of originally nature has been
removed—both times through long practice and daily
work at a period. Here the ugly that could not be removed is concealed; there it has been reinterpreted and
made sublime. Much that is vague and resisted shaping
has been saved and exploited for distant views...In the
end, when the work is finished, it becomes evident how
the constraint of a single taste governed and formed everything large and small. Whether this taste was good or
bad is less important than one might suppose, if only it
was a single taste![23]

It is what Isak Dinesen called chic and found exemplified in Masai warriors—

A Masai warrior is a fine sight. Those young men have,
to the utmost extent, that particular form of intelligence

21

which we call chic;—daring, and wildly fantastical as they seem, they are still unswervingly true to their own nature, and to an imminent ideal. Their style is not an assumed manner, nor an imitation of a foreign perfection; it has grown from the inside, and is an expression of the race and its history, and their weapons and finery are as much part of their being as are a stag's antlers.[24]

Is it any wonder that the psychology of urban man should spring, or rather, renew itself, in Austria, the very name of which derives from auster, which means south wind, and where, in the soul and in the streets, Teutonic toughness mixes with the Southern Italian vivacity and joy. Vienna served also as the Eastern outpost of the Empire of Charlemagne, so Austria knows the *fleur-de-lis* as well. Just as Adlerian psychology features the ingredients of Viking, courtier, and knight, from which contents Adler melded something new, so Austria, and so Vienna, worked the same volatile and fragile alchemy from the materials of historical experience. In many ways Adler simply immortalized the achievements of the Austrian melting pot. He elevated Vienna manners into a philosophy of life. These same manners once astonished Teddy Roosevelt, who was something of an urban man himself. When asked once what had most *delighted* him (Roosevelt's favorite word) in all his many travels, the great bull moose replied: "The manners of the Austrian gentleman."

Another name for urbanity is eloquence. Hence, another name for the tradition of urban man might be the rhetorical tradition. In the aftermath of the humorless denunciations of philosophers, such as Locke:

> I confess, in discourses where we seek rather pleasure and delight than information and improvement, such ornaments as are borrowed from them can scarce pass for faults. But yet if we would speak of things as they are, we must allow that all the art of rhetoric, besides order and clearness; all the artificial and figurative ap-

plication of words eloquence hath invented, are for
nothing else but to insinuate wrong ideas, move the
passions, and thereby mislead the judgment; and so are
perfect cheats.[25]

—and Kant:

Rhetoric, so far as this is taken to mean the art of
persuasion, i.e., the art of deluding by means of a fair
semblance [as *ars oratorial*], and not merely excellence
of speech (eloquence and style), is a dialectic, which
borrows from poetry only so much as is necessary to
win over men's minds to the side of the speaker before
they have weighed the matter, and to rob their verdict
of its freedom....Force and elegance of speech (which
together constitute rhetoric) belong to fine art; but oratory [*ars oratorial*], being the art of playing one's own
purpose upon the weakness of men (let this purpose
be ever so good in intention or even in fact) merits no
respect whatever.[26]

—rhetoric is not so much in vogue today, being viewed, rather as
another name for a wash of aimless, ornate vocables that have no
purpose save delight, or instead, we perceive it, in the hands of ad-
vertising wizards, as a devilish instrument for outright manipula-
tion. By rhetoric, so we assume, mendacity and pretense outpace the
bare bones life of truth. The word itself has been so travestied as to
sack all former meaning. But once it shone with matchless glory. It
produced great names and powerful intellects. It had its advocate
and heroes. Marshall McLuhan here presents a roll call, while also
historically addressing our dilemma.

This tradition has been a continuous force in European law, letters, and politics from the time of the Greek
sophists. It is most conveniently referred to as the Cice-

ronian ideal, since Cicero gave it to St. Augustine and St. Jerome, who in turn saw to it that it has never ceased to influence western society. The Ciceronian ideal as expressed in the *De Oratore* or in St. Augustine's *De Doctrina Christiana* is the ideal of rational man reaching his noblest attainment in the expression of an eloquent wisdom. Necessary steps in the attainment of this ideal are careful drill in the poets followed by a program of encyclopedic scope directed to the forensic end of political power. Thus, the *doctus orator* is, explicitly, Cicero's sophistic version of Plato's philosopher-king. This ideal became the basis for hundreds of manuals written by eloquent scholars for the education of monarchs from the fifth century through John of Salisbury and Vincent of Beauvais to the famous treatises of Erasmus and Castiglione.[27]

McLuhan's list may be supplemented with the encyclopedists of France and the mannerists of Spain and Italy. And indeed these are great names, venerable and luminous, deserving of respect; and yet, regrettably, that is all they are, great names, whose works are little read or much remembered except through the hostile medium of philosophers who collectively stigmatize them as eclectic and derivative, endowed with cleverness and astonishing associations, but deficient in that "importance" that will repay study with a wealth of truth. As rhetoric sullies truth, so study of the rhetoricians retards the philosopher's ascent towards truth.

And yet, when these names are sounded in unison, and their correspondences are noted, we begin to suspect that more is housed here than mere cleverness. Whether in the study or on the stump, whether at parties or in parliament, these orators advanced a coherent philosophy that looked at man primarily in his political and social nature. In Adlerian language, we might say that these "philosophers" suavely, tactfully, but rigorously oriented man towards *gemeinschaftsgefuhl*. As a style of education, rhetoric emphasized the wisdom of the poets, all of the arts and forms of speech, manners and the martial skills, the training of a prodigious, expert memory, historical precepts and examples, and a broad exposure to the realities of life. The object was a sublime equipage in speech and knowledge that adapted man to social living. And when such training was by good fortune grafted onto a natural resourcefulness and savvy, the tradition flowered into the often dandified and theatrical figure of the gentleman, the sophistic philosopher-king.

> The encyclopedic ideal of "Renaissance man" was consciously and explicitly that of Cicero's orator, whether exemplified in a fourteenth-century Italian humanist, or a sixteenth-century Spenser, Sidney, or in Shakespeare's *Hamlet* or *Henry V*.[28]

By eloquence and manner, by versatility and wit, such graduates elevated politics into statesmanship, sublimed private intelligence into a corporate good.

Adler has been linked with many forbears, numberless traditions, the multiplicity of which prove nothing so much as a flaw in understanding. Mairet recalled Confucius; Way invokes Socrates; Sperber and Ansbacher lodge him with existentialist and humanist; Hillman tries to turn him into a witty Neo-Platonist; Ellenberger promotes a background in the enlightenment and Stoics; Stepansky brands him as a reactionary socialist somewhat comparable to the authoritarian socialisms found in the regions of the French rococo. I see a different Adler, Adler who is an orator—

> To begin with, I would say I was born a very weak child suffering from certain weaknesses, especially from rickets which prevented me from moving very well. Despite this obstacle, now, nearly at the end of my life, I am standing before you in America. You can see how I have overcome this difficulty. Also, I could not speak very well early in my life; I spoke very slowly. Now, though

you are probably not aware of it in my English, I am supposed to be a very good orator in German.[29]

Adler, I would argue, belongs body, heart and soul to the rhetorical tradition. But as therapist and thinker, I count him as an orator. The rhetorical tradition is the Adlerian tradition.

Historically the rhetorical tradition has been pitted against the dialectical tradition. No sooner had the sophists won the soul of Greece, than Socrates, a barefooted fat man, appeared to goad and chastise them. To the humorless ear of the dialectician the rhetorical flights of the orator seems so much gratuitous puff which true philosophy should not accommodate.

Glitter all you will, says the dialectician, but we will gild you. In place of the old rhetorical ethos the dialectician substituted an entirely different approach toward truth, a conflicting tissue of values and meanings. Whereas rhetoric aspires to be encyclopedic and eloquent, dialectic is specialized and nominalistic. Dialectic is rationalistic and logical; it prizes clarity and method; loves all that is distinct and clear. Its advance toward truth is step by step, based on verifiable evidence ordered by logic and whatever it discovers dialectic is content to cram into a lumbering, spiritless prose style that envies mathematics more than literature. The battle between rhetor and dialectician surged for over two millenniums. It is Sophist against Socrates; humanist against scholastic; ancient against modern. As McLuhan writes,

> ...these...two radically opposed intellectual traditions...have been warring since Socrates turned dialectics against the rhetoric of his Sophist teachers. Socrates turned from rhetoric to dialectics, from forensics to speculation and definition, raising the issue which pitted Plato and Aristotle against their formidable rival Isocrates, and which pitted the forensic Cicero against Carneades and the Stoics. The same quarrel as to whether grammar and rhetoric, on the one hand, or dialectics,

on the other, should have precedence in organizing the
hierarchy of knowledge is the key to an understanding of the Renaissance from the twelfth to the seventeenth centuries. Just when the quarrel, both within the
Catholic Church and outside it, was reaching its term,
representatives of both parties in the quarrel migrated
to America. The schoolmen went to New England, the
quasi-humanist gentry to Virginia.[30]

For most of our history, the outcome of this struggle has seemed
in doubt. Rhetoric triumphed for a while; then dialectic returned to
conquer. But during the modern epoch, dialectic has seemed to de-
cisively win the upper hand, which it has done, in part, through the
rise of modern science, but the decisive blow was struck, perhaps,
by Gutenberg, in that it was the dissemination of the rapid and swift
and universal possibilities of print medium which has structured
consciousness in such a way as to make the assumptions of dialectic appear to be the very definition and condition of consciousness.
And yet, this victory too may be provisional, because the preeminence of print has more and more been relativized by a recrudes-
cence of the old rhetoric made possibly by the invention and spread
of new technologies in which the ear and hand figure as centrally
as the eye.

So the battle perhaps is always with us. Psychology resurrects
it in the guise of the controversy between Freud and Adler. On so
many issues and even more so, in manner and style, Freud enacts
the dialectical agenda in the tradition of Copernicus and Darwin,
whereas Adler speaks for rhetoric. Freud's values rehearse the values of dialectic, whereas Adler's sympathies echo the rhetorical attitude. And thus, Freud's presumed superiority over Adler may con-
ceivably reflect a mutable historical condition, which is the triumph
of dialectic over rhetoric. If in our age the preeminence of print is
truly fading as our culture grows increasing disenchanted with the
constraints of what appears to be a superannuated world view, than
Adler assumes a fresh importance. He may emerge in time as victor

over Freud, though even a smattering of historical consciousness reveals that such a victory cannot hope to be permanent.

And yet, insofar as psychology is concerned, the conflict between Adler and Freud, rhetoric and dialectic, may be something of a detour that obscures the real conflict, the ominous and destructive one, which is the battle between the orator and the magi, between the rhetorical and hermetic tradition. The issue may be posed as Adler versus Jung (and in this battle Freud may be conscripted as an ally). The danger here is especially acute because in so many dimensions rhetoric and magic blur and overlap, so that in both we find the same emphasis on story, history, memory and speech. But oratory and magic are not identical, not in the philosophy nor in their history as Frances Yeats makes clear.

> I must first of all define what I mean by "the humanist tradition." I mean the recovery of the Latin texts, of the literature of Roman civilisation in the Renaissance, and the attitude to life and letters which arose out of that recovery. Though it had many antecedents in the Middle Ages, the chief initiator of this movement, so far as the Italian Renaissance is concerned, was Petrarch. The recovery of the Latin texts, the excitement about the new revelation of classical antiquity which they brought, belongs to the fourteenth century and continues into the fifteenth century. It was very well advanced and had reached a stage of sophistication *before* the next great experience of the Renaissance—the recovery of the Greek texts and their ensuing new philosophical revelation in the fifteenth century. It cannot, I think, be sufficiently emphasized that these two Renaissance experiences are of an entirely different order, using different sources in a different way, and making their appeal to different sides of the human mind. Let us draw up some comparisons...

The two traditions appeal to entirely different interests. The humanist's bent is in the direction of literature and history; he sets an immense value on rhetoric and good literary style. The bent of the other tradition is towards philosophy, theology, and also science (at the stage of magic). The difference reflects the contrast between the Roman and the Greek mind. Again, in the Latin humanist tradition, the dignity of man has quite another meaning from that which it has in the other tradition. For Poggio Bracciolini, the recovery of dignity consists in casting off bad medieval Latin and dreary medieval and monastic ways of life, and the attempt to emulate in his person and surroundings the social pre-eminence, the sophisticated grandeur, of a noble Roman. For Pico, the dignity of man consists of man's relation to God, but more than that in Man as Magnus with the divine creative power.[31]

The philosophical and historical gulf that separates oratory from magic is too immense ever to be spanned.

We now return to Adler as a reader. If Adler read as an orator, then how do orators read? The answer to the question will naturally reveal something about Adler. If urban men aspired to an encyclopedic learning, then the question arises: how did they acquire such learning?—other than the dear school of experience. In other words, what method formalized their madness? They learned by reading and by developing a consistent style of reading which was structured by a specific objective. *Urban man reads for power!* One masters a text, or samples it, in order to ingest its life stuff.

Devouring is truly the appropriate word. Of course, a certain savagery accompanies this, together with the priceless courtesy of men in combat. The style originated with the Sophists who also typify it, in that instead of reading the poets either as oracles of truth or erring fables (which is the duty of the "true" philosopher to obliterate or else interpretatively redeem), the Sophist honored the poets as savvy, knowledgeable authorities on life. For the Sophists, the great Homeric epics served as metrical encyclopedias into which, besides the virtuoso cadences and dazzling similes, were lodged an entire system of ethics, politics, history, religion, and even technology, so that from study of them one could harvest all the formulas of love and war. The poets yielded information as diverse and necessary as how to ship a cargo, pour libations, forge a sword, make love, make war, make peace. Alexander read for power when each night, amid the silks and crackling camp flames, he bedded down with the heroes of the *Iliad* whose example filled him with an unconquerable ambition that did not dim until it had civilized the world. During the reign of the jade eyed Fairy Queen, when Essex and Raleigh flourished, men likewise read for power:

> The age of Shakespeare was not addicted to education. It had little Latin and less Greek, more of Italian and French. It read books avidly but rapidly, rushing to test them with experience. It went to school to live, and talked back to its teacher with unheard-of insolence.[32]

Montaigne belongs to this breed when he writes:

> In books I only look for the pleasure of honest entertainment; or if I study, the only learning I look for is that which tells me how to know myself, and teaches me how to die well and to live well.[33]

While also revealing too much of its habits:

> When I meet with difficulties in my reading, I do not bite my nails over them; after making one or two attempts I give them up. If I were to sit down to them, I should be wasting myself and my time; my mind works at the first leap. What I do not see immediately, I see even less by

persisting. Without lightness I achieve nothing; application and over-serious effort confuse, depress, and weary my brain. My vision becomes blurred and confused. I must look away, and then repeatedly look back; just as in judging the brilliance of a scarlet cloth, we are told to pass the eye lightly over it, glancing at it several times in rapid succession. If one book bores me, I take up another; and I turn to reading only at such times as I begin to be tired of doing nothing. I do not take easily to the moderns, because the ancients seem to me fuller and more virile; nor to the Greeks...[34]

By defining even interpretation itself as a form of the will to power, Nietzsche celebrates this creed.

Because urban man aspires to power, he especially prizes history and poetry. "History is my favorite pursuit, or poetry, for which I have a special affection," Avers Montaigne. For urbanity, history is a toil and a delight. In the first place, history is a great laboratory in which numberless experiments have been performed, with the results available to every eye that cares to linger. Every strategy and character has been tried. Every success and failure is recorded. History, therefore can teach us about what succeeds; what fails; what miscarries; what aborts. It kindly offers guidance in all affairs. But history does more than save time and testing because it also blazes with lofty tales and fabulous examples whose very lives were such as to quicken our pace along the brilliant paths of virtue and of courage. It whispers, cajoles, exhorts, commands. By precept and example, it catalyzes valor; prowess; courage; nobility; magnificent largesse. After reading Plutarch, Heine said he felt like sweeping up on a stallion to ride forth and conquer France. And even when history fails as inspiration, it always succeeds as warning; for, if nothing else, knowledge of the past frees us from the bondage and the doom of mindless repetition.

As we said, urbanity woos poetry as well, but to what advantage? First poetry consumes us because of the splendor of its phrases. So often what was wordlessly felt and meant and daringly intended is bodied forth in poetry with such a spirit and precision that it indelibly impresses memory; and though memory loses many things rarely does it forfeit the embryonic cogitation perfected in an immortal phrase. This has the obvious reward of supplying us with a glittering stock of images and sayings that enliven social intercourse. But we profit mortally too, for when the sentiment is noble and the poem is true, then recollection of it is intrinsically ennobling. Often it is the memory of a line or commonplace phrase that functions as the pillar of the soul during days of crisis. Thinking also profits, in that so much of thinking is an effort, a plodding climb up endless stairs, which we ourselves must first construct out of the intractable materials of language. By giving us so many of these stairs already made and polished, poetry can convert that climb into a gracious and nimble ascent. Thought grows spry and sportive. Do we not, perhaps, misread the Middle Ages when we assume the syllogism to be a point of logic rather than a poem? Perhaps the most sublime logic is the most beautiful poem, which is a datum towards which we may be tentatively groping in an age when it becomes increasingly difficult to draw a frontier between a Wittgenstein, say, and Ezra Pound.

Further, there are the psychological enhancements available through the conduit of rhythm. The first effect of rhythm is a lotus-seating one: it allays our darkest fears and most anguished torments. Under the rhythmic sway and chant, the repetitious motions, our muscles gradually relax; the dispirited, harried soul begins to peacefully uncoil. As the tartness dissipates, so too do the more imprisoning of our constraints, the ones we impose upon ourselves so as to maintain our fronts of flawless affable conformity, which releases both our angels and our devils, but our devils here are artfully contained, the savage beast is soothed, so that only our angels are left to crowd the solitary air. By reading poetry, by delivering ourselves up to the charming lullaby of iambs, the gallop of an anapest or the solemnity of spondees, we spontaneously self-medicate, where after the consequence is nearly uniformly a heighted-renewed vitality.

The oratorical, the Elizabethan, the troubadours, the Adlerian style of reading is to read for power. But this is not power as transcendence or power as control, but power as *gemeinschaftsgefuhl*, the power to serve the sovereign and the city. It is the power to bring learning into life, form into matter, so enlightenment into the world. As an emblem for this style of reading, let us turn to Dante and to the second circle of the inferno where Dante and his master, Virgil, encounter Paulo and Francesca who, with dazzle poignancy and life recount their tragic tale while tossed about by ceaseless winds.

> No greater grief than to remember days
> Of joy when misery is at hand...
> One day for our delight we read of Lancelot,
> How him loved thralled.
> Alone we were, and no
> Suspicion near us.
> Ofttimes by that reading
> Our eyes were drawn together, and the hue
> Fled from our altered cheek
> But at one point
> Alone we fell. When of that smile we read,
> The wished smile, so rapturously kissed
> By one so deep in love, than he, who ne'er
> From me shall separate, at once my lips
> All trembling kissed. The book and writer both
> Were love's prevailers. In its leaves that day
> We read no more.[35]

Let us take beautiful Francesca as an image of the soul itself, and see in Paulo an image of the ambition of the world; and let us see in the pages of the chivalric tale an image of the kind of stylized, passionate, and empowered style of reading by which the two unite.

———

Having shown that Adler was a reader, we can now read Adler, as he read his *authorities*, that is, not as a dead letter but as a live spirit, having situated Adler in a tradition, let us now address his theory about which he writes quite clearly—

> The sense of inferiority, the struggle to overcome, and social feeling—the foundations upon which the researches of Individual Psychology are based—are therefore essential in considering either the individual or the mass.[36]

Adler's *archai* then are *inferiority, social interest* and the *striving for significance*. They are his "commonplaces"; his rhetorical *topoi*. In terms of them he conceptualized the dynamics of the individual, culture and ultimately the cosmos itself. Clearly, then, to understand Adler requires comprehension of these three principles in all their amplitude and scope.

Inferiority, first, because it was first with Adler. As background for our considerations, let me collate a few passages:

> The method of Individual Psychology—we have no Hesitation in contesting it—begins and ends with the problem of inferiority.[37]
>
> Inferiority feelings are in some degree common to us all....[38]
>
> But the feeling of inferiority is not a disease, it is rather a stimulant to healthy normal striving and development.[39]
>
> The feeling of inferiority rules the mental life and can be clearly recognized in the sense of incompleteness and unfullfillment, and in the uninterrupted struggle both of individuals and of humanity.[40]
>
> ...the historical movement of humanity is to be regarded as the history of its feeling of inferiority and of its efforts to find a solution of its problems.[41]

Indeed it seems to me that all our human culture is based upon feelings of inferiority.[42]

A long time ago I emphasized the fact that to be a human being means to feel oneself inferior.[43]

Though returning again and again to the theme of *inferiors*, as these passages reveal, Adler's most brilliantly radical excursion into inferiority occurs already in his first book, *The Study of Organ Inferiority*, where Adler's reflections are governed by the image of the *organs*. Even in his later formulations, which at times seemed Delphic in their opacity and richness, the image of the organs persist as a kind of guiding fiction or root metaphor. Perhaps, then by imagining the organs and their significance we best absorb the full nutrient of Adler's thought.

So what then are the organs? Imagine. First, the organs are the freaks of the body. At the level of the organs we are all grotesque; all misshapen creatures, horrendous cosmic parodies of our proper form. Even though our surface glamour be almost flawless, with every hair in place, with every wrinkle smoothed, somewhere, in the recesses of the body, we all conceal a hunchback liver or a cleft-lipped lung. In his presentation of the organs Adler appears the Velasquez of the body, the painter whose eyes dwell on the deformities of the human flesh and whose sensitive pen illuminates them. To enter, with Adler as our guide, into the fleshly wilderness of what we cannot see, is to pass behind the carney's curtain, where amid the urine scented sawdust and the glass jars of pickled country spontaneous abortions, we gawk at hairless wonders, alligator men, great mustachioed fat ladies, armless rubber men. In uncovering the inferiorities of the organs Adler recovered the freak that is the nucleus of psychological life; he rejoined the elephant man to the company of the living.

Second, the organs compose a supersensible realm. Under normal circumstances, this "world," his "region" can't be touched, sensed, smelt or eyeballed, except by violating some unconsciously

35

acknowledged norm. What, really, is more shocking to the senses: the visitation of a "spirit" or the graphic spectacle of open heart surgery? Like heaven, perhaps, in some sense, the space of the organs— the heart and kidneys, the liver and the gut—are simple *there*, not *here*, co-present and co-existing with us, but always someplace else. A great divide disjoins us, a divide as impassable as the one separating life and death, mortals and immortals. In this place that is no place, that is, within the "insides" of our own body, there swells a pandemonium of powers, impalpable entities, existing beyond the reach and government of the will. Like gods, these "belong," never taste the indignity of normal food, but instead feed upon the refined essences of the earth transmitted to them through the blood. And like the gods their only superior is fate. And further like the gods, the organs do not stay within their own world, but instead move back and forth, ascending and descending into our dimension, where, sometimes they merely go bump in the night, emitting rumbles of some insistent moveable feast, while at other times, they do come for us via the sharp sting, thud, choke of a heart attack or the convulsive agonies of cancer, and transport us into their own realm where there is nothing save the wordless rhythms of the earth. The organs are completely and overwhelmingly autonomous. The inner sanctum of the body, the world of pulsing tissue, stuffed with quivering meat, is truly a great beyond, an invisible world, more so even than the heavens perhaps, with the organs sometimes transcending even gods, since most of us would claim some special revelation about the goings on in heaven while being more than happy to admit our dismal ignorance of the habits of the kidney. We know more about the gods than we do our livers. Though Moses looked upon God face to face, who has had a similar experience with their liver?

Third, the organs have a sacred character. In eons past the gods themselves were thought to dwell on the subterranean depths of the viscera—gods whom the Egyptian priests preserved by embalming the organs in temple jars. In the West the soul was housed in the liver, while in the East, where the Tao prevailed, it was seated in the kidney. The organs transformed the body into a divine ground, a sacred space upon which we trespass at our peril. The body is Artemis, a Medusa, whose naked, seething insides must be protected from unsanctified excursions. Because of the organs the body becomes a temple, as it was for St. Paul, a vessel rich with sacred fluids. It is a cave, each bodily orifice a sacred cave where a priestess raves and mysteries dwell. As in Norse and Chinese mythologies, the body itself becomes a cosmos, the giant divine stuff out of which the world was made, great chunks of flesh molded by the morning gods into visible geography.

Fourth, the organs belong to the opaque, material zone of the body where the body is a garden of delight, desire, sensation and disease. This is the body that breeds and breathes, squats and straightens, stuffs in, voids. It is the body ruefully remembered by Delmore Schwartz as the heavy bear that goes with me, and rhapsodically proclaimed by Robert Duncan as the sacred body. Not only do the organs belong to the body, they are synonymous with the body. They *are* the body as stuff and secretion. Further this stuff is the body as *nothing but* body—the body in its most brutish, mindless, inanimate form where it approaches the condition of a machine so that machines can sometimes do duty for the organs. If the organs had eyes those eyes would be the vacant stare of those whose lives had been reduced to maintenance by machines.

Fifth, there is something tremendously and sensually auto-erotic in the inferior organ, so that it comes to resemble a flesh-sunk, invisible narcissus who is always wordlessly enraptured with the dazzle of his image. A habitual pleasure seeker, it remains impervious to the necessity of work. As Adler says, the inferior organ shirks culture: in the case of the inferiority of the organ, the participation of the organ and its activity in the demands of culture remain behind. The function then does not follow the required cultural paths, but is predominantly engaged in pleasure seeking. Lush and pulpy, tropical and Southern, the secret life of the inferior organ is very much, I suspect, like life along the Ganges, with its polymorphous gods, its mass of filth and beauty, its sensual magic and torpid rhythms and its hum of self-absorption in the alchemy of the self.

Sixth, inferiority evokes the family. Our inferiority reaches us through the family, through our inheritance of inferior organs. Our families reach us, live in us as inferiorities. Before the family is a system or a sociological fact or a moral good, the family lives as an inferior organ, a fate or destiny, handed down through generations. The family lives as a thin skin, weak liver, hair lip, flat breast, small penis, a defect in the heart. We are all branches on a family tree, sons of our fathers, members of a royal house. We are all Claudians, Antonines, Stuarts, Tudors; we all have the Hapsburg lip; the extravagance of the Wittelsbachs; the madness of the Merovingians. Inferiority reminds us that relatives aren't really relatives at all; instead they're absolutes.

Seventh, next come the Dead. Our organs house the dead. Through the organs, through our inherited inferiorities, the dead come to reach us, milling, teeming, thronging, begging for a chance to taste the blood, the fat ripe sweetness of our lives. Every inferiority is a chalice from which the dead draw sustenance. In struggling with our organ weaknesses we are like Jacob wrestling with an angel or a daimon or a thing, a sacred wound.

Eighth, the organs speak of Fate. Through the organs comes a fate and snares us. The character of our organs is our fate. The organs then are like Dame Fortune, or the Norns who sit under the World Ash; Clotho, Lachesis, Atropos, shaping, spinning, binding, weaving our lives into eternal images, the indestructible patterns of *heimarne*. They are the incurable, unchanging, timeless ground of human nature.

Ninth, the organs speak. The kidneys spell. The heart enthuses. If the psyche is a muse, then every organ is a poet, a blind rhapsode who bodies forth some wordless essence. Sometimes this language is sharp, crude, bold, unsavory as in the sulphurous fuming of a fart; while, in other lighter moments, it stains toward lyric as in the timid, pretty blush that stains the cheek. In the organs mutterings—the burps, gurgles, flushes and secretions, the terrible deformities, the maladaptive functions—Adler heard something more than meaningless errata. Instead he heard the elements of a speech, that is, a language that could with patience, and through practice be convincingly deciphered. The random forms and happenings express the totalities of life, so that blocked bowels often spell closed minds; a lazy penis, a detumescent fantasy; in the gasp of asthma we might hear a suffocating spirit; sapped muscles bespeak lost courage; weeping sores an inner sadness; itching skin a desire to get going; etc. Organs then are misrepresented by saying that they speak because they themselves are speech.

May I sum up then? For Adler, inferiority evokes the freak, the monstrous obscene part of us that comes sniveling or down on all fours; it consists of the supersensible; claims a sacred character; lives close to the stench filled richness of the body; is aflame with desire, autoeros, the dazzle of the glass; constellates the eternal verities, the great cosmic themes of fate and family and especially death, the ancient being whose blazing torch points downward; and, finally, inferiority has a tongue, its own language, rich, rude, perversely irrepressible.

When inferiority is imaged in this way, it corresponds to what in the Jungian tradition has been called soul or psychic. According to the Jungians, the realm of the soul is the realm of the gods. Like the organs, the gods were sometimes freakish; supersensible, sacred, the mediums of fate, etc. At the same time Adler's idea of inferiority closely approximated what the Existentialist call death in that both were somehow holes in being, images of the Void and darkness.

Perhaps, then, in this regard, Adlerians, Jungians and Existentialists share a common ground in their conceptions. And yet it seems to me inferiority is the superior formulation, more precise and durable. By speaking of inferiority, we avoid the spiritual inflation that is often promoted by the idea of soul. Soul may be too grandiose a term. Further inferiority maintains the focus on the Now of present experience whereas we can only have knowledge of our death, we can experience our inferiority, the immediate sensation of a flaw within our strength.

Nevertheless I want to stress the commonality of views between these various perspectives, so as a compromise I propose to adopt the term psyche following Adler's note in a letter to Lou, where I identify psyche with inferiority. Inferiority then is Adler's name for psyche, that dominate in our nature that creates freakishness and narcissism, that is involved with body, fate, family and death, and finally speaks its own language.

The second idea is social interest or gemeinschaftsgefuhl. Let me again begin by collating relevant passages.

> It takes a certain effort to throttle one's social interest, to push it aside.[44]

> Social interest is not inborn but it is an innate potentiality which has to be consciously developed. We are unable to trust any so-called "instinct."[45]

> Freud starts with the assumption that by nature man only wants to satisfy his drives—the pleasure principle— and must therefore, from the viewpoint of culture be regarded as completely banned...Individual Psychology, on the other hand, states that the development of man... is subject to the redeeming influence of social interest, so that all his drives can be guided in the direction of the general useful. The indestructible destiny of the human species is social interest...man is inclined toward social interest, toward the good...if one has clearly comprehended this difference, one will not be able to think that these two theories have anything more in common than a few words. That much any theory has in common with any dictionary.[46]

> Social interest is an intrinsic part of our extending interest in the surroundings.[47]

> It is almost impossible to exaggerate the value of an increase in social interest. The mind improves...the feeling of worth and value is heightened, giving courage in an optimistic view, and there is a sense of acquisition in the common advantages and drawbacks of our lot. The individual feels at home in life and feels his existence to

be worthwhile just so far as he is useful to others and is overcoming common, instead of private feelings of inferiority.[48]

...difficult children, neurotics, psychotics, suicides, criminals, prostitutes, alcoholics, sexual deviants...are all characterized by a lack of social interest.[49]

Social interest is the barometer of a child's normality. The criterion which needs to be watched...is the degree of social interest which the child or adult manifests.[50]

The feeling of belonging together, the social feeling... extends in favorable cases not only to the family members, but also to the clan, the people, all of humanity. It may even...extend to animals, plants and inanimate objects, ultimately to the cosmos at large.[51]

Social interest means...feeling with the whole, *sub specie aeternitatis*. It means a striving for a form of community...as...if humanity had reached the goal of perfection. It is never a present-day community or society, nor a political or religious form.[52]

From this collection, social interest emerges as an extravagant idea. It is a queer concept, at the very least. With a touch of melodrama, Adler introduced it as "that for which philosophy has no name." Back from the horrors of a military hospital; lounging with friends amid the darkening and rubble of a once proud civilization; the lights lambent; the evening chilled; the cakes and coffee rationed, Adler announced a major ideational shift: no longer would he waver between Marx and Nietzsche but instead would henceforth orient his though in accord with a new concept: social interest, *gemeinschaftsgefuhl*. The innovation irked the brainier of his colleagues. They judged the notion awkward, jejune, unstately; while behind their flurry of objections cowered a fear of intellectual dethronement at the hands of so egalitarian a notion. The Marxists too were awfully nonplussed, since such a cracker-barrel concept could hardly fuel sufficient indignation to rouse the masses. But against the winds of dissension and disappointment, Adler held firm: *gemeinschaftsgefuhl* would serve as goal and guide.

When presented in the guise of "that for which philosophy has no name"; social interest resembles Derrida's *undecideables* or the *savage being* of Merleau-Ponty, both of which are spirited excursions beyond the borders of philosophy, raids on the inarticulate. Like an *undecidable*—the *pharmakon*, graft or *difference*, social interest is a mocking, happy, visionary spirit, pregnant with Lost Dutchman's treasure, that haunts Adler's system, destabilizing orthodoxies, disarming certainties, barring seriousness, so that all stays gilded with irony and humor. And also like the *undecideables*, social interest arises out of the effort to think through and beyond dualism, in this case a dualism which Adler had himself constructed—I refer to the inferiority-superiority paradigm. Jonathon Culler's close analysis of Derrida's strategies may very well be a window into the workings of Adler's mind during these critical months.

> To sum up, one might say that to deconstruct an opposition, such as presence / absence, speech / writing, philosophy / literature, literal / metaphorical, central / marginal, is not to destroy it, leaving a monism according to which there would be *only* absence or writing or literature, or metaphor, or marginality. To deconstruct an opposition is to undo and displace it, to situate it differently.[53]

As social interest is a marginal concept, so it has only marginal success. It is in part successful, because it unsettles Adler's thought. It adds the jolt and crackle necessary to resist embalming as has befallen Freud and Jung. Adlerian psychology has not as yet attained the status of officialdom. But it is also in part a failure in that the foundation on which all of Adler's system ostensibly reposes is in fact a swampy, shifting mass, about as dependable as a punch line. The consequence is a complete monstrosity. Social interest really is a monstrous notion, but in this too it emulates the undecideables. As Derrida explains:

> Here there is a kind of question, let us still call it histori-cal, whose *conception, formation, gestation,* and *labor* we are only catching a glimpse of today. I employ these words, I admit, with a glance towards the operations of childbearing—but also with a glance toward those who, in a society from which I do not exclude myself, turn their eyes away when faced by the as yet unnamable which is proclaiming itself and which can do so, as is necessary whenever a birth is in the offing, only under the species of the nonspecies, in the formless, mute, in-fant, and terrifying form of monstrosity.[54]

Let us say that social interest slouches.

Monstrous, or invented by monsters? Rather than one of Der-rida's undecideables or the pseudo-poetry of phenomenology, might we not prefer to think of social interest as a poetical character, in-vented by one of Vico's Titans, muscled and endowed with a vigor-ous imagination? Social interest is a glyph, a beam, a visionary pil-lar whose purpose is empowerment, the empowerment that springs from the clap of thunder and shaft of light that together discloses some fresh and unsuspected feature of reality. Social interest really is the punch line of Adlerian psychology.

The psycho-genesis of the term in Adler's thought and work re-flects a central ambiguity. It bred up slowly and eclectically. With his customary thoroughness, Ansbacher[55] shows that Adler waffled about its meaning sans any final reconciliation. During the first stage of his career—roughly 1928-1937—which corresponds with a hur-ried, active engagement with the city—public lectures, case demon-strations, the founding of child guidance centers, Adler conceived of social interest as a counter-force to the will to power. It played *yin* to power's *yang*. Where its enlightenment prevailed, the will to power submitted to a greater good, the life of the community. But to tentacular and aggrandizing was the will to power, that Adler feared that social interest would often bow, or else be throttled. We might say that in these early years Adler was still working more or less psychodynamically.

During later years, when he was shuttling back and forth from America, Adler re-arranged his thought so as to accent the cognitive element of social interest. Discarding psychodynamics, he matured as a cognitive psychologist. The shift dates from a crucial power where he identified social interest with empathy and identification.[56] In this fresh conception, social interest crystallizes as an innate aptitude that must be consciously developed so as to confer direction on an ethically neutral striving for perfection. Failure to develop this attitude mars existence with neurosis, so that the definition of neurosis is an underdevelopment of social interest, which is reversible by encouragement.

The porous, indeterminate condition of Adler's thought delights the leftist who considered it decisive proof of his authoritarian disposition. If the sense of *gemeinschaftsgefuhl* is allowed to remain wholly indeterminate, then the outcome of the development of social interest implies only a flawlessly submissive conformity to existing institutions, with their racism, inequalities, educational institutions, with their racism, inequalities, educational pabulum and unjust laws. No, no Adlerians say, "social interest aspires to an ideal community." "So what?" shoot back the leftists. "Still, you must be specific. You must construct a model as has every political thinker since Plato and Aristotle. Give us a utopia if you wish, but even that utopia must have names and places, identifiable institutions, normative laws." If the virtuous action is defined as one conditioned by social interest, and if social interest equates with the interest of the community, then in the absence of an descriptive model from which we might take our bearings, the development of social interest means little more than "Slaves, obey your masters." The transcendentalists are happy too, since it allows them to audaciously enthuse with bogus metaphysics. They applaud its sorcery. Farau even yokes Adler to Jung.[57]

The transcendentalist impulse converts social interest into a Coca Cola commercial in which everybody sings.

The Marxists say social interest signifies nothing. The transcendentalists respond that it incorporates everything, a dreamy measure of our discontent. They are two sides of the same coin.

I take a different tack. It seems to me that we touch the root of the matter by shifting our attention from form to function, from information to process. What Adler consistently stressed through his long career was the *civilizing function* of social interest. The development of social interest heightens all the civil virtues. What then is the content of social interest? Its content is symbolic. *Gemeinschaftsgefuhl* is *topoi*, a piece of rhetoric, an image, a symbol; it is the high talk of rhetoric. Quickening and animating the "idea" of social interest is the image of the *urbs*, of *urbs* as *orbs*, the eternal city, the City that traditionally symbolizes the formal perfection, the good life, for which all men ache. Thus Adler's vision of *gemeinschaftsgefuhl* fuses with the City of God in Revelation, which glows with a mass of gold and precious gems; with Blake's visionary London; with the living City that Wordsworth glimpsed from atop Westminster Bridge:

> This City now doth, like a garment, wear
> The beauty of the morning, silent bare,
> Ships, towers, domes, theaters, and temples lie
> Open unto the fields, and to the sky;
> All bright and glittering in the smokeless air.

With the golden trees and mechanical birds of Yeats' Byzantium; with Eliot's "infinitely tender, gentle thing"; with Pound's city of Dioce "whose terraces are stars": with Auden's "well-marbled cities";

with the Earthly City, heavenly city of Robert Duncan; with the "civil beauty" of Robert Kelly, that "clean, passionate order of words." As these poets unitedly confess, simple contemplation of the image of the City is intrinsically ennobling. The *City*: contemplation of it can arouse the most beautiful, passionate, ardent heroics from the most prosaic breast. For the sake of Athens or of Sparta, for the glory that was Rome, for Paris burning, or London bombed, men and women have often made the most supreme of sacrifices, dying face down in the mud. Thus the appeal to social interest is an appeal to the best part of our natures, to the lion and the lamb in man.

It should come as no surprise that Adler should resurrect the City as the cornerstone of his thought, for Adler was a quintessential Viennese. To understand Adler we must imaginatively fly back in time to the city of Old Vienna. Adler came of age during a span of years (1880-1900) when Vienna stood at the peak of European civilization. The other great capitals—Paris, Rome, Berlin, London—could only bow before her. Vienna shone with an eminence that the Great War would blot out. Under the sometimes cumbersome machinery established by the old Emperor, whose whiskers, sober habits, fortitude in the face of tragedy, and saintly dedication to duty, was a standard for all of Europe—certainly warranted the dynasty a better fate than the doom that eventually befell it—Vienna flourished as a nucleus of culture, commerce, beauty.

For centuries, amid threat and turmoil, the University kept alive the flame of knowledge, faithfully passing on its torch. By Adler's time, it stood at the forefront of learning. It typified the very spirit of scientific research, which was then advancing on all fronts. The Viennese home reinforced this cultural supremacy, since as often as not the drawing room was a place where music and artful conversation commingled and excelled. Commerce thrived in Vienna. Her banks, which were the most trusted in all of Europe, bulged with the fruits of vision, shrewdness and common sense. If the Viennese possessed anything as a congenital endowment, it was common sense. The beauty of Viennese women, together with their skill in all the arts of courtesy and love, won the city fame as well. Beauty everywhere met the eye. Archdukes glittered in the streets, where attired in full uniform, with jingling spurs and rattling sabers, they escorted their ladies to ballrooms almost magical in their beauty. Diamonds sparkled; mirrors flashed; colors gleamed; waltzes pulsed at midnight. And though the Viennese aristocrat might be singled out by noble birth or massive riches, he was bound both by common faith and humor to cab-driver and cook.

Fellow feeling prevailed. The Viennese were a civilized folk, even at the poorest levels. The Viennese appeared exempt from the envy and bigotry which often over took their Northern cousins. Tolerance and freedom was the rule rather than the exception.

If the city shone, it shone most brightly in the cafés that lined the streets. Here tables would be pulled together to speed the spread of delicious gossip—aristocratic scandals, duels, love affairs and suicides—and here the humor would fly from lip to lip while glasses clinked, a waiter hovered near, and coffee brewed, thick, rich, fragrant. Adler loved the cafés: the rituals of quip and drink absorbed him and warmed his genius rather than distracting him. He spent so much time in the cafés, repairing there at every opportunity that friends fretted that he might leave the wrong impression with his students. But Adler paid no heed: he never wavered in his love for the cafés and for the friends who flocked there to share a joke or to profit from a parable. During Adler's student years, he could be found in a cheap café near the University. Then after graduation, he shifted to the Café Dom which served as a haunt for struggling intellectuals. Later years saw him as a regular first at the Café Central, where poets and scientists mixed too, and then, to the scandal of his more proper colleagues, to the Whiff of Tobacco. Finally Adler took to the Café Sill, where the crowds who came to hear him could be accommodated.

Love—such a strange and overrated word, bandied about with so much fake enthusiasm. But Adler did love Vienna. In beautiful, eloquent language, Phyllis Bottome recalls his last day at Salmannsdorf:

Often in those lonely New York years, in his hotel sitting room, close to the great hurricane of Broadway, the silent hills and the blue and silver Danubian plain must have flashed upon Adler's "inward eye which is the bliss of solitude."

My husband and I, at his request, spent his last day at Salmannsdorf with him. Adler never *shared* his sadness with his friends; still I think he liked to have them with him when he *was* unhappy. It was summer-time, and the mountains were close and clear; Vienna shone like a handful of jewels flung carelessly out upon the smooth green plain.

We spent most of the day in the garden. A spoilt little boy of five years old, who was staying in the house, clung to us, although Adler took very little apparent notice of him.

There were many things that Adler had to settle up, and give away; but the sunny hours seemed long. To my husband he gave his most treasured book of collected songs; and to the writer the last of his roses.

When we left, the little boy ran after us down the road, crying out to Adler: "Come back—and stay forever!" ... After the Nazis took possession of Vienna, Salmannsdorf was left empty—hat house and garden which was once the house most populated and most prized, most thought of and planned for, most visited and used for giving, in or about Vienna, stands now "like a forsaken bird's nest filled with snow."

After he had left it, Adler never again possessed a home, nor did he return to Vienna. From this time on, he had no "continuing city" until his far-flung pilgrimage came to its abrupt and peaceful close.[58]

In asserting the ennobling power of contemplation of the City, Adler merely confirmed a truth known by his own experience. And if the serene and beautiful enchantments of the City, ennobled him and drew forth his blazing genius, so the same emotions and experience, when recollected in tranquility, or through the medium of history and poem, might produce the same ennoblement in other souls.

The connection with the City illuminates an otherwise obscure rhetorical gesture in Adler's system. In one place, as we have seen, he describes the metamorphosis caused by social interest in such a way as to suggest that it might resolve all problems. On the surface of it, this idea ranges somewhere between the absurd and the intriguing. And yet it is phenomenologically credible, for the City can bestir such change. But to experience this change we must first awaken from that slumber caused by the City being too much with us. Familiarity does much more than breed contempt, it also, more destructively, blunts the faculty of delight and appreciation. In order to overcome this block, we must step off the train or airplane: we must imagine ourselves as a fresh arrival from the outlands of the backwaters, come to the city to make our fortunes or perhaps to lose even the few dollars we have stuffed inside our belt.

We must taste and see, and ramble. Or we need to see ourselves set down by supersonic jet in Paris, where we will dawdle in the dusk; or arrive in the color and bustle of Rome to make a pilgrimage to St. Peter's. At such a moment our heart sets sail. We are stirred from slumber to be different than we were, if only for a moment. The City forms us in its image, so that we come to share its virtue and its spots; the eyes brighten; the feet pick up their pace; and perhaps we develop a special taste for exoticas of vice. When nurtured in the soul, or experienced in the flesh, the City can truly cause a kind of Great Awakening and, I suspect, it was just this kind of alteration, in pulse and visage as well as attitude and soul that Adler was referring to. In such a great awakening, Adler says, lies, if not our salvation, exactly then at least the betterment and hope of man.

If contemplation of the City, can affect real changes, then perhaps a phenomenology of the City, can tell us more about the kind of change it wrought. Thus we may enlarge Adler's terse description. What then comprises what Adler once called "the poetry of the big city."[59]

As the preachers warn, the City is a flesh pot. It caters to the senses. There are spas; parks; vegetable stands; bands, symphonies; lawns; bars; red light districts; lights; squeaks and stinks; and the delicious curves of fashionable physiques. So let us say that social interest roots our life in things; in sensate, material pleasure. It builds a world from steak and steaming vegetables.

Every city has limits: city walls; pillars; boundary stones. As Hilaire Belloc once observed: "Our boundaries have always been intensely sacred to us. We are not passionate to cross them. In that enormous story of Rome, from the dim Etruscan origin right up to the end of her thousand years, the Walls of the Town are more sacred than the limits of the Empire." Where social interest governs, then, there will exist an instinct for limits and restraints, for generational lines and interpersonal boundaries.

Reflection: every city shines with multiple reflections: there are lakes; blue pools; fountains; and also jewelry and tall buildings made of glass. On a hot summer day the city smokes like an inferno of glitter. Some of these scenes are lovely; some of these are not. A crimson gem may sparkle on a sleek white neck; but so too does a silver wrapper wafting in the wind. In emulation, social interest will always involve reflection, the mirror in the moment. But knowing the source of some of its reflections, it will not make a god of mirrors, but instead will both look and leap.

Another trait, activity: the city soul is always in motion; the pell-mell, the hustle bustle; the perpetual to and fro. Adler made activity the hallmark of mental health. So emergence of social interest will always set the soul in motion. Look and then the arching leap; pacing; rhythmic; up and at them, walking, working, go go, quick quick, and always in the right direction. Ready to take a hike or strike out in a new direction.

Cities also house the dead. Every City is a cemetery. As Lewis Mumford writes: "The city of the dead antedates the city of the living."[60] The Greeks and Romans encompassed their cities with cemeteries, so that the first greeting to a traveler was a row of graves. Social interest, therefore, signifies according a place to the dead in the decision of the living. Social interest can tolerate the eros whose torch points downwards. It venerates the illustrious dead.

So in sum, to expand on Adler's description. Social interest does not work wonders. It turns us into concrete men of flesh and bones, who take the side of things, respecting limits, taste and boundaries; reflecting, carefully, then hastening to act, to move with the times, to sometimes stand against them, when the times betray the wisdom of the dead, the teaching of the ancestors. And then one final somber note: the City is perverse: red lights and blue angels; pick-ups and porno; mobsters, con men; bully boys; peddlers and pimps. Social interest then entails that we accept that nothing human is alien to us; that all these things of darkness I acknowledge mine.

By exalting the City, Adler proves himself the superior mind to Freud and Jung. On what grounds? Here I make an appeal to the preeminence of metaphor, enlisting the entire final chapter or Robert Romanyshyn's path breaking *Psychological Life*[61] as an eloquent background to which I refer the reader for a more comprehensive treatment of our time. First, what is a metaphor? While there are many definitions, which date back at least to Aristotle, the most plausible comes from Kenneth Burke who defines a metaphor as a *perspective*.[62] A root metaphor then, is a comprehensive perspective that shapes an entire discipline. According to my thesis, every discipline is anchored in the substrate of a root metaphor that not only structures its "knowledge" but also invests that "knowledge" with an emotional appeal. Through the agency metaphor "facts" are transformed into meanings that matter, that is, intelligibilities to which we extend an emotional attachment. A discipline advances thanks to a refinement or shift in its paradigm; while a discipline is "founded" with a discovery of a fresh metaphor together with a demonstration of fruitfulness and viability.

Now, Freud and Jung have been apotheosized primarily because to them have been ascribed the discovery of a new metaphor for man, that is, the unconscious. The richness of the metaphor is a stimulus to both self-understanding and therapeutic change substantiates their genius. Whereas Freud and Jung gave us wisdom—the wisdom born from the creation-discovery of a new reality, Adler gives us only commonsense.

But does this thesis really stand up to scrutiny? Is the unconscious, or, more poetically, the soul, the root metaphor psychology? I wonder if it is not the City, instead. What documents a root metaphor? Three traits it seems to me. First, the adjectives that in a normal content are assembled around a term also occur in connection with the favorite god in terms of a discipline. In response, we note that the adjectives that in common conversation collect around the city—corrupt, unnatural, poor, neglected, polluted, plural, feminine, teeming with imagination, outcast, barbarian, civilized, cultured, an infinitely gentle, suffering thing—also gravitate to the ideas of the unconscious and the soul. Second, despite its fittingness, few thinkers are disposed to entertain it, even though, to an outsider, the resemblance might seem obvious. Here, the analogy between the city and the soul seems obvious to everyone but psychologists. The City is one of the oldest images of the soul, or better said, humankind has often imagined itself on the analogy of the palpable reality of the city. A third earmark is that in spite of everything, it will pop up. And the City does emerge in the most surprising and conspicuous places, as, for instance, in the dream of Jung, whose images, he said conferred upon him his personal myth: "I found myself in a dirty, sooty city. It was night, and winter, and dark, and raining. I was in Liverpool. With a number of Swiss—say, half a dozen—I walked through the dark streets. I had the feeling that we were coming from the harbor, and that the real city was actually up above…"[63]

I'll only point out the centrality of the city in the dream: it is both present and absent, there and not there, rather like the unconscious, as if the city were the unconscious of depth psychology. Sad is Eros, builder of cities, said Auden upon the occasion of Freud's death. Perhaps Eros was sad because death had removed forever the chance for adequate acknowledgement.

But the City is acknowledged in Adlerian psychology, acknowledged with wordless elegance. It becomes the very goal of man, the object of his noblest aspirations. Indeed for Adler, for Adler as both thinker and therapist, we cannot rest until we rest in the city.

We come now to the third of Adler's governing principles: to what he calls the striving for significance. Adler's first adaptation of the idea is his description of the sanguine individual—

> The sanguine individual is one who shows a certain joy in life, who does not take things too seriously, who does not worry easily, who attempts to see the most beautiful and pleasant side of everything, who on sad occasions is sad without breaking down, and who experiences pleasure at happy events without losing his balance. A detailed description of such individuals shows nothing more than that they are approximately healthy people in whom harmful tendencies are not present to any great degree. We cannot make this assertion of the other types.
>
> The sanguine individual appears to be the one who, in his childhood, was least exposed to the feeling of inferiority, who showed few noticeable organ inferiorities, and who was not subjected to strong irritations, so that he could develop undisturbedly, learn to love life and to come to friendly terms with it.[64]

As the following passages indicate, Adler's formulation of this idea underwent extensive revision, but always there's the common thing of a great drive upward, a sort of *élan vital*.

> I begin to see clearly in every psychological phenomenon the striving for superiority. It runs paralleled to physical growth and is an intrinsic necessity of life itself. It lies at the root of all solutions of life's problems and

is manifested in the way in which we meet these problems. All our functions follow its direction. They strive for conquest, security, increase, either in the right or in the wrong direction. The impetus from minus to plus never ends. The urge from below to above never ceases. Whatever premises all our philosophers and psychologists dream of—self-preservation, pleasure principle, equalization—all of these are but vague representations, attempts to express the great upward drive.[65]

We all wish to overcome difficulties. We all strive to reach a goal by the attainment of which we shall feel strong, superior, and complete...But whatever name we give it, we shall always find in human beings this great line of activity—this struggle to rise from an inferior to a superior position, from defeat to victory, from below to above. It beings in earliest childhood and continues to the end of our lives...

I should like to emphasize first of all that striving for perfection is innate. This is not meant in a concrete way, as if there were a drive which would later in life be capable of bringing everything to completion and which only needed to develop itself. The striving for perfection is innate in the sense that it is a part of life, a striving, an urge, a something without which life would be unthinkable.[66]

The human soul, as a part of the movement of life, is endowed with the ability to participate in the uplift, elevation, perfection, and completion.[67]

Following Adler's link between the sanguine temperament and striving for significance, let us say that the striving for significance expresses the psychology of the blood. Amplification of the symbol of the blood, then, may reveal something about the ultimate nature of Adlerian psychology.

Blood evokes the idea of *passion, vitalism, zoe, élan vital.* In traditional lore blood is linked with wine and flowing juices, and with the ecstasy that carries us beyond ourselves, beyond the confines of our isolated loves and vengeances. In Christian symbolism the Blood of Christ symbolizes the divine power and grace which courses through existence. Blood connotes the passion of the Lord. Alchemy and heraldry speak of the blood of the lion or dragon as synonymous for passion and concupiscence. Greek myth presents the image of the Centaurs blood which when handled rightly may be used as an aphrodisiac to generate passion. A psychology based in the blood and in the attempt to restore its keenness is a psychology rooted in passion.

To discourse intelligently about passion is by no means a simple task, for it requires the suspension of the very tenacious assumption that passion equates with either physical arousal or a unique state of being in love where all is wings and flowers. In response to the question of what is passion: we might reply that it is something on the order of being deliriously hung up upon some present lover.

Although an overwhelming erotic attraction may furnish a perfect symbol for passion, it is not the whole story. The substance of passion is much more elusive. Passion is not a sexual noun; instead it is the universal adverb in that we may do anything with passion: eat, drink, be merry, love, fight, or even pray. Just as blood spreads throughout the body and nourishes every limb and cell, so passion may color any piece of behavior. Like the blood it is an invisible, invigorating substance that may penetrate any action or emotion and transmute it into a magnificent fable with large and noble characters. When in the arms of passion every act of love makes sky and earth; indeed we do not love but instead ascend into a holy place suffused with thrill. When in connection with passion we do not work but instead enter into a rhythmical transformative communion with the generosity of the earth. We do not pray but are swept away in transport. Depression becomes anguish. Happiness, joy. Under the influence of passion, philosophy recovers its primal wonder, poetry waxes lyrical in boundless rapture; war takes on the shape of chivalry.

As the blood is always present so long as life perdures, so is passion a crimson force that can be drawn upon for the enrichment of existence. Passion is enthusiasm, divine delirium, complete desire, luminous aspiration. What distinguishes a passionate experience from an ordinary one is the sense that it is something undergone or suffered, as the etymology of the word suggests, in which case passion incorporates the idea that we are subject to various circumstances over which we exert only minimal control. In a passionate life we succeed through luck instead of through skill.

As Heinz Ansbacher has so cogently demonstrated—beyond any grounds for objection it seems to me—the striving for significance is the most inclusive concept in Adler's system. To adopt a language now in vogue, it is Adler's root metaphor, the cornerstone in his conceptual architecture. But if we associate significance with passion, which is what we have been doing here, then perhaps *Adlerian psychology can be defined as the psychology of passion.* Whereas Freud rehearsed the vicissitudes of instinct; and whereas Jung charted the motions of the soul; Adler addressed the life of passion. But not just any passion. We must tread carefully here, for Adlerian psychology consists of the drama and description of the passion bridges soul (inferiority) with city (*gemeinschaftsgefuhl*).

> The continuous striving for [significance]...urges toward the overcoming of the present reality in favor of a better one. This goal of perfection must bear within it the goal of an ideal community, because all we value in life, all that endures and continues to endure, is eternally the product of social interest.[68]

To be Adlerian is to move from inferiority to social interest via the striving for significance. To be Adlerian is to move from soul to city via passion. The passion for significance is both the connecting link and the medium through which and in which soul and city are conjoined.

Perhaps Adlerian psychology is the passion that refounds the city in the image of the soul, so that whenever we try to link soul and city we are being Adlerian; and whenever we reflect on the nature of that linkage, we best turn to Adler for direction. Adler's aspiration was to rejoin soul and city; he assumed the Dantean task of returning poetry to our civil institutions; soul to drab, deserted streets; imagination in a thousand and one ways: through political involvement, which is what many Adlerians elect to do; through impassioned rhetoric or poetic splendor that unites the community in a common task or vision, which is the Dantean course; through philosophic vision whereby the common stock of wisdom is enriched, which is the old Catholic idea of a treasure house of merits; through work or one's self in therapy, which is the notion of a well ordered state reposing on a well ordered soul; or through something so simple as the simple, tactful ongoing creation of an atmosphere which not only encourages others to feel at home but stirs and enchants them, causing them to bloom. How many quiet friendships provide such nourishment, which is perhaps why Aristotle called friendship the soul of the city. The essential thing is that the Adlerian agenda requires some concrete expression. Or is it more a way of seeing than it is the literal mode of action, a mode of seeing that is supremely conscious of what one might call the ecstatic dimension of human dimension, whereby we finger the fact that all authentic human being is being soaked in *gemeinschaftsgefuhl*?

We live passionately, bridging soul and city, through ways of being as much as having, through ways of seeing as much as doing. We may understand this seeing as a rejuvenation of the life-world which occurs through a passionate imagining of the City as the noblest attainment of the human soul. Golgonooza. Byzantium.

Once again all roads clearly lead to Rome. Once again we meet the urban character. Adlerian psychology culminates in the creation of an urban consciousness. Already, repeatedly, throughout this essay, we have unfurled his banner. So let's add only one more flourish. Perhaps behind all other goods, urban man thrills to beauty—the sort of beauty and refinements that are most commonly available in the company of women. And so, by natural inclination, urban man gravitates towards courts and salons where women rule because there he finds an atmosphere where dress becomes flamboyant; wit, inspired; manners, polished; and conversation, an amorous, sportive game. Urbanity responds to grace and matures most quickly in the school of love. McLuhan stresses:

> Finally, there is basic in any tradition of intellectual and social passion a cult of feminine beauty and elegance. A feeling for the formal, civilizing power of the passionate apprehension of a stylized feminine elegance, so obvious in Southern life and letters, stems from Plato, blossoms in the troubadours, Dante, and the Renaissance Platonists, and is inseparable from the courtly concept of life.[69]

Such an atmosphere existed once at the court of Queen Elizabeth, the fairy queen, in whose jade colored eyes, the Jesuits said one could see the devil. Parisians found the same rich, fragrant, sportive glitter in the great salons, about which even Diderot confesses:

> Women accustom us to discuss with charm and clearness the driest and thorniest subjects. We talk to them unceasingly; we wish them to listen; we are afraid of tiring or boring them. Hence we develop a particular method of explaining ourselves easily, and this method passes from conversation into style.[70]

Adler too displayed his keen appreciation for beauty.

> The writer remembers asking Adler once in a spirit of idle curiosity, "Did you ever see the Empress Elizabeth, and was she really beautiful?" For a moment he was silent, while his eyes seemed to re-create a picture of what they once had looked upon. "Yes," he said at last, gravely, "I *did* once see her; and she was *really* beautiful."[71]

For Adler, perhaps there were only two things in life, Vienna and the Queen.

So where today does beauty lodge? The Great Mistake is to seek it inwardly, to internalize the quest for beauty, so that it becomes a journey into a lushly, mystical interior. This degrades the world and coarsens conduct. Instead we must open our eyes, not close them. We must look outward instead of in. Where infatuation with this anima in the Jungian or Bachelardian sense yields only a fine eye rolling, a chivalrous waiting upon real women—lively, witty, vibrant, wise, enchants society with charm and glow.

Does this not suggest that, as Yeats said, the marriage bed is the symbol of all resolved antinomies, for attainment to beauty requires a lifelong education in the flesh.

Let Rubens then be our guide instead of Dante or some troubadour. Rubens, the Baroque master, courtly diplomat, man of wealth and forms; his brush pulsing with flesh and colors, great curvaceous lines, shades, corpulent and fragrant; Rubens, who lavished his art upon the image of his wife, painting her in every garb and pose; naked, adorned, demure, voluptuous, innocently sensual; as Venus and Maria; garlanded with flowers; flaunting a saucy hat; cradling infants; holding a glove; in gorgeous wedding costume. For Rubens, she was the soul of womanhood. If our quest aspires the beauty of the feminine, who charted the truer course? Rubens was enchanted; Dante, only saved.

━━━

In this chapter we have been looking into Adler to recover both his theory and tradition. We have found a rhetor, an orator, a learned man. What obscures Adler's learning is of course his style. Because we don't think of Adler as a writer, we don't credit him as a reader. In contrast to Freud, suave and modulated clarity commemorate the eloquence of the great classical writers, and to Jung, who crammed his books with Asiatic bombast, Adler's period seem to hurry forward without any sense of overall design. To his friends, he seemed almost phobic about putting pen to paper. Although he may have been a gifted therapist and thinker, and a delight to his friends who could savor the glittering asides tossed off at table, he was screening that favored by the written muse. Even his admirers edit him. And yet the almost disapproval of Adler's "garbled" style reflects more about ourselves than Adler, more about superficiality than his. For in fact, Adler's style has noble precedents. It harkens back to the great baroque masters of the seventeenth century who—

> ...disdained complacency, suavity, copiousness, emptiness, ease, and in avoiding these qualities sometimes obtained effects of contortion or obscurity, which it was not always willing to regard as faults. It preferred the forms that express the energy and labor of minds seeking truth, not without dust and heat, to the forms that express a contented sense of enjoyment and possession of it. In a single word, the motions of souls, not their states of rest, had become the themes...[72]

According to Morris Croll, who is the authoritative writer on the subject, the baroque style in prose aimed at expressiveness rather than formal beauty; and it goes on to sum up the credo that guided their pens—

> Their purpose was to portray, not a thought, but a mind thinking, or, in Pascal's words *la peinture de la pensée*. They knew that an idea separated from the act of experiencing it is not the idea that was experienced. The ardor of its conception in the mind is a necessary part of its truth; and unless it can be conveyed to another mind in something of the form of its occurrence, either it has changed into some other idea or it has ceased to be an idea, to have any existence whatever except a verbal one...[they] deliberately chose as the moment of

expression that in which the idea first clearly objectifies itself in the mind, in which, therefore, each of its parts still preserves its own peculiar emphasis and an independent vigor of its own—in brief, the moment in which truth is still *imagined*.[73]

In its grammatical form the Baroque period is typified by two unique features, the first of which is the curtness of its syntactical members. Under the best circumstances, the Baroque writer tells the reader exactly what he thinks, as he is thinking it, and then moves on, so that the clauses are purged of excess to become all ardor and velocity. But the Baroque writer then moves on with sails set to the imagination rather than logic of dialectic. Croll again—

> We may describe it best by observing that the first member is likely to be a self-contained and complete statement of the whole idea of the period. It is so because writers in this style like to avoid prearrangements and preparations; they begin, as Montaigne puts it, at *le dernier poinct*, the point aimed at. The first member therefore exhausts the mere fact of the idea; logically there is nothing more to say. But it does not exhaust its imaginative truth or the energy of its conception. It is followed, therefore, by other members, each with a new tone or emphasis, each expression a new apprehension of truth expressed in the first...we may compare it with successive flashes of a jewel or prism as it is turned about on its axis and takes the light in different ways.[74]

In late antiquity and the Renaissance, this style was foreshadowed in the idea of a style informed by the Idea of Speed,[75] which is that quality of style that gives vivacity and energy to an oration. According to Hermogenes, a writer may achieve "speed" by virtually the same devices used by the Baroque masters. Curiously enough, the style of speed was linked with Mars, and in a martial rhetoric its centerpiece was courage. The Baroque style, therefore, emerges as the rhetoric of courage.

When set against the background of "the Baroque style in prose" the importance of Adler's contortion and obscurity diminish in comparison with the supreme vigor of his prose. The examples of the Baroque masters illuminate a quality in Adler's style that might otherwise be missed. There is the same ardor; the same effort to relay a thought as it is taking hold of the mind; the same curt periods carried forward by energy of conception rather than logic or dialectic; the same copious illustrations; the same emphasis on courage and the mind in motion; that typify Baroque prose. Although Adler was not a conscious stylist, he was a natural one, who spontaneously adopted the devices of the Baroque style perhaps because they suited his martial, sanguine character. His style is full of thrust and vigor and is altogether sane. It is an expressive of his genius as the contrasting styles of Freud and Jung. Indeed the conflict between Adler and Freud may have one of its many roots in the natural antipathy between the suave, Ciceronian writer and the Baroque or Attic style of prose. This battle reaches back to Greece and will probably outlive us. In this scheme Jung would represent a decadent Ciceronianism, a Gorgian attempt to make magic with the letter.

Adlerians sometimes forget that Individual Psychology exists in at least two dimensions: on the one hand, and perhaps the most significant, Adlerian psychology coheres as a community with a collective memory. We might call his the family tree perspective where the central focus falls on personal knowledge of Adler, where that knowledge expands through ever widening circles, many of which are formalized through institutes, societies, etc. The chief material here is gossip, memories, lore, example, the experience of therapy, the flesh and blood magnetism of a charismatic teacher. The advantages of his perspective are almost palpably obvious, in that without the personal touch and its animating presence, even the best of our knowledge soon hardens into bloodless coda. But these disadvantages are just as evident, for a community compounded exclusively of memorial and personal contact is but a race away from unionism, from the professional ghetto, from the intellectual backwater, from the kind of brainless parochialism that depend upon who you know or where you're trained rather than on what you are.

On the other hand, Adlerian psychology exists as a body of texts, and as such it repulses unionism, because texts are available to anyone and everyone, which is a state of affairs especially abrasive to those who have conferred upon themselves the charge of preserving any particular legacy intact, uncontaminated by any creeping impurities.

Texts reflect and maintain the esthetic dimension of human life, for when a writer sets down to scrawl out essence in the anonymous shadow of the lamp, he transcends himself in an almost involuntary act of *gemeinschaftsgefuhl.* He makes himself available to everyone, to their slings and arrows, to their friendships and their fantasies, which is a humbling, selfless and finally generous procedure. As a text, Individual Psychology will always exceed itself, enriching and ennobling the world in unexpected ways.

Need I point out the disadvantages here, since they are so obvious, in that text means interpretation and interpretation means error and error grows tentacular, fomenting strife and anger. This can eventually destroy a movement by splintering it into the fruitless condition of hostile sects whose mutual fury feeds on itself. The Pharisees and Scribes. And yet at the same time, text forces a movement to remain fundamentally *exoteric,* engaged with the world and open to its influences. Text converts a movement into a kind of medieval kingship, where each of us has access to the source of power rather than that source being in control and mediated by a clerical elite. As a textural reality, Individual Psychology exoterically persists, remains beside itself, suspended in a permanent state of ecstasy. Perhaps more than anything, it is the absence of this ecstasy that enfeebles the movement. Once the scribes stop scribbling, and the typewriters cease to pound out their spasmodic clicks, then thought also, often, stops.

Just as Adlerian psychology exist at two levels, so there are two levels of approach. The first we may refer to as the Way of Dreikurs,

the canny, the cagy, pragmatic therapist, the innovator and insti-
tutionalizer. He worried on his death bed about the fate of his institutional brain child the Chicago Institute. The Way of Dreikurs
immerses the beginner in didactic and experience so that his talents drive him slowly, gradually through the successive stages of development. He or she enrolls, matriculates, absorbs, learns, trains,
counsels, and is supervised, to be finally rewarded by the bestowal of
credentials, which signifies his or her admission into an identifiable
community, the community of Individual Psychology.

The second path, I should like to call the Way of Ansbacher,
where the path is governed by image of the editor, annotated, scholar, bibliophile, the collector of text, author of a serene and tranquil
prose style. In the late '60s, Heinz and Rowena Ansbacher, working more or less outside of the avant-garde tradition, innocent of
avant-garde pretension, created a kind of *wunder text*, so as to make
Adler accessible to the English speaking public. And what an extraordinary text it is, a Borges-like hall of mirrors, informed by what
has been called the poetics of quotation, a kinetic mix, compounded
of glosses, diagrams, extravagant typography, text within text, references, translations, a full scholarly apparatus, essays, interpolations,
biographies, dead and famous names.

Freud might perceive in it a dream book governed by dream logic. Mallarme might sense the logic of the newspaper. The text evokes
the great high modernist works—Eliot's *Wasteland*, the *Cantos* of
Pound; Jones' *Anathemata*; Olsen's *Maximus*; while also recalling the
great medieval *summae*, where syllogisms jostled with history, bestiaries, and treatises on bees. It has been said that the architecture
of the great Gothic cathedrals reflect the logic of the summae and
indeed in my imagination the Ansbachers, the *Individual Psychology
of Alfred Adler* is very much like a cathedral, a spacious, cool, di-
aphanous vault thru which illuminations filter. The high modernists
blazed the way in the struggle to create a form responsive to the subtlest stresses of the postmodern mind. The struggle has since diversi-
fied into adjoining fields—philosophy, psychology, science—to the
point that the discontinues style has become the norm rather than

the exception. But before there was Norman O. Brown's *Love's Body* or Derrida's *Glas* or Minuchin's *c* there was the Ansbachers' work, unpretentious, unassuming, and as focused on accuracy as any objectivist poem. They created the first post-modern psychology book.

Just how important the editor, the way of Ansbacher, might be to a general renewal of Individual Psychology, and through it, a collective life at large, can be appreciated through a simple act of memory, that is, we might recall how central the role of editor has been to the renewal of culture: to the emergency of modernism, for example, the instigator of which was Mallarme, who was himself fascinated with the scribal art of the editor; to the transformation of the old chivalric ideal and to the influential ethic of the gentleman, which was in many ways the work of William Caxton at the Red Inn; to the renaissance when Erasmus worked as an editor at the famous House of Aldus, where most of the real work of the Renaissance was done, the slow, arduous, scrutinizing work of translating the difficult Latin and Greek; and to the survival of the remnants of Classical and Carligian culture during the long dark night of Europe when it was the rhythmical scrawl and buzz of the monks in the scriptoriums as they copied and illuminated that salvaged those ideals.

It is this image that flits across my inner eye as I think of the significance of the Ansbachers' labors in conjunction with the thought that Individual Psychology's most brilliant fixture, by whom I mean Manes Sperber who abstained from the practice of therapy so as to take up the work of editing. In as much as the editors had a great historical role to play, and given that this role has often been to metabolize a renaissance where before there was only the foment of potential, might the recovery and enactment of this image be the very agency to overcome the creeping impotence of a dying movement to create an unexpected renaissance of Individual Psychology. Perhaps, perhaps not.

The absorbing value of the Way of Ansbacher, and of the study of his manner of syntheses in addition to the materials they present, is that it ultimately transcends itself to merge back with the Way of Adler, which is nothing less than the way of the *clinician as intellec-*

tual. The luster of this way has dimmed. But it was not always so, especially before the war—the second one, when we learned enough to number them—before the great exodus to America, which brought in its wake a noiseless almost somnambulistic assimilation into American life, the hustling rhythms of the melting pot, where the premium has always been what works, or what works cleanly, efficiently, and verifiably.

Adlerians have always flourished in the clinic and so they have flourished here, if not exactly in the sense that the Adlerian movement itself has prospered, winning funds and chairs, than in the sense that the basic Adlerian framework has been almost universally adopted. Structural, strategic, systemic, and cognitive-behavior therapies all have their roots in Adler, regardless of whether those roots are acknowledged or not. And psychodynamic work was long ago Adlerianized, sometimes openly, more times not. But in addition to the clinic, Adlerians once flourished elsewhere, in touch with contemporary developments in anthropology, metaphysics, politics and the arts, not to speak of culture, to which Adlerians made vital contributions in cultured prose. (Adler's essay on Dostoevsky might serve as the example here, surely the most beautiful prose style he accomplished.) Gertrude Stein once said that in the beginning poetry was everything. The same could be said of Individual Psychology. Therefore, to the precise extent that Adlerians have narrowed their vision to an almost monocular concern with clinical gimmickry, they have strayed from Adler, forfeiting an inheritance that is lined with treasure. So let me end this chapter with a vision, for just as Adler dreamt of a *gemeinschaftsgefuhl* that extended even into the cosmos so I dream of a renewed Individual Psychology whose interest would move retentively beyond the clinic into the larger field of culture. I suppose I dream then of a cultural psychology, which is a name Adler early on affixed to his distinctive blend of inspirations. Culture—an old word and a noble one, in response to which Herman Goering reached for his gun, and in defense of which Baron von Stauffenberg laid down his life, gunned down in headlight glare by Gestapo murderers. And for a model in this enterprise I look to

Heinz and Rowena Ansbacher, and also to the other luminaries, the master spirits—as Milton called them—Brachfeld, Way, Neuer, Sperber, etc., whose work needs to be recuperated. This then is the outcome of my first looking into Adler.

CHAPTER TWO

Know that when all words are said
And a man is fighting man,
Something drops from eyes long blind,
He completes his partial mind,
For an instant stands at ease,
Laughs aloud, his heart at peace.
Even the wisest man grows tense
With some sort of violence
Before he can accomplish fate,
Know his work or chose his mate.

— William Butler Yeats

There is a Venusian experience within Mars itself.

— James Hillman, "Wars, Arms, Rams, Mars"

Adler's first foray into the psychology of power evolved as a reflection on what he styled the "aggressive instinct." In 1908, while still attending Freud's Wednesday night gatherings, Adler published a paper where he posited a superordinated dynamic force in the mind. He named it the aggressive drive and conceived of it as the initiator and coordinator of the other drives. To this attempt to re-think psychological life in terms of *eris* instead of *eros* Freud responded—

Alfred Adler, in a suggestive paper, has recently developed the view that anxiety arises from the suppression of what he calls the "aggressive instinct," and by a very sweeping synthetic process he ascribes to that instinct the chief part in human events, "in real life and in the neuroses"...I am nevertheless unable to assent to [this view], and indeed I regard it as a misleading generalization. I cannot bring myself to assume the existence of a special aggressive instinct alongside of the familiar instincts of self-preservation and of sex, and on an equal footing with them.[1]

Freud, however, at least in part, eventually adopted the Adlerian thesis, although introducing it with more the poetic, evocative and cosmologically rich name of Thanatos. Since that time Freudians have sometimes tried to compensate for Freud's belatedness, by arguing that Adler subsequently dropped the aggressive instinct from his model of the mind because he was unable to exploit his own discovery. But as Ansbacher explains, the aggressive instinct was never discarded by Adler but only subsumed into a more comprehensive framework.

The crucial change in Adler's theory...was that aggression was no longer regarded as an independent innate drive but was subsumed under the larger concept of striving for overcoming, under which aggression was only the abnormal form which occurs when social interest is not properly developed...[2]

Adler here sums up the shift in theory, while also recalling the initial aspiration:

In 1908 I hit upon the idea that every individual really exists in a state of permanent aggression, and I was imprudent enough to call this attitude the "aggression drive." But I soon realized that I was not dealing with a drive, but with a partly conscious, partly irrational attitude towards the tasks which life imposes; and I gradually arrived at an understanding of the social element in personality.[3]

If Adler's first brush with the will to power gave rise to the idea of an aggression drive, then we ought to scrutinize the concept carefully, for in the life of a daimonic man the first appearance of the daimon takes an especial importance. Was the aggression drive truly the awakening of Adler's daimon, the initial stirrings of what was to function as his great idea? I think it was, for even in its first appearance, while Adler was still a relatively young man working together with Freud in a bond somewhere between the position of a pupil and a partner, the idea rang with a clarity and comprehensiveness to which lesser thinkers vainly aspire. The notion blossomed with a fury, attaining maturity almost instantaneously, so that I expect it dazzled Adler as it dazzles anyone who upon first looking into Adler discovers the complete psychology mapped out in a hundred lines or so. In this section I propose to devote some space to it, examining it in exhaustive and perhaps exhausting detail, with the hopes of establishing a sound textual infrastructure for our subsequent re-working of Adlerian themes.

In addition we should note here that Adler's interest in aggression is of a piece with his lifelong focus on experience, for "experience" is a word that comes down to us charged with martial reminiscences. What a strange intelligence is lodged within this familiar word! Having become a cliché it nonetheless towers with a critical significance. The word originates in the Latin *ex* (to come out of) and *per* (to go through). Already at the root we hear rumbles of ordeals, contests, etc. Together ex and per compose the word *experior* which means "to try" or "to put to the test"; thus Caesar's military employment of the word; thus Cicero's customary usage of the word where *experior* signifies "to measure one's strength with another" and "to try in a hostile manner." In classical Latin the word betokens "trial by combat." In Medieval Latin the word retained its old military import of "trial by arms" while also acquiring the larger sense of "trial by learning or experience." With this we have commenced the generalizing evolution of *experience* into experiment, and a primarily scientific-naturalistic meaning. The flags are fading to be replaced by the strict neutrality of science, but still the echoes rumble of war chariots and the beating of a drum.

If we entrust our reflections to the tutelage of etymology, which is a long accepted move, sanctioned by, among others, Plato, Vico and Heidegger, then to turn to *experience* is to return to aggression as the ground of all experience. Adler here emerges as the proto-phenomenologist, which is an interpretation sustained by the course of his career.

Labeled as superficial by some, Adler was a psychologist of surfaces, an exegete enchanted by the luster of phenomenon. Unlike Freud and Jung who both bogged down in elaborate theoretical constructions, Adler kept a nose for facts, for the facticity of Dasein, for the corporeal limits of a body saturated with the "savage being" evoked by Merleau-Ponty. He stuck to things, a way of getting unstuck in the narcissistic self. By keeping his theory makeshift, Adler remained faithful to experience, which tends to be fluid, iridescent, shifty, a shimmer of illusive reflections. Although some have faulted Adler for his inconsistencies, without them he would never have matured into the theorist that he was. His contradictions are his crown not his cross.

Further if the word or concept of experience comes already saturated with military connotations, then a true psychology of experience must be a martial art at home in the dazzle of the *agon*. It must be polemical, strife torn, divisively even, an intellectual trial by combat. For me, Individual Psychology is such a martial art.

To aggression then. According to Adler aggression is first of all a style of consciousness.

> The aggression drive also dominates consciousness....
> It directs attention, interests, sensation, perception,
> memory, phantasy, production, and reproduction into
> the paths of pure or altered aggression.[4]

As a dominant of consciousness, aggression may be entrusted with all the features of primary and secondary ego autonomy. Perhaps the best entry into the aggressive style of consciousness is by simply taking note of the war-like essence of the mind. Strife is the father of all, said Heraclitus. "War has always been the grand sagacity of every spirit which has grown too inward and profound; its curative powers lies even in the wounds one receives," said Nietzsche. "Operations of thought are like cavalry charges in battle," said Whitehead. Thinking is itself a macabre activity, a trait of the most violent breed of animal. To think is to sunder, separate, divide. Its symbol is the sword held bright and gleaming, poised above the head. Since we cannot think except in terms of objects—consciousness is always consciousness of, said Brentano, the father of phenomenology, and at whose lectures sat Husserl, Freud and Rudolf Steiner—we must assume that every act of consciousness depends upon some earlier crime, some primal act of violence whereby the original unity of subject and object is sundered. Myths of genesis in nearly every land recall this original act of separation whereby day and night are separated, above and below, earth and air, Adam and Eve. The big bang theory of the creation of the cosmos continues this translation. Whether or not these stories recall some actual event is not here germane: regardless they capture an important truth about consciousness. The mind reposes on a primal crime. And then this violence is perpetuated through continual acts of abstraction that shatter the existential unity of things in order to concentrate upon a single quality or trait. We murder to dissect. And even when we try to preserve that unity we nonetheless replace the rich, corporeal unity of living things with the shadow brother of their concept. There is simply no way to bypass the carnivorous quality of consciousness. Since reflection is such a violent activity, is it any wonder that poets such as Poe and Baudelaire chose the horror story and tales of the macabre as suitable vehicles for their fables of consciousness.

Of course, if consciousness is violent, it is also handsomely erotic. *Thinking requires a reciprocal act in which subject and object are held apart by being held together and held together by being held apart.* As consciousness divides so it unites. The Romans knew this and always thought of Mars—*Mars Gradivus* as the brother of the bright god Eros. In astrology Mars rules over both love and war. "Already in Antiquity," says de Rougemont, "poets used warlike metaphors in order to describe the effects of natural love."[5] During the high Middle Ages writers were keenly sensitive to the interplay of Mars and Eros. Eros shoots fatal arrows. Women *surrendered* to men and men *conquered* brides and virgins. Lovers *besieged* their ladies, made amorous assaults and pressed them closely. One of the most beautiful images of the union of Mars and Eros, war and love, is the poetic image of the rose-colored blood. Common sense connects the two in numberless phrases about the battle of the bedroom. Thus in moving, with Adler, in to the cosmos of aggression we must take care not to eliminate the torch of Eros. *We must keep armour with amour,* for otherwise we will lose the gist of aggression.

Like Venus herself, who comes radiant and gleaming from the blood of her father's genitals, the mind is born on a wave of impersonal violence. And having crated consciousness through an act of violence, a dynamic opposition whereby an antithesis is born, subject and object existing in an eternal dynamic tandem, the aggressive instinct will persist in employing this device of the antithesis as its characteristic mode of thought. By fashioning antitheses—binary pairs, dualities, opposites, paradoxes, and tandems—the aggressive instinct comprehends the world. It thinks through opposition. Philosophy itself is full of antitheses employed in explanation of the mysteries of the universe: Parmenides, swept up to heaven, hailed the One and the Many; Empedocles, at the foot of his volcano, spoke of Attraction and Repulsion; and Plato drew attention to the dynamic of Forms and Matter. The list goes on and on, from existence and essence to the ego and the id. Where there is no strife, there can be no thought, no thought as we have come to use the word. Indeed one wonders if "logocentric" thought—in the sense of Jacques Derrida—is itself a creation of the aggressive instinct, a child of Mars.

Adler reflected often on the problem of the opposites; and he arrived at the conclusion that "antithetical thinking" is tantamount to neurosis. We must tread carefully here, for it is easy to misread Adler on this point, and to assume that he was a kind of proto-deconstructivist, whose intention was to discredit the oppositional or "agonic" thinking as a whole, as if the opposites themselves were at the root of our troubles, and in fact concealed a covert hierarchy where through the very idea of the opposites one term dominates another. No, the reverse is true: Adler thought antithesis is a very useful device for coming to terms with the world. What distinguishes neurosis from *gemeinschaftsgefuhl* is not the opposites but our attitude toward them. Whereas social interest will enlist the opposites as heuristic fictions, the neurotic reifies them. Adler writes "The neurotically disposed individual has a sharply schematizing, strongly abstracting mode of apperception. Thus he groups inner as well as outer events according to a strictly antithetical schema, something like the debit and credit sides in bookkeeping, and admits no degrees in between."[6] In the neurotic approach towards reality, the various schemes of opposites rigidify into fixed categories and thus ultimately betray the fluid, dynamic shape of reality.

One way of distinguishing neurosis, then, from *gemeinschaftsgefuhl*, which is the Adlerian definition of mental health, is that the neurotic is just too serious, whereas social interest plays. Adlerian consciousness is *homo ludens*, in Huizinga's famous phrase. Perhaps he plays with the opposites as well, playing them off against each other, as in a contest. So we might wonder if the authentic form of the aggressive style of consciousness consists of viewing life as contest. Is it not simply a *datum* of experience that whenever the aggressive instinct is given sufficient play it will create a contest, both for its own and other's pleasure?

The *agonistic* mind—for let us call it so as a spryer synonym for "the aggressive style of consciousness," which is a mouthful—delights in contest, match, struggle, the spectacle of the agon. This is its root metaphor, paradigm, its guiding fiction in Adler's sense. The love of contest is deeply rooted in our tradition. Huizinga comments: "The Greeks used to stage contests in anything that offered the bare possibility of a fight. Beauty contests for men were part of the Panathenae and Thesean festivals. At symposia, contests were held in singing, riddle solving, keeping awake and drinking. Even in the last-named the sacred element is not lacking....[bulk drinking and drinking neat] formed part of the Choen festival—or feast of pitchers. Alexander celebrated the death of Kalakos by a gymnastic and musical agon with prizes for the doughtiest drinkers, with the result that thirty five of the competitors died on the spot, six afterwards, among them the prize-winner."[7] Nietzsche writes:

> Every talent must unfold itself in fighting: that is the command of Hellenic proper pedagogy, whereas modern educators dread nothing more than the unleashing of so-called ambition....and just as the youths were educated through contests, their educators were also engaged in contests with each other. The great musical masters, Pindar and Simonides, stood side by side, mistrustful and jealous; in the spirit of the contest, the sophist, the advanced teacher of antiquity, meets another sophist; even the most universal type of instruction, through the drama, was meted out to the people only in the form of a tremendous wrestling among the great musical and dramatic artists. How wonderful! "Even the artist hates the artist." Whereas modern man fears nothing in an artist more than the emotion of any personal fight, the Greek knows the artist *only as engaged in a personal fight.* Precisely where modern man senses the weakness of a work of art, the Hellen seeks the source of its greatest strength.[8]

But this love of contest was by no means limited to the Greeks, as Burckhardt apparently thought. It appears throughout our history, in the medieval tournament, for example, which summed up all the dazzling currents of medieval life, and which is one of the most beautiful expressions of the agonistic mind. Insofar as the West is concerned, this view of life as contest seems to be a common phenomenon; perhaps it is universal as Walter Ong has suggested in a recent book which explores the whole topic.

> Contest is a part of human life everywhere that human life is found. In war and in games, in work and in play, physically, intellectually, and morally, human beings match themselves with or against one another. Struggle appears inseparable from human life, and contest is a particular focus or mode of interpersonal struggle, an opposition that can be hostile but need not be, for certain kinds of contest may serve to sublimate and dissolve hostilities and to build friendship and co-operation.[9]

The view of life as contest, which we are claiming comprises the "root metaphor," paradigm, basic attitude or lifestyle of aggressive consciousness, quickens every aspect of social intercourse. Our lives are bathed in its crimson hue. We all desire to be first in strength, knowledge, riches, splendor, beauty, liberality, number of children, even the color of our hair. We'll bet and compete at anything: games, songs, riddles, academic achievement, races, crossing the mall. Breathes there the man with soul so dead that never to himself hath said, "I want to be first," and tried to be first by matching himself against another who may be foe but may also be friend?

Now there are three things I want to note about the metaphor of life as contest because each of these three things foreshadow elements that are fundamental to Individual Psychology, at least as we are here working out that psychology. When life is viewed as contest, *things* become vitally significant. In competition, the participants usually compete for *something*, which may, of course by symbolical, but is often literal: a medal, trophy, shilling, dollar bill, gold cup, jewel, or the king's daughter's hand in marriage. When we compete, we all want a prize or what was / is sometimes called a "gage," a word meaning the symbol of a challenge. Etymologically this word is bound up with a cluster of meanings evoking ideas of passion, chance, risk, daring and the capacity to endure tension.

76

It is as if the view of life as contest attributes a special significance to *things*, finding in them a stimulus to great deeds and heroic effort. Whereas art makes culture by transforming things into artifacts, contest makes culture by turning them into prizes and trophies. As the artistic vision of a form concealed in matter will catalyze enormous energy and perseverance, so does the vision of things as trophy call for discipline and deed.

Second, the view of life as contest steers Adlerian psychology away from preachiness and do-gooders, for the traditional idea of contest allows a place to various forms of trickery, deceit, fraud and opportunism. As Huizinga reminds us that although "to our way of thinking, cheating is a means of winning a game robs the action of its play-character and spoils it altogether...."

> Archaic culture...gives the lie to our moral judgement in this respect, as also does the spirit of popular lore. In the fable of the hare and the hedgehog the beau role is reserved for the false player, who wins by fraud. Many of the heroes of mythology win by trickery or by help from without. Pelops bribes the charioteer of Oenomaus to put wax pins into the axles. Jason and Theseus come though their tests successfully, thanks to Medea and Ariadne. Gunther owes his victory to Siegfried. The Kauravas in the *Mahābhārata* win by cheating at dice. Freya double-crosses Wotan into granting the victory to the Langobards. The Ases of Eddic mythology break the oath they have sworn to the Giants. In all these instances the act of fraudulently outwitting somebody else has itself become a subject for competition, a new play-theme, as it were.[10]

Adlerian psychology, practiced in the light of life as contest, would take a decidedly worldly view of our daily falls from the summits of perfection. Manes Sperber puts the poem quite eloquently.

To the individual psychologist, moral compunctions are usually something fabricated by the guilty in their search for additional moral benefits. A fundamental distinction between psychoanalysis and individual psychology manifests itself here, and it has anthropological implications. In the demonology of Freud's interpretation of dreams, and in psychoanalytical neurosis studies, all the cases concerned patients who concealed their own murder wishes from themselves and nevertheless suffered from oppressive guilt feelings which caused them to lose their equilibrium. As if hunted by the Furies they vainly sought refuge in self-castigation and tremulous anxiety. Today, after two world wars, several revolutions and counter-revolutions, the rise of totalitarian dictatorships, and a boom in injustice, torture and murder, the daily perpetuation of monstrous acts has been transformed into a sort of official policy carried out by office-holding criminals and countless millions of silent accomplices. Yet the total feeling of guilt has not increased one iota—on the contrary! Fear of their own ruthlessness, and of their deserved punishment, *should* be just as excruciating for those actually guilty of these crimes, if not more so, than if they merely subconsciously plotted and imagined the deeds, but it is not. Morality has very little to do with psychology.[11]

Where light goes, there too is shadow. Such a genuine tolerance primes the springs of human compassion and understanding which are so important to therapy. To view life as contest is to exalt tolerance as a cardinal virtue.

A third quality of contest that is worth noting revolves around the idea of winning, which, as Vince Lombardi said, is not the most important thing, it is the only thing. But winning is not so much a product of the will to power, conventionally conceived, as it is the consequence of the will to excel, the will to be honored for one's excellence.

Huizinga states flatly: "the competitive 'instinct' is not in the first place a desire for power or a will to dominate."[12] Thus the agonistic view of life already presents in *status nascendi* the distinction between *superiority* and *significance* that was to become so importance in Adler's system. Contest teaches that distinction on the level of the body, the heart, the instincts. During the first few grueling hours of preparation for any contest, we realize that a wide gulf separates superiority and significance. If power as superiority is the goal, then there are far easier ways to obtain it than the endless, agonizing hours of training that are the condition of success in any authentic contest. If genius is 99% perspiration and 1% inspiration, the ratio for successful competition is even higher; inspiration hardly enters into it at all, and even the advantage of the gift of talent means very little unless that talent is disciplined and formed through training. Training for Adler was the secret of life. The contest fosters striving for significance; the agonistic view of life is itself the essential form of this great upward drive.

And just as we learn about significance and superiority through contest, so we grasp, on the level of experience, the complex relation obtaining significance and social interest. When we triumph in a contest, we obtain honor and esteem which will usually also pass to the group we represent. New York wins the Super Bowl and the entire city waxes proud. Thus we may say that any genuine striving for significance will work to the benefit of the community, adding a cohesiveness and vigor that might not have otherwise existed. Striving for significance will always contain an element of social interest. And yet this striving is pre-eminent as it was in Adler's theory, ultimately, as Ansbacher and others have made clear. Or in Huizinga's words again, "Here we have another very important characteristic of [contest]: success won readily passes from the individual to the group. But the following feature is still more important...the desire to excel..."[13]

The agonistic mind, the aggressive style of consciousness, cannot think except in terms of other as adversary, foe or opponent.

From at least the time of Socrates until very recently the natural desire to "best" an opponent in argument or intellectual achievement has been widely acknowledged as an entirely natural and basic human instinct and therefore enlisted in the search for truth. In his extraordinary *Art of Teaching*, Gilbert Highet, one of our century's most eloquent and brilliant teachers, points out "....competition is a natural instinct in the young." After remarking that "competition keeps a class from being merely a group of faceless nonentities, and gives it something of a diversity of life," Highet goes on to praise the Jesuits who used the spirit of competition as a way of sparking the deep, hidden, vital instincts for knowledge, which in the absence of competition will sometimes remain completely dormant.[14] Both Walter Ong and Johan Huizinga have written superb histories of the agonistic heritage of academia.

Huizinga writes that "all knowledge—and this naturally includes philosophy—is polemical by nature, and polemics cannot be divorced from agonistics. Epochs in which great new treasures of the mind come to light are generally epochs of violent controversy."[15] Ong shows how the study of learned Latin, which has been the language of learning though most of our history, was itself a kind of rite of passage, filled with contest and calculated hardship from which the student emerged with a sense of *esprit de corps* and a feeling that together they had suffered through a kind of combat where they had completed the *conquest* of the world of knowledge.

Ong links "philosophy as polemics," and thereby what we are calling the agonistic mind, with rhetoric in the oral tradition, while suggesting that when the tradition of winged words is superseded by print culture, then agonistic consciousness will always fade to be replaced by structures that as yet are not altogether determined. Ong declares that the old agonistic style of consciousness was "conspicuously decadent almost a century ago."[16] By remarking this decline, Ong helps, incidentally, to illuminate the meaning of Adler's famous defection from Freud. Although numerous theories have been offered in explanation of why Adler split from Freud, none, it seems to me go to the heart of the issue. We approach that heart by noting that just as the old rhetorical tradition was losing its ascendancy in intellectual arenas, it reappeared to take psychology by storm. Psychoanalysis was consistently and self-consciously a *talking cure*, a rhetorical exercise. In language that might have made the sophists blush, Freud praises the witchery of words.

> Words and magic were in the beginning one and the same thing, and even today words retain much of their magical power. By words one of us can give to another the greatest happiness or bring about utter despair; by words the teacher imparts his knowledge to the student; by words the orator sweeps his audience with him and determines its judgments and decisions. Words call forth emotions and are universally the means by which we influence our fellow-creatures. Therefore let us not despise the use of words in psycho-therapy and let us be content if we may overhear the words which pass between the analyst and the patient.[17]

Psychoanalysis was rhetoric revised but one essential element was missing, that being the polemic, agonistic, aggressive style of mind. Preferring to model himself after the newer scientific tradition, where truth was supposed to be a privilege of isolated minds in communion with clear, distinct ideas, Freud disliked polemics, even to the point of forbidding the discussion of papers at psychoanalytic congresses because such discussions might spill over into verbal conflict. Freud wanted the appearance of a universal movement in service of a universal truth, which is something quite foreign to the clash of ideas that is typical of rhetoric.

By defecting from Freud, Adler changed all this, in that he introduced polemic conflict, the clash of views and all the accoutrements of agonistic consciousness into the history of psychology. By temperament, he was entirely suited to do this in that contemporary descriptions often stress his contentiousness. When Alphonse Maeder met him, he summed up his impressions:

After I read my report, Adler came to me and holding each button of my waistcoat, one after the other, started to explain his ideas to me. He wanted to win me for his theories...there was something unpleasant in his manners....He was rather peculiar, not handsome, and had nothing winning in him.[18]

Ernest Jones ground his axe—

My own impression of Adler was that of a morose and cantankerous person whose behavior oscillated between contentiousness and sulkiness. He was evidentially very ambitious and constantly quarrelling with the others over points of priority in his ideas. When I met him many years later, however, I observed that success had brought him a certain benignity of which there had been little sign in his early years.[19]

Friends of Adler seem at times to regret this, but Adler had the sanguine temperament characteristic of his ethos. He was rhetor, or orator pure and simple. When he broke with Freud, he recovered for psychology the full depth and resonance of the rhetorical tradition and made psychology the vehicle of its return. Had Adler towed the line with Freud, psychology would never have become *psychological*, that is, agonistic and rhetorical; and would have remained instead a scientific project that might, because of its work with words, on occasion have reached the condition of poetry, but a poetry devoid of wordly import, that is a poetry devoid of rhetoric. Because of Adler, psychology developed in the form of *schools* which many have found to be reminiscent of the ancient schools of Greek philosophy. But the rhetorical spirit of the schools has always been opposed by the equally powerful desire to make psychology a science. I suggest that this is largely because it is through identification with "science" that psychology becomes a business, profitable, organized, respected. The aspiration to honor and excellence that is characteristic of agonistic consciousness has always been conspicuously absent from the business ethos, where the competitive instinct is almost neutralized by being conscripted into the service of the bottom line. In business money substitutes for honor while the completed sale does duty for the thrill of excellence. Largely because of Adler's work, depth psychology has remained true, in structure if not always in content, to an ancient tradition which the liberal arts have for a century now been struggling to transcend, and this despite the lure of the glittering spoils of financial success. And yet today the business *ethos* has reached the stage of an almost complete and overwhelming triumph, which would finally spell the end of agonistic consciousness and thus the negation of one of Adler's most impressive contributions, his phenomenology and personal enactment of an agonistic style of mind.

As there is an aggressive style of consciousness, so there is an aggressive style of behavior, which takes multiple forms and is especially evident in infancy.

> The aggressive drive dominates the entire motor behavior, its motor irradiations being unusually clear in childhood. Crying, fidgeting, throwing oneself on the floor, biting, and grinding one's teeth, are simple forms of this drive which are not infrequently found again later in life, particularly in hysteria.[20]

It is curious that Adler should associate aggression, which at the time he was presenting, *contra* Freud, as the motive force of the psyche, with the hysteric, the *la Passionele* of Janet's and Charcot's medical theatrics, who has, in turn, been linked with the maenads of antiquity who followed in the train of Dionysus. The association is at least as old as the Renaissance, when it appeared in the work of Rabelais, and as recent as the work of E.R. Dodds, the classicist, who compares Dionysian rebels with the portraiture of hysterics assembled by nineteenth century French psychiatry. The kinship has become a commonplace in depth psychology, *a la* Hillman and Brown.

Already, in 1908, while Adler still belonged to the Freudian circle, Dionysus is evoked and with him the idea of *zoe*, becoming, motion, the *élan vital*. For the Greeks Dionysus was the spirit of motion, the vitality of matter, the spirit of the air. At the heart of the Dionysian world is motion. His dismemberment is the birth of motion as Plutarch describes it:

> When the god is changed and distributed into winds, water, earth, stars, plants, and animals, they describe this experience and transformation allegorically by the terms "rending" and "dismemberment." They apply to him the name Dionysus...[21]

Already, in 1908, years before he came into his full maturity as a thinker, Adler appears as an apostle of becoming, which idea he grappled with throughout his long career, struggling to avoid the fate of Pentheus and to bring Dionysus into the city, so that the wild blood of nature might enrich the holy stones of culture. The fact that the idea of Becoming is present in his phenomenology of aggression gives the lie of the belief that Adler was ever truly a disciple of Freud, a pygmy whom a giant made great. Adler's daimon chose him from the start.

But our purpose here is not so much to remember Dionysus as to describe the typical aggressive forms of behavior. If crying, biting, etc. are simple forms, a more complex form is the *boast*. Indeed I would argue that boasting is the true type and flower of aggression as Adler understood it. And I would note as an aside that the destruction of Thebes, which Dionysus wrought may be read as consequence of a refusal to boast. Dionysus entered the holy city *boasting* of his celestial paternity, and then devised the destruction of Pentheus because Pentheus failed to do him homage. What Pentheus should have done is answered with a more extravagant boast and challenged the divine lord to a drinking bout. Had boast answered boast the city might have flowered.

Boasting has a very complex phenomenology which also offers a concrete illustration of Adlerian theory. What happens when we boast? What happens when, over drinks, before the fire, on the playing field, or in the presence of a girl, we boldly announce, with strut and taunt, that "I can do anything better than you." When we boast, we release the upward flaming aspect of our spirit, the divine youth, the world shaker, whose accomplishments cry out for epic homage. When we boast, we are, at least in our fantasy, the companion of the gods. Boasting is thus a concrete instance of the striving for significance, the desire for elevation and perfection, which Adler took to be the basic drive to man. But as Adler says, such striving never arrives at authenticity unless it be shaped by social interest. And in boasting we don't go up alone but instead extend a hand to our competitors. Not just "I can do anything" but, "I can do anything better than *you*." Boasting is dialectical, dialogical, it posits a beautiful and dazzling I-Thou relationship which is purged of every token of sentimentality. For boasting is really flourish, it requires a rival, who may also be a friend, who tries to top us with grander tales of exploits and potential. Boasters swap stories and dares. Unable to boast alone, we together climb the ladder of being outrageous rung by outrageous rung, until in tandem we create an ideal community where anything is possible and where tall spirits dwell in the shade of the tree.

At the conclusion of a round of boasting two or more spirits may dwell there in a kind of vital, perfect union which we may take to be the community of *gemeinschaftsgefuhl*, which Adler often speaks of while insisting that it is a fiction, a place apart. And though this "Vanilla" may seem like a state of superiority, it has a comic side as well which will swiftly undercut any stirrings of presumption. True boasting always entails an element of play, so that while we swap and dare, smile and lie, we are perfectly aware that these spirit twins, whose accomplishments are legion, are something quite different from the actual men of flesh and bones who sit here drinking and lying to the amusement of their friends. To boast is to swell up bullfrog-like in an airy mix of pride and laughter. Thus the ideal community that boasting creates is accepted as a fiction, an image of all that we would like to be and perhaps will strive to be on the basis of our boasts. In boasting our goals remain completely fictional, a constant pull and prod that keeps desire flowing. This is how Adler understood the purpose of a goal. A goal is meant to challenge, to spur and fuel, but never to be realized, since realization would end its power to move the psyche, which movement, Adler, as did Aristotle, took to be its essence.

The boast is a universal phenomenon; it appears in all cultures, at all times, and at all stages of human development. Huizinga writes "It is remarkable how large a place these bragging and scoffing matches occupy in the most diverse civilizations."[22] Two boys playing catch upon a playground, the white ball skimming swiftly across the asphalt, will spontaneously create a slanging match wherein each tries to top the other with exaggerations of prowess until the boast slips off into nonsense and giggles. Two knights, the flowers of chivalry, would often do the same in order to enliven the time away from combat. Legends tell us that on their visit to Byzantium, Charlemagne and his twelve companions found couches prepared for them, upon which, at Charlemagne's suggestion, they held a slanging match before going off to sleep. The Emperor himself began, whereafter followed Roland who said "Let King Hugo lend me his horn and I will stand outside the town and blow so hard that the gates will fly off their hinges. And if the king attacks me I will spin round so fast that his ermine cloak will vanish and his moustache catch fire." These exchanges were the art of *Gaber*, gap meaning mockery or derision, particularly as a prelude to banquet or combat: The old Germanic languages contained the equivalent word, *gelp*, which also conveyed the notion of a bragging ceremony. When Beowulf arrives at the court of the Danish king, he is challenged with taunts to recount his former exploits. Remus jumping over Romulus' wall at the dawn of Roman history also belongs to this tradition. The Greeks too enjoyed the ceremony of festive challenges, stares, boasts. If it is true that the agonistic style of consciousness manifests itself in the behavior of the boast, then that instinct lies at the very root of human civilization. Not only Eros builds cities, so too does his brother Mars.

We might also note that animals too delight in boasts, in mutual displays of prowess, contest, strutting, showing off, prancings,

preenings and pretense. Watch a pair of young pups in the freshness
of the morning, while, with bristled backs, they snap and strut and
bare their teeth and pretended to growl; watch a pair of coal black
crows as they stage mock combat in a bright sky above a corn field;
watch two young bulls in a summer pasture as they toss their horns
and paw the dust and charge, only to pull up short of the furious
impact and crash of actual combat. So much foolishness has been
written about re-connection to our animal psyche that it is perhaps
worth noting that we best connect to the animal, the mammalian
wisdom of deep blood and deep bone, by taming the animal in ourselves. In the case of boasting we become like animals only through
refinement, manners, ceremony, which once accomplished allows
us to resemble them. We become more animal-like by stylizing behavior until we join with Charlemagne and Roland into a courtly,
civilized existence.

> Aggression, says Adler, is also a style of phantasy. The
> excited but contained aggression drive creates the cruel
> figures of art and phantasy...[23]

As was the case with our investigation of agonistic thought
forms, the entry into agonistic fantasy is by noting just how dark and
fierce a thing imagination is when it is considered in its nature. Far
too often in circles where fantasy is taken seriously it is the form-
producing qualities of imagination that are emphasized to the complete neglect of all its horrors. But the imagination is a horror-laden
thing. To experience a full revelation of its power is to be completely
terrified. Every child know this, as he lies awake at night, teeth chat-
tering and awash with sweat, afraid to bother mom, and so remains
prey for hours to gruesome shadows who hunger for his soul. Nothing is so terrifying as the depths of our own mind. Perhaps because
they were in communion with the child's deep knowledge, the great
Romantics recognized the violence of the imagination: one thinks of
Blake's tiger in the forest of the night; Coleridge's sacred rivers in cav-
erns measureless to man; Shelley's Wild West Wind; of Steven's fire

cat and his Prince of Peacocks. In the best phenomenologies of the imagination, we also find this stress of deformation (Bachelard); de-creation (Simone Well); derealization (Lynch); pathologizing (Hillman). If the imagination is feminine, then its embodiment is dark Kali, about who Heinrich Zimmer writes—

> She appears as an emaciated, gruesome hag of boney fingers, protruding teeth, unquenchable hunger…(feeding) upon the entrails of her victim. And who among beings born is not her victim. She cleaves the belly and draws out and gobbles the intestines—that is what she is fond of—steaming with the last breath of expiring life.[24]

If the imagination is an animal, it is *draco caelistis*, Typhon, Hydra, Behemoth, the huge black dragon who bites his tail, the Midgard serpent, a subterranean being, a being of the depth, a wretch who will be on the side of demons and monsters in the final battle. If the imagination is the repository of ancient truths, then those truths are the Furies, who require blood payment for every debt. In its essence, the imagination is an elemental force, fierce, dauntless, horrific. The horror, the horror, says Marlow, having glimpsed its bestial floor. It is more sleeping beast than sleeping beauty. To idolize the imagination as the source of all beauty and order regardless of how imagination is employed is to completely betray its nature.

For this reason Adler opens a long list of occupations that the aggression instinct creates, while also showing the place of the aggressive instinct in the symbolic products of our cultural imagination.

> The stronger aggression drive creates and chooses a large number of occupations, not to mention criminals and revolutionary heroes. The occupations of judge, police officer, teacher, minister, physician, and many others are taken up by persons with a larger aggression drive and often show continuity with analogous children's games.

> Some children's games, the world of fairy tales and its favorite figures, the sagas of the various peoples, hero worship, and the many cruel stories and poems of children's books and readers are created by the aggression drive for the aggression drive.[25]

By the aggression drive, for the aggression drive. The move is psychological, self-reflective. Adler is trying to remind us here that the imagination has a dark, bestial, aggressive side, which is quite evident, say, in children's fairy tales. The aggression instinct produces cruel, frightful images in order to remind itself of how cruel, frightful and aggressive the imagination can often be. When we lose this sense of the violent nature of the imagination as is done in Jungian psychology, for example, where the *anima*, the archetype of the imagination, emerges as a flighty, iridescent, shining, magical thing, who is miles away from Kali and who shows little appetite for sheer destruction, then the violence of the imagination slips underground where it does not diminish but intensifies. *The repression of the violence of the imagination releases that violence to symbolically destroy the world.* Ironically, repression gives the imagination free hand to symbolically and psychologically accomplish what it can never attain in the real world: complete, absolute destruction of the materiality of the world. On the individual level this results in a vague, though unbudgeable, conviction that the "real" world is simply not important; that what really counts is the exploration of the soul; while on a collective level this leads to a metaphysical devaluation of everything entailed in the idea of "the flesh," so that it ceases to play any role in philosophy or religion. The flesh may either be completely denied as grave, cell, prison, etc., or it may be radically indulged in an eternal sensual repast. Since the body is not real anyway, it makes no difference what we do with it. De Sade looms near.

Once we realize that violence of the imagination; once we truly come to terms with its hooves and sexuality; then we see the necessity to integrate the imagination into a developing pattern of *gemeinschaftsgefuhl.* We see the necessity of connecting imagination to the world. This is a vision of the world where the form of our relationship with others becomes a paramount importance. Critics who have sensed this dynamic in Adler's thought have labeled him an "ego-psychologist," but if we must use the alien terminology of Freud and Jung, let us call him a *persona* psychologist, a thinker convinced that the true goal of human existence is to enrich the communal bond. The decisive evidence for this interpretation of Adler is his vision of the City rather than nature as the perfection of human existence. The founding of the city symbolically represents man's discovery that the deep natural violence of the soul must be tamed, civilized and snared into a cultural order, if man is to attain the perfection that is possible to his nature.

Like any instinct, aggression needs to admit to stylization, if it is to be absorbed into culture. As Adler says: "Its refinement and stylization lead to sports, competition, dueling, war..."[26] Consider dueling, for instance, which from Hector and Achilles to Hamilton and Burr has been a vital theme in culture and the subject of a lavish ritual. In 1836 one of the most curious products of the Age of Dueling appeared in the form of a book, *The Art of Dueling*, published anonymously, by "*A Traveler.*" Besides dealing at length with such predictable matters as choice and care of weapons, the book also gives elaborate instructions on how the duelist should pass the evening the night before his rendezvous with fate. The author warns against the onset of depression. Avoid gloominess at all costs, he says: "A man should not allow the idea of becoming a target to make him uneasy; but treating the matter jocosely, he must summon up all his energy, and declare war against nervous apprehension;" and recommends that the duelist "ought to invite a few friends to dinner and laugh away the evening over a bottle of port, or, if fond of cards, play a rubber of whist." And if, at midnight, he cannot drift off, he must take some amusing book—one of Sir Walter's novels, if a lover of the romantic; or Byron's *Childe Harold*, if he delights in the sublime; and read until he drops asleep."[27] The book continues with other advice on when to rise, the type of pistols, appropriate garb and courtesy and the need for an attendant physician.

Above I said "vital," by which I meant that the ritual of dueling has added story and song to culture and in many cases diminished the actual cost of life, as in the various "royal" duels that have substituted for an actual clash of armies. To even speak of dueling, now, seems quaintly ludicrous because dueling is an extravagant gesture in service of one's honor; and neither extravagant gestures nor a keen sense of honor have been welcome in our culture for many years. And yet, in the absence of dueling, and the attempt to civilize aggression that dueling and other grand, though often bloody, customs often represent, are we any more civilized or any less murderously inclined? Whole nations war now instead of kings in single combat; and death is still a sport on city streets, though the body count is higher.

One of the most beautiful and successful attempts to civilize aggression is the *potlatch* practiced in various archaic cultures. The potlatch is a solemn feast, during which two groups, with lavish pomp and ceremony, exchange gifts on a large scale, with the expressed purpose of winning glory, honor and renown. Any important event may occasion a potlatch—wedding, funeral, construction of a house. Amid songs and dancing, the recitation of the spirit lore, and drama with the masks, one clan will squander all its goods, distributing them to rival clans in a lavish, reckless, act of generosity. But by taking part in the potlatch rival clans incur the obligation to make a grander feast in the future. Failure to do so results in total loss of honor, badges, totems, civil and religious rights. The consequence of this round of events is circulation of the possessions through the tribe, although there is an element of risk and adventure bound up with this particular form of the invisible hand. A potlatch theoretically can fail, in which case a whole clan may fall into poverty and ostracism.

According to Huizinga, "The potlatch and everything connected with it hinges on winning, on being superior, on glory, prestige and, last but not least, revenge. Always, even when only one person is the feast-giver, there are two groups standing in opposition, but bound by a spirit of hostility and friendship combined."[28] Huizinga goes on to demonstrate that the potlatch always has an element of combat about it, so that it takes place in a world of pomp, challenge, honor, braggadocio, which is also the world of chivalry, where pride, combat, noble lineages and illustrious names bulk large. The duel also belongs to this world, and is perhaps its most durable expression. The underlying principle of the potlatch and the entire realm of chivalry is agonistic consciousness, that is, the aggressive instinct. The potlatch must "be regarded first and foremost as a violent expression of the human need to fight."[29] But we also see how the potlatch tames this violence and puts it into service of the community. Thanks to the ritual of the potlatch the archaic world remains lively, rich, just and fair, and above all, fully human, in that it accommodates the full and sometimes violent range of our humanity.

In addition to the duel and the potlatch, there are many other ways to civilize aggression, many of which we touch on in various places of this consideration of Adler's phenomenology of aggression. My point here, and Adler's point as well, is to indicate that aggression can be stylized in ways that are not inimical to the community; and to also illustrate some of the means that have been historically employed to do this. In its most beautiful and civilized forms, aggression, or agonistic consciousness, can be a rich, alluvial nutrient for the growth of culture in the same way and with the same unconsciousness stamina as iron nourishes the blood.

Adler identifies aggression as a typical form of pathology. Before asking about the pathology of aggression, we must first inquire into its perfection. Further, the phenomenological world of actual description must be preceded by rigorous ideational effort. Prior to examining the most vital expression of aggression, we must ask what is its most vital way of conceiving of itself.

What Adler meant by "aggression" is best conceived as *thymos*. Under the rubric of aggression Adler intuited what the Greeks called *thymos*, and the Latins, *animus*. While Individual Psychology was still in the white-hot heat of original conception, Alexander Neuer grasped the connection between the spirit of Adler's work and the spirit he was trying to transmit to others, and the ancient Greek idea of *thymos*. By restoring courage to the central existential place that it had occupied for nearly all of Western history, Adler recovered *thymos*. Neuer writes:

> The nature of the mind (soul, spirit, psyche) may be incomprehensible as a thing-in-itself, but it may be understood in relation to community. Aristotle calls man a *zoon politikon*, a social animal. For this universal social quality of consciousness, Adler uses the term *Mut*, that is, courage. The spirit that springs from and lives from community—in Adler's terminology, this is the courageous spirit, *die mutige Seele*. Often before in the history of philosophy the word "courage" did duty for the idea of "mind." In Greek, for instance, *Thymos* means both courage and mind.[30]

Unfortunately, Neuer never exploited his insight, never advanced along this particular front. Even so, he flagged a site for future work and Adler's enthusiastic support for Neuer's insights lends a special authority to this attempt to mine that site. By looking at *thymos* we may derive a classical paternity for Adler's thought, a matrix for future considerations.

So what, then, did the Greeks count *thymos*? In *Psyche*, his monumental excursion into the depths of the Greek mind, Erwin Rhode discounted every definition of *thymos*, because he was convinced that, with respect to *thymos*, the Greek experience is simply beyond modern comprehension. Rhode simply calls it an untranslatable word. Richard Onians, on the other hand, claims, on the basis of massive evidence that *thymos*, "should, mean vapour. Whence? From what liquid but blood, the hot liquid which is in fact concentrated in the heart and around it in the lungs ($\varphi\rho\acute{\varepsilon}\nu\varepsilon\varsigma$). The latter are filled with blood and breath that interact, giving and taking from each other.[31] *Thymos* compares with the Latin *fumus*, Sanskrit *dhumah*, which means "vapor," or "smoke," with the Old Slav *dymu*, "smoke," *duchu*, meaning "breath" or "spirit" etc. "The $\Theta\acute{\upsilon}\mu o\varsigma$ is not the blood-soul as opposed to the breath-soul nor indeed mere breath but breath related to blood, not mere air but something vaporous within, blending and interacting with the air without, something which diminishes if the body is ill nourished."[32] *Thymos*, then, is the vapor of the blood, the hot keen spirit coagulated in the heart, the visible steam that is given off when the blood boils and rages in the grip of strong emotion. It is steam, vapor, boiling substance, the wild dew of the heart.

Onians' emphasis on *thymos* as the *suspiration* of the blood when the usual definitions simply chalk it up as "blood soul" points to something psychological, since air, froth, dew, vapor, etc. are traditional symbols of fantasy. It points to the idea that *thymos is the blood soul's fantasy of itself*, that is, through the idea of *thymos* the agonistic style of consciousness articulates its own reality. In other words, *thymos* is the blood soul's unique means of imagining its own inward spirit. From the *thymos*, then, we learn about the blood, about the psychology of the blood. Adler's attachment to the blood soul can be gleaned, de-constructive style, from the material of his first book, *A Study of Organ Inferiority*, which gained him a solid reputation among psychoanalysts, although it was rejected at the university on the grounds of being too *geistreich*, that is too clever. On page one of his book Adler reflects on the nature of the kidney; he catalogues its various ills. Now the question arises as to why the kidney and not some other organ, the liver, say, or the lungs? While there may be many obvious reasons for this choice, there is a subtle one as well. There is a psychological reason which may be gleaned from a simple straightforward description of the kidney.

The kidneys are a pair of bean-shaped organs which sit down river in the body, where they are posted like two sentinels. Tradition ascribes a certain nobility to the organs, even in its afflictions, which unite men into a proud company described by Montaigne:

> I feel everywhere Men tormented with the same disease: and am honor'd by the Fellowship, forasmuch as Men of the best quality are most frequently afflicted with it; 'tis

a noble and dignified disease. And were it not a good office to a man to put him in mind of his end? My kidneys
claw me to a purpose.[33]

The kidneys are almost weightless; together they top the scale at
barely one half pound. Rich with ducts and tiny arteries, the kidneys
shape their body space with the spine and the bulk of the liver. They
do their work quite naturally, unassisted by directives from the cra-
nial mass of the brains. Put quite simply, the business of the organ is
the filtering of the blood. They separate waste matter from the keen
stuff of the blood. What is judged and found wanting is discharged
into the bladder while the re-invigorated blood is channeled into the
hungry veins and far reaches of the body. The function of the kidneys then is to restore the richness of the blood.

If Adler's work is kidney shaped, shaped in the image of the kidney, then it is a work charged with the directive to restore the sanity,
vigor, keenness, the wealth and richness of the blood; and all the
verities evoked by the blood: the passion of *amour* and friendship,
the *fama* of the family, courage, boldness, dignity, endurance, the
flow of compassion, the wild lyric of utmost loyalty that is rendered
unto death. From the very beginning, then, Adler's work was quickened with the desire to restore the ancient rites off the blood soul;
from the very beginning it exalted the hero; from the very beginning
it was situated in the heart; from the very beginning its seat was the
thymos. As it did with Montaigne, the afflictions of the kidney set
Adler dreaming of a noble company, the *urbs aeterna*, which was
eventually to materialize as the very goal of human existence, the
ideal community of *gemeinschaftsgefuhl*.

Onians insisted that the *thymos* "thinks"; it is itself a way of
thinking. "How do Homeric notions of the main processes of consciousness differ from our own? A good deal is explicit. Thinking
is described as 'speaking' and is located sometimes in the heart but
usually in the…'midriff' or 'diaphragm'…deep reflection is conversation with one's *thymos* or of one's *thymos* with one's self. Thus
Menelaus, deserted in battle, spake to his great-hearted *thymos,*

'Woe to me if I leave behind these noble arms...or why did my *thymos* thus hold converse...'"[34] If *thymos* is a form of thought, and if *thymos* does provide the classical background for Adler's consideration of the aggressive instinct or the agonistic consciousness, then Adler is clearly justified in describing aggression as a style of thought. From Onians' description of *thymos*, we may supplement our earlier description. Since *thymos* depicts itself as a thing-like substance, we may say that the *thymos* "thinks" through the metaphor of things. It "thinks" by transferring both itself and other immaterial realities into things that can be sensed by the inner eye. To think it must be touched and in turn it struggles to touch others, perhaps through rhetoric. As Onians notes, *thymos* thinks in words. Since *thymos* is clearly rooted in the body, being inseparable from its bodily substrate, *thymos* thinking will always be deeply engaged with the matters of flesh, tongue and bone, with what Yeats called the rag and bone shop of the heart. And since *thymos* is curiously increased by intake of food and diminished when there is no external nourishment, we may suspect that *thymos* thinking is extraverted thinking, thinking that requires the worldly substance of sensation and experience in order to reflect at all. Adler was a thinker who had to practice clinically in order to think at all. It is thus Aristotelian thinking, for which there is nothing in the mind that was not first in the sense. As psyche needs an epistemology, so too does *thymos*. Where Plato wrote the first, Aristotle furnishes the second. Need we still wonder that Adler described himself as a student of Aristotle, the meaning of which description has continually eluded even the most brilliant of Adlerians?

Both historically and psychologically, *thymos* has a subtle linkage with what the Latins called *animus*. The connection further hammers down the idea that *thymos* describes a mode of reflection. Onians argues that throughout Latin literature the *animus* was the principle of consciousness.

> Consciousness with all the variations of emotion and
> thought is a matter of *animus*. To contemplate some ac-

tion is "to have it in one's *animus*"; to turn one's attention to something, an idea within or an object in space,
is "to turn the *animus* towards it"; courage, despair,
etc., are matters of animus; to feel faint, to be on the
way to losing consciousness, was in the Plautine phrase
quoted "it goes ill with one's *animus*"; when a man loses
consciousness his "*animus* leaves him"; to collect one's
faculties and spirits is "to collect one's *animus*"—and so
we might continue.[35]

The *animus* also has the connection with chest, breath, heart,
etc., that are characteristic of *thymos*.

> *Animus* was originally some "breath" in the chest; also
> *animus* was the stuff of consciousness, and the con-
> sciousness was in the chest; therefore *animus* was breath
> that was consciousness in the chest. What breath was
> there in the chest? The ordinary breath of respiration,
> the breath in the form of which pride, spirit, etc., i.e. *ani-
> mus*, appears, and in the form of which—words—con-
> sciousness issues forth, thoughts are uttered.[36]

Onians sums up his findings: "*Animus* thus appears to have
been the same in origin as Θύμος, the breath that was consciousness in the chest."[37]

If *thymos* stands behind the Adlerian project, which project first
took the form of a phenomenology of aggressive instinct, then Adlerian consciousness is consciousness as *esse in animus*. This puts us in
a position to understand the paroxysms of fury that Adler tends to
excite in leftist critics such as Jacoby, Marcuse and Stepansky. Almost
frothing at the mouth, barely able to contain their fury, these "critical realists" vilify Adler as the snake in the polymorphous garden of
love's body. In their eyes Adler replaced Freud's psychic depth and
discovery of a radical, deep, instinctual, erotic consciousness with a
celebration of the ego.

If the history of psychology is the history of forgetting, Adler was the first, but by no means the last, to forget. His revision of psychoanalysis was a homemade remedy to assuage the pain of the unfamiliar: psychoanalysis. The notions that he, and the neo-Freudians, would champion were borrowings from everyday prattle: the self, values, norms, insecurities, and the like. They were offered as antidotes to Freud's illiberalism. Yet just this constituted Freud's strength: his refusal to bow to reigning wisdom; his exploration of a tabooed and erotic psychic underground that officially did not exist. The subjectivity and social factors the revisionists added to correct Freud's excess did the trick; they brought psychology back into the fold.[38]

But here Jacoby is only warming up. Let me collate a few more comments:

> (Adler) betrayed the revolutionary core of psychoanalysis for common sense.

> Adler repressed psychoanalysis by liberalizing it. He diluted its position, negated its power.

> Adler's later thought succumbs to the worst of his earlier banalization. It is conventional, practical, and moralistic.[39]

In faulting Adler as the father of "ego-psychology," these critics make an entirely illegitimate equation between the *animus* or *thymos* and the ego. To an extent they are victims of their own Freudian ideology which cannot grasp the idea of consciousness except as a quality of the ego. For the most part, Adler eschewed the ego in his conceptual apparatus and so was able to transcend the Cartesian tradition with its monads, egos and footless *cogitos*. Adler's genius was that he found a way to subsume the "ego" and "ego" psychology into a larger framework which allowed for "thinking," "acting," "functioning," "willing," "adjusting," with the heart instead of with the head. If anything the ego is but the shadow of the *animus, thymos*, striving for significance. It is a pale shadow of a scarlet substance. True this style of thinking does give rise to a typical politics to which the left will always be in total opposition. But elaboration of this point would take us too far afield. Suffice it to say that such a politics is not the politics of ego-enrichment, monads fighting over the trickle down crumbs of an invisible hand. It is something altogether different.

> In antiquity both the *animus* and *thymos* were deemed to be the seat of particular virtues.[40]
>
> Upon a man's "spirit" or "breath-soul" depend his fierceness or energy (μένος) and courage (θάρσος). He breathes them.[41]
>
> The gods place boldness to the *thymos*, so that in warriors before a battle 'no pity was there through their lips (οἶκτος οὔτι ἦν διά στόμα), but the iron-lunged [thymos] (σιδηρόφρων) θυμὸς breathed flaming with valor.'[42]

The image of *thymos* "flaming" reveals its fiery, sulfuric, combustible nature. It easily ignites. Its colors are the red and gold of a sunburnt sky. *Thymos* also affects the senses, molding them in its image. Seeing especially was thought to be the work of *thymos*.

> In actual seeing, something—what is received through the eyes—is "breathed" from the objects seen...What is received...was recognized in light (differentiated by colour and form), thought of as gaseous or confused perhaps with the air through which it passed...The same though will explain the Latin use of *aura* of a ray or gleam, radiance.[43]

Thymos then transforms actual sight into vision. To see through *thymos* is to be a visionary perceiver, to see a universe in a grain of sand, to be a Dante or Petrarch, whose heart leaps up in glad response to the colors and shades of beauty. To see with *thymos* is to drink to thee with mine eyes. And finally, *thymos* is emotion.[44] In antiquity it was linked with the strongest of emotions. There were certain experiences that constellated thymos. As Onians says, "it is θυμός [*thymos*] which is most mentioned when...describing emotion...For the Homeric Greeks the θυμός [*thymos*] is the 'spirit,' the breath that is consciousness, variable, dynamic, coming and going, changing as a feeling changes."[45]

From Onians discussion it is clear that certain experiences are fraught with *thymos*; and further, that he believes that such experiences are accessible to us today. When they occur, we usually describe them in an idiom of air. To pant with eagerness, to gasp or whistle with astonishment, to snort with indignation, to sob with grief, to yawn with weariness, to laugh with mirth, to sigh with sadness or relief, or some of the more marked variations of breathing that have found distinct expression in everyday speech. The "breast heaving with emotion" is a common place. We "catch our breath" at a sudden sound, "hold our breath" in suspense, "breathe more freely," and so the list might be continued. The sudden changes in the breast signal the presence of *thymos*, its entry into the realm of human experience. On the basis of Onian's definition of *thymos*, together with his indication that *thymos* continues to form a part of the modern existential world, we are now in a position to describe the typical modalities of *thymos*, the way it appears in actual experience. To cast it back in Adlerian language, we are now positioned so as to enjoy an unobstructed gaze of the experience of the aggressive instinct. But since we have adopted the language of *thymos*, we shall continue to employ it. One advantage of the word is its strangeness, its uncanny ring, for this keeps it from being absorbed back into the circuit of conventional associations that crowd around the word aggression.

Thymos appears in anger. As Adler says "We find pure expressions of the aggression drive in temper tantrums."[46] In speaking of anger we are not referring to the garden variety of getting mad, although even there the presence of thymos is deeply felt, a twin-plumed spirit passing through the mind. Rather, the reference is to something much more profound. Where thymos emerges, the fists will clench, the arm strike out, the foot sweep up in vicious kick, a baleful glance grimaces the face. Let us name it rage. The Romans knew and feared it as the battle lust that sent the Celts moiling into battle, naked, painted, with swords encrusted with glittering jewels and hot with murderous intent. The Japanese call it kamikaze and know that it can heighten the senses into a frenzy of perception, so that each detail of the enemy is noticed: the chill blue color of his eyes; the ivory pall of his cheek; the precise pitch of his death cry. We should remember that this rage went hand in hand with aesthetics and a cult of chivalry, and a high level of cultural refinement. Rage belongs to subtle civilizations. The passage of anger into rage is large-ly a matter of ritual and cultural support. Most of us would gladly deny anger any vessels for its shaping. But when rage is not accepted, not countenanced as a normal part of life which needs refinement and stylization, anger does not simply disappear, but instead slips underground to smolder until erupting into ineffectual tantrums or cold, fatal violence. Nations with rich martial tradition—pomp and circumstance, medals and the heroic dead—often have a very low level of random violence. The opposite of a soldier is not a paci-fist, but a terrorist. Even when life ends with a whimper instead of a bang, end it does nonetheless. In determining the rank of thymos among other psychic realities, it is good to remember that our long Western saga commences with "Sing, Muse, of the wrath of Achilles." When we exterminate that wrath, we lose connection to our history, our Tradition and perhaps to the springs of poetry itself.

Although we are trying to grapple here with Adler's daimon as it originally appeared to him; and are deferring, for a moment, dis-cussion of its subsequent development, we should in fairness note that Adler himself was not so kind to anger. Generally, he viewed it as a disjunctive emotion which evinced an underlying superior-ity complex. Whether in adults or children, an outburst of temper tantrums reflects an asocial nature. Rage sins against the common good. Adler writes—

> The disjunctive emotions (*trennende Affekte*) such as anger, sorrow, or fear, are not mysterious phenomena which cannot be interpreted. They appear always where they serve a purpose corresponding to the life method or guiding line of the individual. Their purpose is to bring about a change of the situation in favor of the individual...Through such heightened effort his own person is placed into the foreground and made victorious. Thus, as there is no rage without an enemy, this emotion can only have victory over him for its goal. It is a popular method, still possible in our culture, to assert oneself through such increased movements.[47]

And then goes on to expand on ager in particular, the consequences and pathology thereof.

> In an outburst of temper the individual wishes to overcome his imperfections as quickly as possible. To hit, accuse, or attach another individual seems to be the best way. The anger, in its turn, influences the organs. It mobilizes them for action or lays an additional stress on them.[48]

Now in this passage we should note that Adler recognizes that present day culture often sanctions anger and rewards it with the laurels of significance. Thus in our society, as it is presently constituted, anger can belong to a more or less normal striving for significance. Anger can be a positive force perhaps a token of social interest. To argue otherwise requires a wholesale condemnation not only of our own society, but most of the classical tradition, which begins with wrath and is largely agonic in structure. Surely such a condemnation would itself reveal a deficient social interest. At the very best it would be disloyal.

In Adler's description of how anger affects the organs, we may read an evocation of the "iron body," the minerals in the blood, the wolf and scarlet headed woodpecker, the animals of Mars. All the beauty and the lore of armor is itself an extension of this inner "iron body" that Reich intuited as body armor, although he entirely misread its significance, and that Adler in another place calls the body of courage:

> A courageous individual will show the effects of his attitude in his physique. His body will be differently built up. The tonus of his muscles will be stronger, the carriage of his body will be firmer...The expression of the face is different in the courageous individual, and, in the end, the whole cast of features.[49]

Armor is itself the glittering mirror of this psychological reality. When we cast away this honor, we cast away our souls as well, our potential to enter into a genuinely Adlerian form of consciousness. No matter how ingenious the technique, no matter how comprehensive the form of education, no matter how good intentioned the inspiration, true rage cannot be eliminated from the compass of the psyche or from the field of civilization. By trying to do so, we turn something vital into something vicious. The same poet whose wild mind produced the fearful symmetries of the tiger burning bright also knew the consequences of the attempt to not know the depths of our own anger.

> I was angry with my friend.
> I told my wrath; my wrath did end.
> I was angry with my foe.
> I told it not; my wrath did grow.
> And I watered it in fears
> Night and morning with my tears
> And I sunned it with smiles
> And with soft, deceitful whiles

And it grew both day and night
Till it bore an apple bright
And my foe beheld it shine
And he knew that it was mine
And into my garden stole
And when the night had vailed the pole
In the morning glad I see
My foe outstretched beneath the tree.

When we try to domesticate or chain the wolf, an unconscious Lupercalia soon results. At Rome there was a cult of wolfish brothers who at their festival, which fell in February, would slaughter a goat and then spatter themselves with the fresh blood while skinning the animal. They would then run naked around the city in a wild festival of taunts and crudities aimed at rivals and pretty women in the crowds. They would then converge upon the Palatine, the she-wolf's den around which they would circulate in a lewd, mystical and bloody frenzy. This circulation "cured" them perhaps because they had symbolically enacted a return to the Wolf, the deep source of rage and anger, and expressed a desire to be suckled there as were the founders of Rome, Romulus and Remus. The Lupercalia represented an attempt to affirm rage as a fundamental element of our social living. While there may be something that can be suckled from and mined, other Roman myths depict this truth in the image of Mars as an ancient agricultural deity long before he ascended to the place of god of war. When rage is affirmed, then "war" itself can become a civilizing force as it was in Rome. Psychologically, this means to sense the connection between contest and civilization, between rage and culture. Indeed outrage may be one of the best ways to awaken a dormant sense of *gemeinschaftsgefuhl*. "I'm mad as hell and not going to take it anymore," may be the right weapon for destroying that network of injustice that works against the true nature of the charity.

A second stimulus to *thymos* is Herculean effort. Because Vico realized this, he made Hercules the symbol of his cultural psychology. This includes even those wretched times when it takes a Herculean effort even to survive. Whenever we extend ourselves so as to truly confront our limits, just then *thymos* may appear to carry us past those limits and into a dazzling space where time does not exist. All is rhythm there, magnified into a low, delicious sound. This is the kingdom of the heart; it has become available through the conquest of both impulse and the squalid call of sloth. What we accomplish during such a time may seem a miracle because it is a miracle wrought by *thymos*, the power of the heart. I think of Ezra Pound stretched out in a cage near Pisa, with his mind hanging by a grass blade, an old man subjected to dust, glare and savage indignities, but hanging on to write some of the richest poetry ever to crystallize in air. *Thymos* fed this poetry, nourishing it with crystal springs. The peasant in his timeless, ancient work, in new mown fields of hay; the mystic with his hair shirt and midnight prayers; the soldier, posted on the frontier or dying in the trenches; the athlete dying young: all know the mystery of *thymos*. Of *thymos* they are all compact.

Closely related to heroic, Herculean effort is the sudden crisis that springs on us unaware to require a serene clarity of action of which we did not think ourselves as capable. *Thymos* will surge in an instant of travail, as it did for Odysseus as he floated on a raft in the middle of a wide dark sea. Suddenly a storm blew up which was summoned by Poseidon, earth shaker, who carried a vendetta in his heart against Odysseus. Night sprang from heaven. The sea was dark and death was near. During that moment, Odysseus had an experience of *thymos* as an unconquerable will that flamed up from his chest and with whom he could take counsel. He addressed his heart who in turn sustained him. *Thymos* stirred and throbbed, focused and directed, until culminating in a revelation of beauty and skilled decision which took the form of a woman. Leukothea appears, a nymph, and gives him a celestial garment on which he floats to safety.

We all compare Odysseus, in that at certain times when the risk is great, to either the sanctity of the soul or the health of the body, something within us leaps up to stiffen resolve enough to carry us through the immediate crisis. Glassy eyes become all glass, new windows of the soul illumined by an unconquerable flame that burns within, while we slip out of our everyday roles to become something large: and grander, discovering new depths of personality that allow us to embrace the moment as a chance to prove ourselves, or allow us to say No, even at great cost. A small boy, who is pushed too far, may suddenly discover self-respect as he lobs a skinny punch into a bully's face; a spineless man may quit his job because it compromises decency and thus recover the timeless wealth of pride and dignity; a single mother, sitting exhausted at 4 a.m. within a darkened kitchen, may find the courage to go on. Such courage may seem a gift of fortune, a celestial aid, a miraculous garment like the one delivered to Odysseus from the depths of the sea. It is what we are calling *thymos*. As with Odysseus, such moments often climax with a visitation of overwhelming beauty. Leukothea comes; or Petrarch's Laura; or Dante's Beatrice; and there upon our hearts are driven wild. As Dante says, writing of his first glimpse of beauty "...the spirit of life, which hath its dwelling in the secretest chamber of the heart, began to tremble so violently that the least pulses of my body shook."[50] These divine ladies, who often appear in poetry and life, are the revelation of *thymos* to itself. Through the agency of Beatrice, Dante learned about the state and possibilities of his own soul. By asking us to reflect, these ladies are mirrors who catch the burning blaze of *thymos* and deflect that blaze back on its source, so that the *thymos* can glimpse itself and discover its own rude and native beauty. It is as if the lady were to tie a golden scarf around a lance, whereby her fancy knight discovers that his own dark, bloody trade is somehow beautiful, or becomes beautiful once he acquires the eyes to see it. What we are saying here is nothing less radical than that the celestial dames reveal that violence itself is beautiful, that it houses an immense aesthetic appeal. Violence is beautiful, the sword a charm that dangles from a ruby encrusted belt. Poetry itself begins a celebration of the beauty of violence. As David Jones comments "...for us in the West the arts and the arts of war have been in a rather special relationship."[51] War is an art: it is this the lady shows. Upon the presentation of beauty Dante's whole

106

spirit began to tremble violently as if the whole purpose of Beatrice's visitation was to show that violence itself may be a *via regia* to the vision of the Rose. For the most part, however, we all recoil from even the vague suggestion that there is something fair or beautiful about a violent act. And yet war itself is beautiful, as Robert E. Lee once said, the most chivalrous of soldiers, and on a lesser scale even school boys will flock around a fight, happy and at home with the idea that the trickle of blood may soon disgrace a face; adolescents flock to films that describe in almost loving detail every conceivable way a body can be maimed, speared, spiked, beheaded, mutilated and undone, sitting there with popcorn and cokes and planning back seat escapades; and even we adults, meek, responsible, raised upon an ethic of nonviolence which we praise as one of our highest values, will rubber neck along the highway hoping to catch a glimpse of the victim as he lies there amid the blood and shattered glass. Although every nerve and fiber of our civilized consciousness rebel against the thought, there is an immense beauty housed in violence. In the East they understand this. Aggression and aesthetics seem bound together in a kind of inner blood wedding in which we all are bridesmaids and groomsmen at least in our instinctual reactions even if not in our consciousness.

The Romans realized this connection, and so made Venus into a god of war. As Venus *victrix* or Venus *armata*, she was an ancestral goddess of the Julian house. Appearing on the gems and coins of Caesar and Augustus, she symbolized the beauty native to the act of war. So too did the condotierre, whose vitality and energy so fascinated Ezra Pound. The English company of John Hawkwood, one of the most famous condotierre, received the name of the White Company because of the incredible polish of their armor which turned every battlefield into a symphony of light. De Rougemont describes the "professional soldiers in the service of princes and popes, the *condottieri* were much less given to making war than to ensuring that war did not take a toll of lives. They were not only adventurers, but skilled diplomats and astute traders."[52] While Burkhart describes their style of combat—

Fighting invariably takes place on horseback, the soldiers being protected by arms and assured of preserving their lives if taken prisoner...The lives of the defeated are nearly always spared. They do not remain prisoners for long, and their release is obtained very easily. A town may rebel a score of times; it is never destroyed. The inhabitants retain the whole of their property; all they have to fear is that they will be made to pay a levy.[53]

In one of his medals, the condotierre Federico da Montefeltro summed up the Renaissance view of violence as a potentially vital and beautiful form of life which must nonetheless be harmonized with other claims. This patron of the arts placed a cannonball at the center of his medal between a sword and a cuirass, which belongs to Mars, and a whisk broom and myrtle, which belong to Venus. In the rockets' red glare he found an invitation to reflection on the imponderables of life. And even closer to our own time are those scholar soldiers who were fashioned by the playing fields of Eton and the martial traditions of Napoleonic France. In The Face of Battle, John Keegan, one of our most authoritative military historians, reflects upon the romance of soldiering. The romantic soldier, he says, was—...an unusual figure, but not an uncommon one. Fiction knows him well, of course, a great deal of Romantic literature having as its theme the man-of-violence who is also the man of self-knowledge, self-control, compassion, *Weltanschauung*. He certainly exists in real life also, and as often in the army as elsewhere, as the memoirs of many professional soldiers—though few successful generals—will testify. Perhaps—it is only an impression—he is more typically a French or British than a German or American figure, the horizons of the Sahara or the North-West Frontier encouraging a breadth of outlook denied to the Hauptmann or the first lieutenant on dreary garrison duty in Arizona or Lorraine. And although there is a German "literary" literature of military life, it is very much more a literature of leadership, as in Bloem's *Vormarsch*, or the exaltation of violence, as in Jünger's *Kampf als innere Erlebnis*, than of adventure,

exploration, ethnography, social—sometimes even spiritual—fulfillment, the themes which characterize the novels of Ernest Psiachari
or F. Yeats-Brown, or the memoirs of Lyautey, Ian Hamilton, Lord
Belhaven, Meinertzhagen and a host of other major and minor ser-
vants of British and French imperialism in this century and the last
who, by design or good luck, chose soldiering as a way of life and
found their minds enlarged by it.[54]

In the Roman soldier, the life of the Renaissance condotierre,
and in the meditations of empire troops, we find a keen sense of the
beauty of war and a decision to live with it so as to diminish its more
destructive components.

For the aggressive instinct to truly be integrated into consciousness is probably too large and difficult a task to be accomplished,
given the current climate of opinion, which fears nothing so much
as war. But is it war that we fear or is it the paradox of a warless war,
that is, a war where there is no opportunity for beauty, chivalry or
courage. It is sometimes said that the bomb will mean not only the
end of humanity but the end of all human things, especially culture.
But the presence of the bomb has already ended one vital part of
culture: war and the imagination of war. Any genuinely psychological accommodation of the aggressive instinct; of *thymos*, requires as
a first and indispensable condition that we realize the inner beauty
of aggression. Aggression must be given a chance to know its own
beauty through the medium of tournaments and other ritualized
contests. When these contests are affirmed as a vital part of culture
and not an anachronistic expression of machoism and chauvinism
and the savage mind that ought at all costs to be eliminated, stamped
out on playground, in classroom, in work, and most perniciously, in
therapy, then aggression may flower into chivalry, attaining to the
flame colored heights of *thymos*, where the hearts sings and a star
stirs and a fire brings light and illumination to the darkness of the
human condition.

We come now to the pathology of agonistic consciousness, of
the aggression instinct. Robert Sardello addressed this problem in
a classic piece which serves as inspiration to this entire work. Seek-

ing to understand the temper tantrums and random violence that have become the American pastime, Sardello resurrects cyclothymia, an illness whose phenomenology has been neglected because of the dominance of hysteria, schizophrenia, and manic depression. In 1936 Kretschmer describes the illness as a variation of the cyclic personality temperament, while offering this description.

> People of this kind have a soft temperament, which can swing to great extremes. The path over which it swings is a wide one, namely between cheerfulness and unhappiness...there is, however, another swinging path which is very little used, namely that which leads in the direction of nervous excitability...
>
> The cyclothymic is a person of quick temper, a knightly hot-bloodedness...who flares up all of a sudden, and is soon good again. They cannot halt behind a mountain; when anything gets in their way, they see red at once, and they try to get their way by making a row.[55]

It is striking how closely this description resembles Adler's portrait of anger as a disjunctive emotion. Sardello finds cyclothymia at work in the American family, where it leads to "ineffectual sacrifice," "blood split," "Hiroshima in the Family," "the Great Conflagration," ending with a jump and imitations of Empedocles, into a volcano.

The cure for all this? Beauty, says Sardello, the aggression instinct realization that in itself contains a feminine component. What Sardello calls feminine, we might even label narcissistic. If aggression is to be healed, Mars must learn to preen, to accept his own desire to be beautiful, to wear the white armor of Hawkwood's company, the red cross of the crusader, the lyric heraldry of medieval knights. During the Middle Ages the knights loved to fight, but they loved to dress up just as much or more.

This fondness for all that glitters reappears in the general gaudiness of dress, especially in the excessive number of precious stones sewn on the garments...Transferred to the domain of hearing, this partiality for brilliant things is shown by the naïve pleasure taken in the tinkling or clicking sounds. La Hire wore a red mantle covered all over with little silver bells like cow-bells. At an entry in 1465, Captain Salazar was accompanied by twenty men-at-arms, the harness of whose horses was ornamented with large silver bells. The horses of the counts of Charolais and of St. Pol were altered in the same way, also those of the lord of Croy, at the entry of Louis XI into Paris in 1461. At festivals jingling florins or nobles were often sewn onto the dress.[56]

It may be that the cure for violence is in the cult of the dandy as if the glory slaughter of the battlefield were but an afterthought to the splendid, colorful marshalling of forces which preceded it. Perhaps the aggression instinct falls to killing because it is afraid that its own innate love of beauty would somehow mark it as effeminate. But is not beauty, art and the shock of the new, the greatest violence?

Is not power truly the imagination? Has not the "violence" of modern art been telling us this for over fifty years? In the classical tradition beauty is defined as that which arrests motion. Might this not extend even to an advancing army? Was not Paris saved because it was so beautiful? Beauty may be the only way to stop blitzkrieg, in which case we must say that beauty is more powerful than a tank. And in therapy are not the most effective interventions usually the most aesthetic? Let violence only accept its narcissism and it may be healed or at least partially contained. Perhaps we see red so much because we can't see crimson. In medieval tournaments red predominated. At some princely entries all the accoutrements were in red. And the purple reserved to the emperors was really a deep crimson.

Give the soldier in us a sash and medal and he may not go to war. As Frederick the Great said—

> The soldier polished his rifle and accouterments, the cavalier his bridle, saddle, and even his boots; the manes of horses were dressed with ribbons...If peace had lasted beyond 1740, we would probably now have rouge and beauty spots.[57]

—of his invincible army. A close reading of history confirms our view, for during the latter days of chivalry, the aggressive instinct did indeed lose much of its ferocious edge, so that the tournament, which had always been the centerpiece of knight errantry, and which had only been little more than a bloody free-for-all evolved into a virtual form of theater. Skill and symbol superseded violence. The world of the tournament became a world of—

> ...burnished hauberks, emblazoned shields and banners, rich mantles and costly furs...It was only natural that the knightly world which listened to their stories [the chroniclers] should seek in turn to infuse into its sport and ceremony some reflection at least of the romantic interest with which these were charged in fiction. To put it in this way is inevitably to oversimplify, for the interplay of life and romance is always a complex matter, but the importance of that interplay, for the history of tournaments, is not in doubt. From the point of view that we have been following until now, the hurly-burly of such engagements has presented a spectacle dominated by crude and sometimes extreme masculine violence. From the new angle of vision that the romance storytellers open for us, what we see now is a very different scene, in which colour and violence fuse together into the display of the male before the female.[58]

The great Huizinga considered the arcane pageantry to be an indication of the decay of chivalry, its chilling into autumn. My view, however, accords with Maurice Keen who writes—

> Just as the church with its literate priesthood at hand, from the earliest times, found means to express new movements of the spirit in additions to its liturgy and ritual and to visual religious symbolism, so now chivalry could do the same, through the medium of heraldic art and knowledge. And just as in the history of religion such additions to liturgy and observance do not denote a tired spirituality but rather the continuing vigor and infinitely variable range of religious feeling, so in chivalry increasingly complex and symbolic modes of expression and observance do not denote that it has become effete: they are signs rather of its still green growth, of its inventiveness, and of a broad awareness of the richness and potential of its independent tradition.[59]

Rather than being a symptom of decline, the transformation of mayhem into theater confirmed that chivalry succeeded in its stated goal: the civilization of the aggression instinct. For three or more centuries chivalry rewarded aggression instead of suppressing it; and what these centuries of "acting out" produced was the discovery that aggression attains its goal not in murder or destruction but in a dandified display.

We might surmise then that rage "acts out" in an attempt to prefect its outward form. From gore to glitter then. From the hero to the dandy.

This additional courtly and amorous appeal of the tournament was one that could co-exist without difficulty with the other attractions we have been considering: the tourney's value as a training ground for war, its significance as an exercise in which great prizes could be won, and as a social gathering of a certain kind of elite. But it was capable of more elaborate development than they were, and in particular directions—those of ceremony, of theater, and of what anthropologists call play. Perhaps the best early examples of all three combined were the two great jousting tours of the Bavarian knight Ulrich von Lichtenstein, his *Venusfahrt* (1227) and his *Artusfahrt* (1240).

> For the *Venusfahrt* he equipped himself for the role of Frau Venus with a magnificent costume (and a brace of long blond plaits); attired in it, he made his way from Italy to Bohemia, offering a general challenge to all comers to joust with him in honour of his lady. To each comer who broke three lances with him he promised to present a gold ring: but if the challenger was defeated, he was to bow to the four corners of the earth in honor of Ulrich's lady. Ulrich traveled magnificently attended, and broke three hundred spears in a month's jousting (or so he claimed)...Ulrich, moreover, although extravagant, was no lunatic *poseur*, like Don Quixote: he was an able lord and warrior, who enjoyed a long and distinguished career in arms and politics, and has an honorable niche in the history of his native Styria. His fantasies were more exaggerated than most, but they reflect something of the genuine spirit and the tastes of his age and class.[60]

Socrates, they say, prayed to Pan for fairness of the inward souls. For outward beauty, we pray to Mars.

Of all Adlerians it was F. G. Crookshank who showed the keenest understanding of what Adler was taking aim at with his psychology of aggression. Crookshank faulted other Adlerians for favoring what is weak and inferior in the soul at the expense of what is strong. He wrote—

> If we all agree that the inferiority feeling arises from obstruction to the expression in action of the Will to

Power, we are able to see then clearly when Adler and Nietzsche differ as well as agree. Nietzsche, on the one hand, cries for a stronger and ever-stronger exercise by the individual of his will to power; Adler counsels, not so much social activity as a canalization of this will to power, but social co-operation as a source of that feeling of security put in peril by its frustration. I often think that we, as Individual Psychologists, might do well if, whilst always encouraging the weak to gain this security, we more boldly counsel the strong to aid the weak by the exercise, and the social interest, of their own frustrated strength. It seems to me that if, as I have elsewhere said, Greek and Roman society lost much—perhaps every-thing—through ignorance of the social value in dwell-ing in the weak and imperfect, there is no reason why we, in following the Christian path and encouraging the despised and rejected, should at the same time deprive society of the social advantages to be gained by the right exercise of strength by the strong.[61]

We may take this psychologically as a complaint leveled against those who seek to deny strength, boldness, courage, *thymos*, and even violence, their proper place in the economy of the psyche. Crookshank also perceived the connection between Nietzsche and Adler, speaking in one place of a "golden thread" that ties the two. And yet, it seems to me, Crookshank misread his Nietzsche. This misreading had tragic consequences for Crookshank who took his own life long before his thought had independently matured. Crookshank's death together with the other suicides that darken the early years of depth analysis remind us of the perils involved in any brush with deep psychic matter. Although Crookshank misunderstood the work of Nietzsche, he was entirely accurate in this conception of a continuum between Nietzsche and Adler. To clearly grasp what Adler meant by aggression, masculine protest, the will to power, and finally the striving for significance, requires consideration of the notion as it first appeared in Nietzsche. To that task we now turn.

Chapter Three

We are the smirched. Queen Honor is the spotless.
We slept thro' wars where Honor could not sleep.
We were faint-hearted. Honor was full-valiant.
We kept a silence Honor could not keep.

　　　　　— Vachel Lindsay, "Honor Among Scamps"

When Adler's work is considered a detailed phenomenology of the will to power, this closes the loop with Nietzsche, who is, of course, the progenitor of the notion. Most Adlerians begrudge the connection. Lewis Way is fairly representative of the common view when after spending pages in a nuanced discussion of the relationship between Nietzsche and Adler he suddenly recoils by claiming that while Freud may hearken back to Nietzsche, they are both neurotics in Adler's view.

> It seems to me clear that Nietzsche's teaching is in essence the same as Freud's. The criticisms which the great Master of Scorn pours upon the ideal of neighbor-love recalls Freud's wondering query on the same subject, and it would appear to Individual Psychology that the work of both is vitiated by similar neurotic attitudes.[1]

On this same point Brachfeld asserts in his usually pointed prose:

> The stupid assertion has been made, and how often repeated, that Adler "deified Nietzsche's Will to Power,"

117

that he proclaimed and extolled Hobbes' *libido domi-nandi*. Some of Adler's early writings lend a certain color to this erroneous interpretation. In them he speaks of a *Streben nach Nacht* and lays undue stress on the importance of "aggressive impulses" in neurosis and in life in general. But the more he deepened and elaborated the results he drew from the analysis of thousands of subjects, the further he moved from this terminology.[2]

Kurt Adler devotes an entire article to rehearsing the distinctions between power and significance. Even Adler sometimes paces off a wide distance between himself and Nietzsche, declaring in one place that "Regarding the striving for power, we find the misunderstanding that Individual Psychology not only regards psychological life as the striving for power, but propagates this idea. This striving for power is not our madness, it is what we find in others."[3] But on this point we may summon Adler against himself and against the casuistries of some of his disciples. Showing his customary passion for accuracy, Heinz Ansbacher says in regard to what Adler calls a "misunderstanding," "This misunderstanding to which Adler refers here does in fact have some justification in that he at one stage treated the striving for power as the usual manifestation of the basic striving."[4] At least at one stage in his career Adler sanctioned what we have observed to be Crookshank's view, that being, that Individual Psychology and the philosophy of the superman, the flame, the iron, the spirit, are united by a "golden thread." Nietzsche demonstrably influenced Adler. For Adler, at one time he seemed an oracle of truth. And even if that influence ebbed throughout the years, as Adler hammered out the full scope of this new discipline, the influence continued to be mediated by Vaihinger, whose views Adler always endorsed and whom himself identified Nietzsche as a primary source for the philosophy as-if.

To go on wrestling with Adler's daimon requires a look at Nietzsche. If we are to substantiate the thesis that Adler, through the medium of the aggressive instinct, discovered the agonistic roots of culture, then we must demonstrate that Nietzsche was enacting something similar. At the same time we want to understand the roots and rationale of the Adlerian objection.

But how are we to truly understand the will to power when the entire notion has been absorbed into a scholarly tradition, where it has been predictably deprived of its once wild-eyed appeal. The superman was once a dreadful notion that had a powerful impact on the course of European history: it stamped politicians in its image; prompted students and workers to stream into the streets; sent starving, dreamy eyed poets to their desk or the shade of muse inspired trees. It has been said that if Marx fathered the European Left, the Right goes back to Nietzsche at whose feet we may lay the calamity of Fascism. Whether this is an accurate reading either of Nietzsche or of European history is not here the issue: rather my point is to illustrate how powerful the idea of the will to power was once imagined to be. But today all that has vanished to be replaced by calm analysis and chalkboard commentary scrawled out with squeaks. If we are really to grasp the Nietzsche who appealed to Adler, then we must step back in time into the fires of creativity, the dark and colorful flame, where the idea first was forged.

In order to unlock the hidden meaning, the *eidos*, of the will to power, I want to bypass scholarly tradition and employ a personal variation of the Adlerian technique of inquiring into early recollections. Adler describes exactly the efficaciousness of this technique.

> Among all psychological expressions, some of the most revealing are the individual's memories. His memories are the reminders he carries about with him of his own limits and of the meaning of circumstances. There are no "chance memories": out of the incalculable number of impressions which meet an individual, he chooses to remember only those which he feels, however darkly, to have a bearing on his situation...Most illuminating of all is the way the individual begins his story, the earliest incident he can recall. The first memory will show his

fundamental view of life, his first satisfactory crystalli-
zation of his attitude. It offers us an opportunity to see
at one glance what he has taken as the starting point for
his development.[5]

So let us imagine Nietzsche, then, stretched out upon the plush-
ness of the couch, and ask him the following question: "What is
your earliest memory in connection with this strange idea you have?
When you let your mind float free what associations do you have?
What memory or image comes to mind?" In other words, let us ask
Nietzsche to precisely imagine the origin of the will to power, and
then to proceed from there.

We do not know when the will to power first occurred to Nietzsche, but we do have the evidence of an incident, which he later
related to his sister, where the idea seems to have the air of newness.
One evening at dusk, during the Franco-Prussian War, Nietzsche
watched his old regiment ride by on the way to the front. It came
to him then that "the strongest and highest will to life does not lie
in the puny struggle to exist, but in the Will-to-War, the Will-to-
Power." Here in the tragic beauty of men marching off to war lays
the complex origin of the infamous will to power. This passage arrests, given subsequent interpretations of Nietzsche as some kind of
crazed Berserk in thrall to the experience of war, with all its passion
and emptied intestines. Indeed the realities of war are only indirectly
involved in that they lie ahead on the battlefield or behind in the hospital where Nietzsche was working as an orderly. Rather the source
for the idea lies in an almost aesthetic vision of war: the dazzle of
arms, the mane and flank of the war horse, the jingle of spurs and
harness, the shrill rattle of the drum, and all set off by the bittersweet
fires of dusk. In its original Epiphany, the will to power took shape
in the image of the cavalryman, the cavalier, a chevalier, who was all
decked out for war but not actually engaged in killing. How different it would strike us if the idea had seemed to come to Nietzsche
while he was actually charging with a bayonet or wading knee deep
in corpses. In considering this early recollection, we can't help notic-

ing that this is not a memory of war at all; but is instead an image of war, perhaps of war itself as a set of beautiful images for ordering both individual and collective consciousness.

Nietzsche's memory corresponds to the earliest recollection of a poet whose vision has helped to shape the present work. The poet is David Jones, author of "The Anathemata," "In Parenthesis," "The Sleeping Lord," and two critical books of essays, *Epoch and Artists* and *The Dying Gaul*. In an essay called "In *illo tempore*" the poet recalls that his—

> ...first remembered thing was in 1900, or about 1900. I was tucked up in a cot next to my mother's bed, but an unfamiliar sound from the roadway outside impelled me to creep out as cautiously as I could and make for the window, to look between the slats of the venetian blinds; and what I saw and heard was a thing of great marvel—a troop of horses, moving in column to the *taratantara* of bugles. It was in fact a detachment of the City Imperial Volunteers on a recruitment ride through the outer suburbs for the war in South Africa of which I was, as yet, in blissful ignorance. But to me, those mounted men were a sight of exceeding wonder...[6]

Here we have the same complex of imagery that we found in Nietzsche: the beautiful horses, the white dust rising, the Jericho like sound of bugles. The poet goes on to relate how he questioned his mother as to whether or not the soldiers might be angels, to which his mother curtly replied, "not for little boys who disobey their parents."

Who was David Jones? As Kathleen Raine has said in a beautiful essay on the poet, few would not doubt that he was "a very great maker" both in poetry and visual forms, for Jones was also a designer of types and a marvelous painter.

His greatest achievement lies in poetry. His poetic creed was quintessentially high-modernist. He compares with Eliot, Lewis,

Pound, Joyce and the other men of 1914. As was the case with Eliot, central to Jones' art was his religious faith; but unlike Eliot, whose poetic *métier* was the mystical tradition of the fire and the dove, Jones' poetry is governed by the complementary but more terrestrial ethos of chivalry. Unlike the other high-modernists Jones actually knew the blood and overpowering dampness of the trenches. He fought in World War I, and it was there, as a solider that he first was present at the Mass, watching through a crevice in a barn, while a priest celebrated the ancient mysteries. The experience was formative: Christ appearing to a *soldier*, as a soldier. In Jones' poetry Christ is the divine war-duke, a holy knight engaged in battle with the forces of evil. His Christ is Arthur, Charlemagne, the Sleeping Lord who has actually arisen. Like Langland's Christ, which was a favorite image of the poet, he puts on human nature in the way a knight clasps to his armor (*The Anathemata*, 226-231) and jousts in Jerusalem. The disciples are a sacred "war band of twelve" (letter to Rene Hague). Hung up a tree made shining by the purple color of his office (*The Anathemata*, 231), the war-duke conquers death. His sacrifice creates the "spoil-dump" (*The Anathemata*, 213) of grace. The epistemology of the word *sacramentum* delighted Jones. In Rome sacramentum was used to describe the oath of soldiers taken to their *imperator* while in the early Church it received an esoteric interpretation: it became the convenient term for efficacious signs. It was as if the Church itself had chosen chivalry—the symbols of vassalage, loyalty, the pledging of swords, the bending of the knee—to describe its most cherished arcana.

In his vision of Christ as chevalier Jones remembers Hopkins. As with Hopkins the vision of chivalry that flashes in the "air, pride, plume, here / Buckle" of the "The Windhover" underpinned his vision of a redeemed and transformed world. Just as the blood sacrifice of Christ redeems the world, so chivalry can knit human existence into a semblance of the heavenly order. This happened in the past when it created for example the Carolingian Renaissance and the High Middle Ages. Chivalry was then a rage for order that transformed the unruly impulses of barbarian souls into the vital nourishment of a magical order built around the vision of Charlemagne or the myth of Arthur, a "conception of the leader" who is "first among equals— his peers set circularly in their fellowship about him. He, 'chosen by adventure and by grace,' the giver of gifts, the bridge-builder, the war-duke, his protection co-extensive with Christendom."[7] And yet, to be sure, Jones shunned romanticism, in that he realized that this vision was "very remote from the actuality of idealism, legalism and gangsterism that men knew seven or eight hundred years ago."[8] But it was just this realism that enabled the poet to retain his optimism. Ironically, it kept him hardened in the mystery of hope, because if seven or eight hundred years ago, the beautiful images of chivalry were successful in transforming gangsters into knights who at least occasionally dreamt of Grails instead of murder, then there is no obvious reason why chivalry might not flourish amid present circumstances is Jones' art itself, which is surely one of the most significant bodies of work to be produced in this century. In the same way that chivalry fired his imagination, instilling it with nobility and grace, so might it nourish the imagination of our collective soul. So might it become the basis of a renewed *gemeinschaftsgefuhl*?

Both Nietzsche's memory and Jones' early recollection hearken back to one of the most beautiful tales in all of Western history. It is also a tale of chivalry. It is the story of Percival who figures in our history as the hero of the Grail Legend. Percival was born to a royal lady wrought with tears over a husband who living by the sword had also perished by it. And so, deciding that the price of chivalry was too high, since it had cost her the warm embrace of her husband, this woman spirited the child away to a remote palace where he might be brought up shielded from any knowledge about knighthood. The child grows up beautiful and strong. He is also innocent of chivalry. But one day, in the darkness of the woods, he sees two knights ride by splendid in the flash of gold and jewel encrusted armor. He hurries to discover their identity; but when he asks the people of the wood, in whose charge he has been posted, he is told that they are *angels*. Answering that he would be an angel too, he joins their company, to his mother's inconsolable regret. After being knighted at the shining court of Arthur, Percival becomes the Grail Knight, who frees and restores the Wasteland, so that the land and soul are ripe again.

Since Percival is the most beautiful of knights, the very summation of all that is grand and true in the chivalric tradition, then we might expect that through the vehicle of this image we might glimpse the psychological basis of chivalry. In a moment we shall look into this question more extensively.

But for now, the image declares the psychological foundation of chivalry to lie in a vision of the knight as angel: that is, as a presence or form of the imagination. In dreams, myths, fantasies, etc., angels often play this role: they symbolize the angelic powers of the mind, the agent intellect, the imagination itself. At the heart of Percival's story, we find a discovery of war as an angel, a beautiful image, a form, a way of ordering the imagination.

Given the resemblance between Nietzsche's memory and the poet's earliest recollection; and given that both rehearse the legend of Percival, which symbolically depicts the story of a chivalrous soul; might we not assume that the conception of the will to power was at the very least an unconscious attempt by Nietzsche to hurl himself back, together with the dying age he lived in, into the radiant world of chivalry? Nietzsche as Percival. Nietzsche as knight. Nietzsche as Templar, perhaps. Perhaps Nietzsche was reaching for chivalry with the only means at his disposal, which was primarily a Germanic mind steeped in classical scholarship. From Germany to Greece to chivalry, maps Nietzsche's pilgrimage and the results of this pilgrimage, as we shall see, reflects this road. But for now let us simply note that the analytical approach to Nietzsche on the basis of first memories reveals a picture very different from the one exposed by conventional scholarly methods; but that is the rationale for the analytical approach. If scholarship had been a sufficient psychopomp, an adequate mirror to the depths of the psyche, the analytical approach might never have materialized, which it did largely as a compensation for the failures of the Ivory Tower to illuminate the meaning of history and life. As an advocate of the forms of chivalry Nietzsche looks much different from the Cruci-fied One that he believed himself to be, and that scholarship has for the most part been authenticated through the study of his texts. But can a man who described abstract thinking as "a feast, a fren-zy" ever be reached through his texts? Did he not himself confess: "I have dictated for two or three hours practically every day, but my 'philosophy'—if I have the right to call it by the name of something that has entered me down to the very roots of my being—is *no lon-ger* communicable, at least not in print." We've taken Nietzsche at his word, and so resorted to more arcane tools, to discover a more arcane truth.

But we need not be quite so clever to expose Nietzsche's chivalric roots. Ernst Bertram, whose book, *Nietzsche: Attempt at a Mythology*, has only recently been translat-ed (2009) and, in the English speaking world, defended from what appear to be Walter Kaufmann's misrepre-sentations, maintained a similar point of view. In his chapter "Knight, Death and Devil," Bertram writes: "We know of only a single pictorial representation to which Nietzsche remained attached over the course of many long years, only one that he viewed and admired as a better part of himself: Albrecht Dürer's engraving *Ritter, Tod and Teufel* (Knight, Death and Devil), from 1513, the year that Luther, returning from the convulsions of his trip to Rome, was struggling with the slowly growing visions of his future prophecy. It is the only gift, concen-trated within a specific form, that the visual arts were ever allowed to give to the half-blind, sound-obsessed romantic Socrates. And, in a kind of convulsion, he felt it to be autobiographical, a warning to himself, the way one only feels those things that appear to be special con-cretizations, as it were, of points where different curves in one's life intersect, where decisive lines on one's tra-jectory converge."[9]

Nietzsche wrote: "Dürer's picture of the Knight, Death, and Devil is the symbol of our existence." Bertram continues:

> Nietzsche perceived the image of courage in Dürer; he perceived himself while thinking he saw Schopenhauer. Just as the print is the only one that stays with him and dominates his thinking, the idea of a Knight Templar of truth—*that* truth which does not kill, but makes one live.[10]

Bertram's interpretation ratifies an identification of Nietzsche with chivalry. From the beginning to the end of his life, Nietzsche identified with Dürer's Christian Knight: "I identify with this image in a way I can hardly explain." His friend Franz Overbeck wrote to him: "In your expressive portrait you remind me of the bold Dürer knight you once showed me." But for Bertram, Nietzsche's fascination with the image epitomizes a particularly Northern, Protestant, Lutheran steely-eyed, determined chivalry, which may be too confining. Nietzsche abounds with contradictions—"O, for a beaker of the warm South," Nietzsche would have thoroughly understood the Keatisan expression. Bertram admits that Nietzsche's soul was in its essence musical, so that, presumably, his emotional response to his first exposure to Wagner's *Parsifal* may be more revealing even than his fascination for the Dürer print, and, Parsifal belongs to the Grail and Arthurian cycle, a much more all-embracing and cosmopolitan category, than any Lutheran derived "Northern Chivalry" ideal.

This more universal chivalry form Nietzsche himself embraced, though only in sudden illuminations. "*Tanzen wir gleich Troubadourn*," says Nietzsche. Let us dance like troubadours. Nietzsche dreamt of philosophy becoming a Gay Science, *die frohliche Wissenschaft, la gaya scienza* stems directly, as he says, from "...the Provençal concept of *gaya scienza*—that unity of *singer, knight,* and *free spirit* which distinguishes the wonderful early culture of the Provençals from all equivocal cultures."[11] Nietzsche ached for chivalric science, a philosophy that would be erotic, *agonal* and *French*:

Philosophy in the manner of Plato should rather be defined as an erotic contest, as a further development and inward intensification of the old agonal gymnastics and their *presuppositions*....What finally emerged from this philosophical eroticism of Plato? A new artistic form of the Green agon, dialectics.—I further recall, *opposing* Schopenhauer and to the honour of Plato, that the entire higher culture and literature of *classical* France also grew up on the soil of sexual interest. One may seek everywhere in it for gallantry, sensuality, sexual contest, "woman"—one will never seek in vain.[12]

How Nietzsche adored those chivalric poet knights, exalting them as the creator gods of passion and of the idea of Europe itself "...*passion*—which is our European specialty—simply must be of noble origin: as is well known, its invention must be credited to the Provençal knight-poets, those magnificent and inventive human beings of the '*gai saber*' to whom Europe owes so many things and almost owes itself."[13] Nietzsche always thrilled to what he called the "[K]nightly-aristocratic value judgments [that] presupposed a powerful physicality, a flourishing, abundant, even overflowing health, together with that which serves to preserve it: war, adventure, hunting, dancing, war games, and in general all that involves vigorous, free, joyful activity."[14] Nietzsche imagines himself in his war with God to resemble Charles the Bold, chivalric paragon, outraged against his liege lord Louis: "...our attitude toward God as some alleged spider of purpose and morality behind the great captious web of causality, is hubris—we might say, with Charles the Bold when he opposed Louis XI, "*je combats l'universelle araignée*".[15] Finally, when Nietzsche sought to honor his old teacher, Schopenhauer, he could bestow no greater laurel than the tribute "[A] genuinely independent spirit like Schopenhauer, a man and knight of a steely eye who had the courage to be himself, who knew how to stand alone without first waiting for heralds and signs from above."[16]

Even the notorious blond beast passage, where Nietzsche seems to trumpet a barbarian code of values, warrants close re-examination against a chivalric background.

> One cannot fail to see at the bottom of all the noble races the beast of prey, the splendid *blond beast* prowling avidly in search of spoil and victory; this hidden core needs to erupt from time to time, the animal has to get out again and go back to the wilderness: the Roman, Arabian, Germanic, Japanese nobility, the Homeric heroes, the Scandinavian Vikings—they all shared this need.[17]

This passage must be weighed against the equally famous excerpt where Nietzsche insists on the necessity of "giving style to character" and also his love for Frederick II, the Norman king, whom he extolled as the "First European" whose splendid court was a center of grace, lightness, refinement and cosmopolitan knowledge. As Walter Kaufman has observed, the notorious blond beast is not a racial idea at all, not a bloodthirsty Aryan warrior, but a lion, the chivalric emblem *par excellence*. "The blond beast is not a racial concept and does not refer to the 'Nordic race' of which the Nazis later made so much. Nietzsche specifically refers to Arabs and Japanese...and the "blondness" obviously refers to the beast, the lion."[18] Rather than an uncivilized berserk, Nietzsche is commemorating here something like the knight or Samurai, a Richard Lion Heart or Saladin, whose style of life was called chivalry in the West and *bushido* in the East and for which the heraldic lion, blond and bold, has traditionally served as emblem. Where such a style of conduct flourishes (the race and geography are incidental) life flames up with color, boldness, poise, torpor, exultation, with a taste for beauty in all its forms, a relish for the effronteries of contest, and a joy in all that overflows with skill and strength. If on occasions such a man might be too combative and expansive for the confinement and coquettish pleasantries of the *salon*, though here too, more often than not, he thrives, well versed in all the arts of love, like the lion, he prides himself upon his regal bearing, his courtly manners, his gallantry towards friend and foe. In the last analysis, and when grasped against the entirety of Nietzsche's life and thought, the blond beast is the mounted chevalier.

The rather novel thesis that Nietzsche advocated chivalry extends a brilliant intuition of Oswald Spengler who writes—

> The Classical tendency towards making the body the sole spokesman is emphatically not the result of any carnal overload in the race...it was *not*, as Nietzsche thought, an orgiastic joy of untrammeled energy in perfervid passion. This sort of thing is much nearer to the ideals of Germanic-Christian or of Indian *chivalry*.[19] (Italics mine.)

Alone among all great twentieth century thinkers, Spengler divined that the Nietzschean *ethos* is the ethos of chivalry. Insofar as I am aware, Spengler nowhere amplifies this thought. It simply reposes there on the page, as if it were some pre-Socratic fragment that refuses to say more.

And yet, despite chivalry's appeal to Nietzsche as something spotless and immense, he felt ambivalently about it, so that the attraction was thoroughly mixed with fear and even an element of repulsion. Nietzsche's attitude toward chivalry reflected his attitude towards his father, whom he both adored and idolized, and yet at the same time feared. Nietzsche wondered if his father were not in some way dragging him down into a pit, a great hollow grave from which he could not resurface. Nietzsche's father died while he was still a boy. The following dream, which Nietzsche had in January 1850, just before his baby brother died, coagulates his feelings—

> I heard the church organ playing as at a funeral. When I looked to see what was going on, a grave opened suddenly, and my father arose out of it in a shroud. He hurries into the church and soon comes back with a small

child in his arms. The mound on the grave reopens, he climbs back in, and the gravestone sinks back over the opening. The swelling noise of the organ stops at once, and I wake up. In the morning I tell the dream to my dear mother. Soon after that little Joseph is suddenly taken ill. He goes into convulsions, and dies within a few hours.[20]

What fathered the best in Nietzsche also excited dread. It is no coincidence that in Nietzsche's mind his father was associated with a powerful, monumental statue of St. George that dominated his father's rectory.[21] St. George, patron of all Christian knights. And yet St. George immigrated into the West from out of the East, bringing with him—who can say—legends and symbols tainted or perhaps even saturated with meanings entirely alien to the observance of Christendom. Was St. George a Christian Knight or was he a Templar? Nietzsche's ambivalence towards first his father and then St. George and all the confusions while remembering that it may have been precisely them that made Nietzsche into such a strange, enchanted man, misfit and magician. It shall be a delicate enterprise indeed. Through the will to power Nietzsche stepped, unawares, like Percival, into the Castle of the Grail King. And it is by examining chivalry that we can assess the scope and magnitude of this idea.

What was chivalry? In its essence it was a mode of thought; and as a mode of thought it flowered into a host of observances and rites (tournament, hunt, *cortesia*); shaped a unique form of education (centered on the study of heroes and history); fashioned a complex psychology (the science of heraldry); incorporated a political vision (statecraft as soul craft); created characteristic courts (in Burgundy, England); ideal monarchs (Charles the Bold, Elizabeth); generated learned masters (Ramon Lull, William Caxton); and an authoritative text (*The Book of Chivalry*); and, perhaps, most critically, civilized the profession of arms (duels, heralds, ransoms, tournaments, etc.). Chivalry was a set of beautiful images for ordering the soul. I think of the Cult of the Nine Worthies, and the entry of the English King, Henry VI, into Paris in 1431, behind a crowd of banners emblazoned with their heroic standards.

One of the most beautiful images in all of chivalry was the image of the knight as lion. In war, explains one text, the knight should emulate "the condition of a lion." To grasp the symbol of the lion requires what Wallace Stevens once called "a capable imagination." We must summon up the blood of deep inspiration. Robert Edmund Jones, impresario of stagecraft, discovered this upon asking a young stage designer to produce a tapestry decorated with heraldic lions, where after the young designer presently bounced back with a handful of sketches, all of which lacked vigor. Let us think now, mused the master, let us put our soul to work: let us fly back to the past, to a star-pocked hillside, where Richard's army is encamped, the banners flapping in the stiff, cool, dark night breeze, while each fire crackles with an orange silver glow:

> Perhaps Richard, the Lion-Heart, carried this very device emblazoned on his banner as he marched across Europe on his way to the Holy Land. Richard the Lion-Heart, *Coeur de Lion*...What memories of childhood this name conjures up, what images of chivalry! Knights in armor, enchanted castles, magic casements, perilous seas, oriflammes, and gonfalcons. Hear the great battle-cries! See the banners floating through the smoke! *Coeur de Lion*, the Crusader, with his singing page Blondel... Do you remember Blondel's song, the song he sang for three long years while he sought his master in prison? "Oh, Richard, Oh *Mon Roi!*"[22]

This is the lion. This is the lion whose ethical fierceness and bright mane courage, Nietzsche recognized, in the first of Zarathustra's speeches, to be a brother spirit to the laughing warrior, Zarathustra. Like Coeur de Lion, Nietzsche's lion appears in the desert where he is matched against the sparkle of the East.

In the loneliest desert, however, the second metamorphosis occurs: here the spirit becomes a lion who would
conquer his freedom and be master in his own desert.
Here he seeks out his last master: he wants to fight him
and his last god; for ultimate victory he wants to fight
with the great dragon.

Who is the great dragon whom the spirit will no longer
call lord and god? "Thou shalt" is the name of the great
dragon. But the spirit of the lion says, "I will." "Thou
shalt" lies in his way, sparkling like gold, an animal
covered with scales; and on every scale shines a golden
"thou shalt."

Values, thousands of years old, shine on these scales;
and thus speaks the mightiest of all dragons: "All value
of all things shines on me. All value has long been created, and I am all created value. Verily, there shall be no
more 'I will.'" Thus speaks the dragon.[23]

The "I will" conquers the matrix of all values. Before the ferocious war of the lion the dragon flees, back into his timeless sleep
and sparkle.

Who is this dragon, other than the matrix of all value? What does
the Great Wing symbolize in psychological terms? For Nietzsche, the
dragon depicts the almost overpowering temptation to adjust to accepted norms even at the cost of the vital spark of unique individu-
ality. The French symbolic-directive psychologist, Robert Desoille
echoes Nietzsche's estimation. Taking issue with the Jungians, who
fuse the dragon with the archetype of the Great Mother; and presenting a self-consciously Western perspective which he distinguishes
from the Eastern viewpoint, where the dragon would mean something else entirely, Desoille confirms that the "dragon stands for all
the prohibitions imposed on the subject by his cultural milieu. First
of all, there are the restrictions imposed by the family. Then there
are those which arise both from the patient's social class and from

his vocational commitments. Finally, the nation, too, imposes its limitations on the individual."[24] James Hillman, on the other hand, explores an entirely different route in that he views the dragon as the imagination itself, the imagination considered as an instinct, a primal force in life.

> Killing the dragon in the hero myth means nothing less than killing the imagination, the very spirit that is the way and the goal. The dragon, let us remember, is not a snake, not an animal at all. It is a fictitious animal, an imaginal instinct, and thus the instinct of the imagination or the imagination as a vital, instinctual force.[25]

If we allow these two ideas to interpenetrate—which we must, of course, since there are no empirical grounds for rejecting either of them—we might say that the dragon represents the great temptation to conform at all cost, and above all other exigencies, to the power of the imagination, to an imagination unbound by the material limits of things and history. Since historically the dragon came to the West from the East, appearing first on the imperial banners of the Byzantines, let us say that this dragon is the *draco* of the East, the great winged dragon who towers above being, who represents the ease of Oriental torpor, tranquil adjustment to outward norms, so that the soul may travel through its *chakras* and planetary houses, flaming upward in a solitary quest. By East, I mean, in the words of Denis de Rougemont, "an attitude of the human mind which has reached its highest and purest expression in the direction of Asia; this mystical attitude is dualistic as regards the world and monistic as regards fulfillment. Eastern askesis is directed to negation of the Many and to absorption into the One; it looks to a *complete fusion* with a god, or, lacking a god...with the universal One of Being. All that assumes the availability of a Wisdom, of a technique of progressive illumination... an *ascent* from the individual towards that Unity in which he will be lost."[26] By East, I mean *gnosis*.

Since Nietzsche looks to the lion for the means to vanquish the dragon; and since the lion is a universal symbol of chivalry, may we not assume that Nietzsche found chivalry the quicksilver and the gold of transformation, the end and object of Zarathustra's quest? Was not Nietzsche that most chivalrous of gentlemen about whom it was most "surprising that on rare occasions, when he was sufficiently provoked, we find appeals to his old-fashioned sense of honor, even his brief military service and on one point the idea that he must challenge a man to duel with pistols." And was it not Nietzsche who greeted Lou Andreas-Salome with marvelous *cortesia*.

> She was twenty-one when she reached Rome, still not quite well, and when Paul Ree, a young philosopher, introduced her to Friedrich Nietzsche. This meeting, carefully prepared by Ree, took place in St. Peter's Cathedral. It was to have been the beginning of a partnership of three, including a plan to live the student life together. Nietzsche was much older than Lou Salomé, thirty-eight, but he had heard of the brilliant Russian and imagined her a kindred spirit, one whom he hoped to bring up as his disciple. His initial greeting in the cathedral set the tone: "From what stars have we fallen to meet here?"[27]

Of course the lion is followed by another transformation, into a child, which has grave repercussions for Nietzsche's later thought, since that child was to become the divine child, Zagreus, Dionysus, but here we may invoke Nietzsche against himself, for Nietzsche argued again and again that strife is the father of all. The only truths worth living are the ones that have been won in combat; and we note that in this early parable of Zarathustra it is the lion's truth whose Epiphany is brought forth through a crossing of the swords. According to Nietzsche's own determination, this would enthrone the lion above the child. In Nietzsche's personal heraldry the lion belongs with the blue spirit of the eagle in that both are liberating presences who free the soul from submission to the matrix of all values, the dragon of the imagination, the *draco* of the East. The lion fires the courage in the soul that drives it onward as *condotierre* and *conquistador* into new territories of conquest, meaning and exploration. Conqueror, master, flame cored beast, *virtu*, valor, *thymos*: these are the values that both knight and Nietzsche ascribed to the lion: these are the values that they embraced.

Although the medieval knight was the flower and type of chivalry, chivalry as a set of images can no more be confined to the High Middle Ages than monarchy, say or the practice of *cortesia*. The roots run deeper; the foliage, grander. C.S. Lewis remarks on chivalry's background in the experience of the Roman legions:

> We must never forget that the Medieval Latin for a knight is *miles*; that the conception of earthly knighthood and of the angelic knighthood (*militia*) are sometimes connected; and that both pre-suppose the discipline of the real Roman army. It is doubtful whether the whole ideal world of chivalry could have existed unless the legions had existed first...[28]

While Huizinga insists on a fundamental continuity between medieval chivalry and the Renaissance:

> According to the celebrated Swiss historian, the quest of personal glory was the characteristic attribute of the men of the Renaissance...[h]ere, as elsewhere, Burkhart has exaggerated the distance separating Italy from the Western countries and the Renaissance from the Middle Ages.
>
> The thirst for honour and glory proper to the men of the Renaissance is essentially the same as the chivalrous ambition of early times, and of French origin...The passionate desire to find himself praised by contemporaries or by posterity was the source of virtue with the courtly

knight of the twelfth century and the rude captain of the fourteenth, no less than with the *beaux-esprits* of the *quarttrocento*.[29]

This kinship was obvious to the knight, as it was, for example to John Lydgate, who was bound to the traditions of chivalry while also befriending the new Renaissance learning. Lydgate writes:

> Knighthood in Greece and Troy the City
>   Took his principles, and next in Rome town,
> And in Carthage, a famous great country,
>   Record [witness] of Hannibal and worthy Scipio[30]

Historically, as well, there was easy commerce between the old high medieval tradition and the fresh spirit of the Renaissance. At the court of Henry VIII, chivalry and humanism blended to create a handsome, glittering court, full of life and vigor, where Erasmus could be patronized while Froissart, the great French chronicler of chivalry, was being translated at the king's command. While the colors of the court remained profoundly chivalric, Henry also gathered humanists about him, who explained to him the beauties of the classics. In his wide learning and hunger for chivalrous renown Henry was following in paternal footsteps. The easy graft of humanism onto chivalry is symbolized by his father's bestowal of the Order of the Garter, the highest honor in English chivalry, on the Italian Duke of Urbino, who dispatched his personal emissary to receive it. Count Baldassare Castiglione greeted Henry's court in the name of his honored prince. Even Moore and Erasmus, whose very *fama* depended upon the shock of the new, were not so much opposed to chivalry as simply indifferent. "English humanism tended, in fact, to be nonchivalric rather than antichivalric."[31] Chivalry thus comprehended both Caesar and *condotierre*, both antiquity and the present age, and with a potential for the future.

Chivalry, in fact, furnishes a set of images for contemplating Western history as all of a single piece, a great chariot, as Chesterton said of the Church, veering this way and that without every quite losing its balance, at least until the time of the French Revolution. The revolution knocked the chariot into chaos. The evil tide got underway in the late fifteenth century when "[t]he most effective intellectual force operating against the chivalric ideal" was "the spirit of undoctrinaire realism, of practicality and good sense."[32] The tide soon swelled to justify the murder of Charles Stuart at the block, the beheading of an anointed, consecrated king; and then reached flood stage with the bloody ascendancy of the guillotine. The chief villain in the book of chivalry is Robespierre, that dour accountant of right and wrong, the satanic prince. The Age of Chivalry is dead, said Burke, as he gazed across the channel. For Burke, and for all who share his sentiment of chivalry, it was the chaos of the French Revolution that shattered the old world and darkened perhaps for all time the splendor that was chivalry.

Therefore in invoking chivalry as the background of Nietzsche's thought we are by no means asserting that his genius was medieval in contrast to Greek or humanist. If chivalry anchors his reflections, then he was all these things, and more.

Chivalry was founded on a quality called *preux*. As the lion's splendor, *gravitas* and courage are rooted in the blood, so the forms and substance of medieval chivalry pulse with a mysterious reality called *preux*. Though the definition of *preux* may be reserved to those who have attained it, we must attempt one anyway. To shine in valor and honor, this was *preux*; to have the soul magnanimity and the art of love, this was *preux*; to cut a shining figure at the rituals of hunt and court; to be marvelous and skilled at courtesy; this too was *preux*; to laugh at death and bourgeois prudence; to glory in one's vassalage and serve the liege-lord gladly; to conquer one's enemies in the annealing furnace of war; this was also *preux*; and finally, to offer one's sword to the service of Holy Mother Church in her attempts to advance the faith through time and space: this perhaps was the crowning rite of *preux*, the evidence that its own life was as nothing in comparison with the eternal verities bound up in the faith. Jean de Bueil, a fighting knight of the fifteenth century expressed its essence:

It is a joyous thing, is war…You love your comrade so in war. When you see that your quarrel is just and your blood is fighting well, tears rise to your eye. A great sweet feeling of loyalty and of pity fills your heart on seeing your friend so valiantly exposing his body to execute and accomplish the command of our Creator. And then you prepare to go and die or live with him, and for love not to abandon him. And out of that there arises such a delectation, that he who has not tasted it is not fit to say what a delight it is. Do you think that a man who does that fears death? Not at all; for he feels so strengthened, he is so elated, that he does not know where he is. Truly he is afraid of nothing.[33]

In a comment on this famous sentiment, which was the aspiration of every knight, John Huizinga writes "They show us the very core of courage: man, in the excitement of danger, stepping out of his narrow egotism, the ineffable feeling caused by a comrade's bravery, the rapture of fidelity and of sacrifice—in short, the primitive and spontaneous asceticism, which is at the bottom of the chivalrous ideal."[34] In Huizinga's view *preux* equates with courage, and so we may say that courage was the anchor of the chivalrous idea, the psychological factor that explains its resonant images and venerable ideals.

But since this knightly evocation almost trembles with a mysterious bond to others and a delight in friendship, we must say that if courage grounds the world of chivalry, courage cannot be confined to individual prowess shown in battle. For the medieval knight, courage entailed much more than holding fear in check; much more than overcoming the dry tongue, and shaky legs and bowels that know no honor; much more than a Tillich like affirmation of anxiety and willingness to continue on *in trotz dem*: instead, courage involved a rich, powerful, shining element of fellow feeling. In *The Allegory of Love*, C.S. Lewis pays homage to the "lover-like" identity of these chivalrous affections and notes that in "their willful exclusion of other values, and their uncertainty, they provide an exercise of the spirit not

wholly unlike that which later ages found in 'love.'" As a unique way
of striving for significance, *preux* teamed with social feeling, with affection, eros, all the elements of bonding, all the materials of culture.
In Adlerian language, we could say that if *preux* was courage, then
preux, like courage, is the other side of social interest.

Preux looks back to the Greek conception of *arete*. Since nearly all commentary agrees that there is no exact equivalent in any
language for the elusive meaning of this term, we may say at once
that *arete* thrusts us back into a cosmos of distinction, differences,
uniqueness where the focus is on special fate and powers, being
that *arete*, being a distinctive term, connotes a distinctive cosmos.
In Werner Jaegers view the word refers to "a combination of proud
and courtly morality with warlike valour."[35] *Arete* is a whole shining
condition. In its earliest appearances the word seems freighted with
an almost physical index, so that it points to the heightened pulse,
damp pallor and shining eyes that are common on the battlefield.
In Homer the usual reference is to physical prowess, the strength of
arms that is able to dispatch a foe to the realm of Hades. The *arete* of
the hero attains its noblest pitch amid the glare and carnage of battle.
Thus *arete* is an ideal type of consciousness that is grounded in the
blood and bone. To have *arete* is to be "tough," have nerve, warlike
vigor, unconquerable courage, immortal flame. And yet already in
Homer the word ribbons out to incorporate other contexts, so that
it may not be conflated with the ethic of might makes right. Another
element in *arete* is the sophisticated eloquence enshrined by Phoenix, who was both counselor and teacher to Achilles. The noblest
arete, says Phoenix, is to be both a speaker of the words and a doer
of deeds. And what Phoenix exalts, Odysseus embodies, as in his
famous speech before the assembled armies where his words are like
snowflakes. *Arete* is also splendor, the visible wealth of palace, glitter,
trophies, honor, beautiful consorts, comely brides. *Arete* is visible in
"the divine house" of Menelaus. When Telemachus and Mentor are
led into the court "these marveled / as they admired the palace of
the king whom Zeus loved, for as the shining of the sun or the moon
was the shining / all through thus high-roofed house of Menelaus."

Only look, says Telemachus at "the gleaming of the bronze all though these echoing mansions, / and the gleaming of gold and amber, of silver and ivory. The court of Zeus on Olympus must be like this on the inside, / such abundance of everything. Wonder takes me as I look on it."[36] *Arete* also flowers in dignity, for "In Homer, the real mark of the nobleman is his sense of duty. He is judged, and is proud to be judged, by a severe standard."[37] And this dignity is especially present in a special pride in lineage and desire to be worthy of the past. When Glaucous meets Diomede on the battlefield, he first names his illustrious ancestors and then continues: "Hippolocus begat me, and I claim to be his son. He sent me to Troy, and often gave me this command, to strive always for the highest *arete*, and to excel all others."[38] Further, for *arete* to flourish, it must be colored with the glow and richness of magnanimity. It was the survival of the code of *arete* as social glue that saved the Greek cities from the curse of the bourgeois spirit. "...the higher social standards of the *polis* were derived from aristocratic practice; as is shown not so much in any particular precepts of bourgeois morality as in the general ideals of liberality and a certain magnificence in the conduct of life."[39] *Arete* always cries out to be tested; hence the eternal delight in the *aristeas*, the game, content, competition, match. And finally *arete* is not confined to humanity in that it may be found in a horse, eye, axe, all of which may be filled with *arete*. Plato speaks of the *arete* of dogs and horses, eyes, gods, while Homer makes mention of the *arete* of a stallion.

Perhaps the best summation of *arete* is made by Juan Huizinga who situates it in "the whole semantic complex of strength, valour, wealth, right, good management, morality, urbanity, fine manners, magnanimity, liberality, and moral perfection."[40] *Arete* relates to that condition where the body is not bruised to pleasure soul; where words are filled with tusk and fire and the eloquence of snow; where the luster of each thing is valued; where events proceed with gravitas and sacerdotal dignity, in fidelity to the illustrious dead; where ecstasy outweighs economy; and where the world itself has virtue, the best in us responding to the best in it. *Arete* is the sphere of the nobleman, aristocrat, the hero and all that is most noble in ourselves.

Preux also reclaims the Roman idea of valor. Montaigne who was fond of Seneca's aphorism "to live is to fight" voices the Roman ideal when he notes that in addition to military valor, there exists a kind of valor "much greater...and fuller," and a "strength and assurance of the soul, equally despising all sorts of adverse accidents, equable, uniform and constant," for "who is prepared to hear valiantly the accidents of everyday life will not have to swell his courage to become a soldier." Montaigne was perhaps remembering here the Roman general Marcus Claudius Marcellus whose life was consecrated to valor and in honor to whom he erected a splendid double temple at the Capene gate.

What distinguishes the Roman valor from the Greek *arete* is the discovery of a private sphere of existence—what today we would call the realm of *conscience*, while forgetting of course that in their original meaning conscience and consciousness were not distinct, that one could not be conscious without also being aware of right and wrong—where valor might be achieved. In contrast to the Romans, who are often dismissed as insensitive brutes who understood nothing but the necessity of order, the Greeks simply didn't have an inner life, not in any depth or in the sense that we use that word today. They dedicated their inward being to the whimsicality of the gods, to what the romantics would later call the "not I" whose wind blows through me plucking out the distant music of my soul. Nietzsche roundly praised them for their superficiality:

> Oh, those Greeks! They knew how to live. What is required for that is to stop courageously at the surface, the fold, the skin, to adore appearance, to believe in forms, tones, words, in the whole Olympus of appearance. Those Greeks were superficial—*out of profundity*.[41]

And whenever the Greek spirit rises to ascendancy, the emphasis will always fall on visibility, as during the Renaissance when Castiglione rehabilitated the old idea of *arete* and thus advises his aspirant courtiers that when the courtier is "at skirmish, or assault, or battle upon the land, or in such other places of enterprise," he should "work the matter wisely in separating himself from the multitude." Whatever "notable and bold feats" he does, he should undertake them "with as little company as he can, and in the sight of noble men that be of most estimation in the camp, and especially in the presence and (if it were possible) before the very eyes of his king or great personage he is in service withal."[42] The Greek quest for *arete* will always carry the aspirant beyond himself—Socrates into the marketplace, Plato to Syracuse, Aristotle to play the tutor to the king of kings, Alcibiades into Persia, Alexander to the exotic fringes of the map, Castiglione's courtier into the utmost visibility. *Arete* was always a thing to be exclusively achieved within the sight of others. One gained *arete* by triumphing over others but never the stubborn "other" in one's self.

The Romans, however, were a different breed. Their story unfolds according to a different script in that they were always acutely aware of inner demons that lie just beyond the pale of the *logos*. This is evident in Montaigne, whose spirit was entirely Roman, but also in the Stoics, who were the custodians and interpreters of the Roman experience. Whereas Socrates talked and swooned over the bright eyes of a beautiful young boy, Marcus Aurelius pondered; where Socrates invented dialectic, Marcus delivered up an extraordinary bestiary of the human soul. The Stoics were supremely aware of an inner darkness where lurked the death instinct, the *libido moriendi*, which was their contribution to psychology, not Freud's; they troubled over anxiety, disgust, the fear of death, the diminished vitality of depression. Because of their "conscience" the Stoics at times appear beleaguered, overcome with fear and trembling at the shear effort needed to maintain the flame of sanity. In order to conquer the inner demons, one needs valor; thus the Romans understood valor to be a psychological reality instead of exclusively a social one. The Stoic quest for valor was existentially an inner one, private, moral, psychological. To live is to fight. This quest often rewarded them with suffering and it is this suffering that bestowed upon them the famous Roman gravitas, a spirit and demeanor entirely foreign to the Greeks. This gravitas was the outer emblem of inner valor—a valor as real and durable as anything won by the legionnaires on distant battlefields. Its shining was immutable.

The medieval *preux* combines the best of *arete* and valor because together with the stress on flamboyant deed there is also the ideal of private virtue won through moral struggle. In some sense, every knight was expected to be a monk knight. Lancelot, whose renown eclipsed all other knights, succumbed to vice and so is denied completion of his quest for the Grail; while Galahad, who blends grace at arms with inner purity, succeeds to virtue and so is vouchsafed a vision of the miraculous vessel. This second "ghostly chivalry" which pertains primarily to the moral sphere would eventually replace the first with the rise of the cult of the gentleman who need not necessarily win fame in battle in order to fulfill the ideal. But this ghostly chivalry was present from the first, adding a valorous, stoical dimension to the horizontal thrust of *preux*. From Malory's testimony we know that even during the height of chivalry, when the Grail cycle was in full flourish, knights were expected to end their days in seclusion with a hermit, an old wise man, to whom they rendered an account of all that had befallen them. Ensconced within a monastery or the deep woods, in a stone cottage, hut, or at the base of a sacred tree, the hermit would interpret the events so that each became a symbol of the knight's quest for virtue. We may take this as a symbolic depiction of a continuous psychological process whereby the knight is always working out his salvation in the world, consulting his *spiritius rector*, hermit, heart, in short, his conscience, as he attempts to win renown. The object of the quest is fame, of course, but a fame that can be consecrated both to and by the hermit, by keeping, via a vertical axis, the knight in psychological connection to the hermit, *preux* keeps action and learning, fame and conscience, the world and soul together. In the pursuit of *preux*, the knight steers clear of the course of Alcibiades, whose quest for fame knew no moral bounds; while also bypassing the intolerable priggishness that sometimes afflicted the Stoics. Under the code of chivalry the desire for fame and the imperatives of ethics must be harmonized as they were thought to do in Percival.

As *preux* looks back to *arete* and valor, so it looks forward to the ideal of nobility, as it has surfaced in various twentieth century authors, most notably D.H. Lawrence and Ortega y Gasset. Lawrence concludes his *Movements in European History*, a book intended for adolescents which we may take psychologically as a tract addressed to the internal potential for youth in our souls, with a grand plea for restoration of true *Noblesse oblige*, which in Nietzschean fashion he links with power. "*Noblesse* means, having the gift of power, the natural or sacred power. And having such power obliges a man to act with fearlessness and generosity, responsible for his acts to God. A noble is one who may be known before all men."[43] In *The Revolt of the Masses,* Ortega regrets—

> the degeneration suffered in ordinary speech by word so inspiring as "nobility." For, by coming to mean for many people hereditary "noble blood," it is changed into something similar to common rights, into a static, passive quality which is received and transmitted like something inert. But the strict sense, the *etymon* and the word nobility is essentially dynamic. Noble means the "well known," that is, known by everyone, famous, he who has made himself known by excelling the anonymous mass. It implies an unusual effort as the cause of his fame. Noble, then, is equivalent to effortful, excellent.[44]

Ortega then goes on to point out that "nobility does not appear as a formal expression to the Roman Empire, and then precisely in opposition to the hereditary nobles, then in decadence." Nobility, then, is a way of distinguishing that which we have from that which we must attain. Even the superior talent must train that talent and affirm it with a vital yes.

Preux also compares with Pound's robust idea of *virtù* which he deemed to be the basis of all true artistry.

It is by reason of this *virtù* that a given work of art persists. It is by reason of this *virtù* that we can have one Catullus, one Villon; by reason of it that no amount of technical cleverness can produce a work having the same charm as the original, not though all progress in art is, in so great degree, a progress through imitation....

It is the artist's business to find his own...it may be something which draws Catullus to write of scarlet poppies, or orange-yellow slippers, of the shaking, glorious hair of torches.[45]

It is the artist's business to discover his own *virtù*, it is the business of *virtù* to stamp each life with a uniqueness of artistry, a supple flair.

Against the background of *arete* and valor and against the foreground of nobility and virtue the Nietzschean will to power seems more and more to be a power, ecstasy and excellence, a whole shining condition, as we said before, that while inseparable from *gemeinschaftsgefuhl*, from concrete engagement in a literal world, and high, bold passionate exchange with others, it is nonetheless quite distant from the horrors of war and the necessity to dominate others in order to demonstrate one's value. When cast against the background of medieval chivalry, the will to power evokes a world of valorous disposition, of beauty and a keen sense of artistry. The will to power thus becomes a unique signature imprinted on the entirety of a symbolic imagination as it comes to grips with its *potentia* for excellence. Conviction more than conquest is its characteristic mark. The will to power thus become what James Dickey calls the "Dead coaches live in the air, son live / In the ear / Like fathers, and urge and urge. They want you better / Than you are."[46]

Of all ideals, however, both ancient and modern, it is honor that most closely approximates what the Middle Ages affirmed as *preux*. "But if it be a sin to covet honour, / I am the most offending soul alive," says Henry V. (*King Henry V*, Act IV, Scene III). Most commentary on the ideal of honor confirms it to be an inheritance from chivalry, and to be most at home in a hierarchical society that retains a special place for the traditional professionals of war, law, philosophy and medicine. "It would be a mistake, however," says Peter Berger, "to understand honour *only* in terms of hierarchy and its delineations."[47] Drawing on research of J.K. Campbell, who has explored the ideal of honor as it presently exists in rural Greece, Berger shows that while the obligations of honor may differ according to class or gender, they nonetheless embrace the entire community as a comprehensive ideal governing social intercourse. "...the etiquette of everyday life consists of ongoing transactions of honour, and different groups relate differently to this process according to the principle of 'To each his due.'"[48] Honor then is a code, totem, spirit, fiction that is omnipresent in human society, to which it gives a characteristic form that prevailed in the West even unto the age of the bourgeois saints. And yet, it was the rise of the bourgeois, particularly in the consciousness of its critical intellectuals that not only the honor of the *ancien regime* and its hierarchical prototypes were debunked, but that an understanding of man and society emerged that would eventually abolish *any* conception of honor. The new idea emerged as dignity.

Berger distinguishes between honor and dignity both of which are concepts that bridge self and society. Although each has a psychological soil—to which we shall turn in a moment—it is primarily in relationship with the world that both honor and dignity are actualized. Both are objects of a moral enterprise in that there are somethings we must strive for, often amid fierce opposition. To lose them is to forfeit our sense of self. Further, both have an almost magical, contagion quality, since they can be transmitted to the body and to others as in "a dignified carriage" or bringing honor to one's family, regiment, troop or king. In other words both articulate a conception of the Self, which selves are very different. Whereas honor implies "that identity is essentially, or at least importantly, linked to institutional roles. The modern concept of dignity, by contrast, implies that identity is essentially independent of institutional roles."[49] Entry into the realm of dignity requires that we discard all roles, casting away the sumptuous apparatus of name and lineage in order to confront each other as we are, abstracted from any circumstance or color.

When dignity reflects on honor, the result is comedy as in Mark Twain's *Connecticut Yankee in King Arthur's Court*, where Merlin becomes a village crank, Arthur a befuddled fool, and a coat of armor an uncomfortable iron cocoon that prompts one of the most hilarious episodes in all of literature. The Yankee, transported across time and space into the very home of chivalry, ends by echoing Falstaff's famous complaint that "honor is a mere scutcheon." The ethic of dignity signifies demystification of all roles. It penetrates, ridicules, unmasks, gets down to brass tacks, basics, I's and thou's. Although Berger does not make this point, dignity seems compounded of chiefly masculine elements. It enthrones the eye to produce an ethos of seeing though. Honor on the other hand seems feminine, which Berger obliquely recognizes when, in his opening paragraph, he compares it with chastity.

> Honour occupies about the same place in contemporary usage as chastity. An individual asserting it hardly invites admiration, and one who claims to have lost it is an object of amusement rather than sympathy. Both concepts have an unambiguously outdated status in the *Weltanschauung* of modernity. Especially intellectuals, by definition in the vanguard of modernity, are about as likely to admit honour as to be found out as chaste. At best, honour and chastity are seen as ideological leftovers in the consciousness of obsolete classes, such as military officers or ethnic grandmothers."[50]

When honor is forced to confront dignity, it is almost defenseless. Its consciousness is raped as Galileo bragged of raping in his famous letter to Copernicus. The result is tragedy. The result is Don Quixote, the Knight of the Sad Countenance, who in the end "comes to his senses" as did Galileo, and Robespierre, awakening to the fact that all enchantment is madness, to be best chased away like so much silver dream stuff. Don Quixote's death scene reveals his vulnerability, his terrible pathos. He has lost something; he has lost his Dulcinea. "For what did Don Quixote fight? For Dulcinea, for glory, for life, for survival. Not for Iseult, who is the eternal flesh; not for Beatrice, who is theology; not for Margaret, who is the people, not for Helen, who is culture. He fought for Dulcinea..."[51] At the end he loses his Dulcinea, his glory, his aptitude for arms and chivalry, his eye for beauty and the soul of things. And the world hurtles on towards destruction.

It is in this femininity that we catch sight of the psychological foundation of honor. When considered phenomenologically, honor is almost a tangible reality. A palpable chasteness. *Honor is the purity of a man's ideals.* It is the line that won't be crossed; the vow that will not be broken; the pledge honored to the last dying breath. *Honor may be defined as a passionate, daring, exultant commitment to the purity of one's ideals.* And, these ideas must be *pure*—pure in Spirit, as in Blessed are the Pure in Spirit for they shall see God—that is, in continuity with the best of the Greco-Roman-Judeo-Christian tradition and in solidarity with the best, the highest ideals, the sacred High-Mindedness fostered by all of the World's Great Religions and Mythologies. It is as if honor were a man's virginity. Honor is his maiden-head, his shield of innocence, a knightly ensign that he buckles on as if it were a chastity belt that preserves him from entrapment in false designs. In the phenomenology of honor, we meet all the qualities of virginity. In Faulkner's novel, *The Reivers*, which together with being a marvelous yarn, is also a Renaissance courtesy book, on the model of Castiglione, that teaches the art of being a gentleman, the young protagonist describes his honor at the moment before he is "seduced" by Boon Hoggenbeck, a Southern Caliban. It was—

> [S]ecure behind that inviolable and inescapable rectitude concomitant with the name I bore, pattered on the knightly shapes of my male ancestors as bequeathed—nay, compelled—to me by my father's word-of-mouth,

further bolstered and made vulnerable to shame by my mother's doting conviction, I had been merely testing Boon; not trying my own virtue but simply testing Boon's capacity to undermine it; and, in my innocence, trusting too much in the armor and shield of innocence.[52]

Plunging deeper into the idiom of chastity, the youth goes on to evoke the "impregnability of virtue as a shield." Like virginity, honor is a unique state, an almost metaphysical condition whose colors unfold in royal banners of alabaster white. Both virginity and honor wear a snow white robe of purity. Robert Desoille encourages development of magnanimity and coolness, which are perhaps the two chief tokens of honor, by asking his analysands to symbolically mantle themselves with a luminous garment. Honor is reminiscent of virginity in that it requires a certain detachment from impulse if the purity is to be impregnable, closed and vessel-like, or forfeit the special grace of its condition. Honor further resembles virginity in that it may be lost through a fleeting submission to impulse which allows the world to breach it in a manner not sanctified by custom. And finally, in imitation of virginity, when honor is lost it cannot be regained. The ritual of duels, apology, knightly penance, etc., are not so much attempts to restore honor as they are hoped for proofs that honor remains intact, wholly impervious to the insult or stain, because of the strength of its internal purity. Although one can reassert one's chastity or recover one's reputation through penance and change of heart, virginity and honor are ultimately irrecoverable. By defending our honor, we serve our Dulcinea. We establish inward connection with the Virgin whose sanctuary is thereby nurtured together with its cedar groves and miraculous veils. In all the touchiness and pride that are the inevitable accompaniment of a universal code of honor, the Virgin crystallizes in a dazzling magical Epiphany. Like Artemis, or Melissa of the Bees, Joan of Arc, the Martial Maid of Spenser, Faulkner's Drusilla, or the France of Péguy and Bernanos or Charles De Gaulle, she is wild, autonomous, untutored and yet curiously detached from all but the eternal questions of what is due our own and other's honor. We may hazard the opinion, therefore, that honor renews acquaintance with the deep woods of the soul, and the eternal varieties that are present there. The "souls of honor" that we are familiar with in our tradition often reflect this paradox in that while they may be terrifically flamboyant in outward manners— colors, pennons, pearl handled pistols—they nonetheless maintain a psychological state of extraordinary purity. They are marvels of innocence. They may curse like a stable boy but they pray on their knees. And if honor is a kind of maidenhood, then the cult of honor will make us maidenly; and indeed it is the gallant, beau, or dandy who, among all other men, is most apt to show a womanly concern for surface, tone, and etiquette. Bitchiness too belongs here: the kind of bitchiness that can turn even an innocuous word, uttered without any intention of giving offense, into a summons to appear at dawn in the company of your seconds. And finally, as the virgin is a moon goddess, so the cult of honor awakens lunar consciousness, a mind blurred and dazzled and enraptured by the stars, and entirely receptive to the power of rhythms and the numen of the blood.

In traditional mythology the virgin is often associated with the deer. Artemis represents the deer for example. Pausanias explains that the goddess was worshiped as Artemis Elephiaia (*elaphos*, deer) and in the hymn to Artemis, Callimachus reports that she goes out to find deer whose horns shine like gold so that she may harness them to her chariot. The deer is also an emblem of Mary, important in Christian ritual. Baptisteries were often decorated with emblems of deer drinking at the springs.

So then let us take the deer as the very symbol of masculine honor. A ghostly deer will often appear at that awful, ineffable moment when a boy takes possession of his maturity as in Faulkner's beautiful story *The Old People*—

> And he would remember how Sam was standing. Sam had not moved...Then the boy saw the buck. It was coming down the ridge, as if it were walking out of the very sound of the horn which related its death. It was

not running, it was walking, tremendous, unhurried, slanting and tilting its head to pass the antlers through the undergrowth, and the boy standing with Sam beside him now instead of behind him as Sam always stood, and the gun still partly aimed and one of the hammers still cocked.

Then it saw them. And still it did not begin to run. It just stopped for an instance, taller than any man, looking at them; then its muscles suppled, gathered. It did not even alter its course, not fleeing, not even running, just moving with that winged and effortless ease with which deer move, passing within twenty feet of them, its head high and the eye not proud and not haughty but just full and wild and unafraid, and Sam standing beside the boy now, his right arm raised at full length, palm-outward, speaking in that tongue which the boy had learned from listening to him and Joe Baker in the blacksmith shop, while up the ridge Walter Ewell's horn was still blowing them in to a dead buck.

"Oleh, Chief," Sam said. "Grandfather."[53]

This happens in the old lore and in the new lore as well. For example, the movies *The Deerhunter* and *Stand by Me* both employ the traditional symbol. Further when a man seeks to recover the shining innocence of his lost life of honor, he will sometimes in his fantasy take refuge with the deer, as does the old king in Isak Dinesen's story, *The Fish*—

In the window within the fathom-thick wall a small star stood, shinning, in the pale sky of the summer night. The restfulness of this star made the king's mind restless: he could not sleep.

The nightingales, which all evening had filled the woods with their exuberant, rapturous singing, were silent for a few hours around midnight. There was no sound anywhere. But from the groves around the castle came, through the open window, the scent of fresh, wet foliage; it bore all the woodland-world into the king's alcove. His mind wandered, unhindered and aimless, within that silver land: he saw the deer and the fallow-deer lying peacefully amongst the big trees, and in his thoughts, without bow or arrow, and without any wish to kill, he walked up quite close to them. Here, maybe, the white hind was now grazing, which was no real hind, but a maiden in hind's slough, with hoofs of gold.[54]

The revelation of the deer, with its inexhaustible boundless echoes, will always excite a male imagination into transformation. James Dickey's poetry abounds with such moments that leave him dazzled and with an amazement "to last him forever".[55] It is the white stag that announces the Grail in the Arthurian legend. The old Celtic and Nordic kings wore stag horns as their crowns as if the life of honor were the crown of masculine nature.

Just as in traditional mythology the Virgin is associated with the deer, so she has the power to tame the unicorn, the fabulous beast that bulks so large in the Western imagination, appearing in arcane medical lore, bestiaries, histories, and numerous coasts-of-arms. In medieval woodcuts, the wild deer or stag is often pictured with the unicorn, the antlers and the horn either touching of intertwined, as if to show the necessity and the means for attaining psychological harmony. The image itself commemorates the very old idea, which dates back to antiquity that the sole means for capturing a unicorn, whose shaft was prized both as a medicine and aphrodisiac, was by dispatching a virgin to loiter in a poppy laden field. There the unicorn would seek her out, coming to nestle the weight of its regal head in the soft folds of her garment. While tarrying there he could be trapped. Inasmuch as the traditional idea is that the unicorn symbolizes masculine consciousness, being a true expression of instinctual vitality, the hot, wild, sperm-thrust of masculine desire, may we not say that it is the presence of honor in the soul, the emblem of the virgin and the deer, that allows a man to civilize his desire and bring it into the stable, where its high blood and beauty may enrich the life of civilization. Honor is the golden bridle, the dazzling halter that transmutes the overpowering instincts that are seated in the blood. The old shamans recognize this with their image of the stag with the iron skeleton.

Eliade comments that "...the Tungus shamans costume represents a stag, whose skeleton is suggested by pieces of iron. Its horns are also of iron." The image documents the psychological realization that it is the stag, the universal code of honor, that allows us to internalize in a powerful, permanent way, even as the brace and spine of the flesh, the iron in the soul and all the iron symbolically coagulates: masculine desire, red mars riding on a lion, fire, magma, passion, blood, the shaft and glistening flank of the unicorn. The sum of the allegorical teaching about the relationship obtaining between virgin and unicorn, honor and instinct, antlers and horn, is to say that if we care to civilize the deep power of the masculine soul, then we must find the virgin in our nature, the potential for purity; then isolate it within the field of consciousness through meditation, fantasy, reading or prayer, so as to fashion a code of honor, the effect of which will be to bedazzle instinct and put it to work in the noble task of civilization.

We may also deduce from this image that while honor may be a force for restraint and limitation, it is not an agent for repression, in that the virgin not only gentles the unicorn, she also constellates him, drawing him forth from his solitary life in the deep shade of Merlin's wood. The virgin arouses the unicorn; she can turn a nagging impulse, the impulse that is nothing but a nag, into a magical beast full of instinctual vitality. In the code of honor, therefore, we find the means for checking impulse without succumbing to the harsh, debilitating hand of repression. Honor makes us wild, fierce, the mind a nervous sword, ready to battle and enrich, to heal and fertilize. In other words a deep concern for the preservation of one's honor will not blot out masculinity but will instead intensify it to the point of absolute ferocity. Michelangelo alluded to this, I think, when he added horns to Moses' head. Moses' purity and intense dedication to the wisdom of the bush, fire and desert whirlwind, inflamed his presence and imagination with an animal charisma. The stone tables that descend from the Mount didn't destroy instinct; rather than the Ten Commandments created a warrior people, a king who danced before the Lord, the builder of a sacred city. Honor is kinsman to passion not to impotence; song, not silence; it is more likely to make a pirate from a prude. Since the Church Fathers identified the unicorn with the image of Christ, we may say that there is something redemptive in the image of the unicorn. When the unicorn is tamed by the virgin, when instinct yields to honor, it brings the good news, the gospel of redemption to masculine instinct, turns masculine vitality into a redemptive force, into a ghostly chivalry, into whose arms and lances the city may commit its spirit. Like the Crusaders bound for Jerusalem, the unicorn sallies forth under a cobalt banner of the virgin.

Albert Camus once wrote that "there is no sun without shadow, and it is essential to know the night." "Our science is of shadows," said Ezra Pound. As is the case with every psychological reality, honor is dogged by various forms of shadow, that is, pathologies, into which it can elide, and from which is must be discriminated. In Nietzschean language, honor has its ugly man. Of course in actual analytic work the separation of honor from its darker twins is always a matter of nuance requiring the most subtle of distinctions. But even those distinctions require prior generalizations. Let us quickly tick off two pertaining to the pathologies of honor. A first pathology is machismo, which is a vice particularly in Hispanic cultures. Since machismo has lately fallen into such disrepute, let me confess a certain admiration for it. There are many good things to say about machismo: it lends a color and graciousness and high civility to life that ought to be the envy of every Northerner. Machismo flowers in the hidalgo, the knight errant who vigorously defends his right and meets his lady with a bow and a flourish. But machismo is more Stoic than knight, for it requires a man to renounce his feelings so as to attain a state of passionate solitude. Above all other goods the macho male aches to be invulnerable to incursions from the outside world. In his classic *The Labyrinth of Solitude,* Octavio Paz indicates that

> The Mexican *macho*—the male—is a hermetic being, closed up in himself, capable of guarding himself and whatever has been confided to him. Manliness is judged according to one's invulnerability to enemy arms or the impacts of the outside world. Stoicism is the most exalted of our military and political attributes. Our history is full of expressions and incidents that demonstrate the indifference of our heroes toward suffering or danger.[56]

Machismo exalts stoicism, passionate solitude, hermetic secrecy, and so is summed up in the image of the expressionless and featureless mask, the face and voice and gesture that never cracks to reveal an underlying current of emotion. But the emotion is there, simmering, rising steadily in temperature, until finally erupting in the fiesta, the lethal act of vengeance or the blood wedding of the bullfight.

Because of its desire to be closed, hermetic, secret, machismo may seem to evoke the virgin, the still unravished bride of quietness, as its most appropriate external image; and in this way merge with honor. And yet machismo scorns nothing so much as the vulnerability of women. The macho male dreads the epithet of "girl." Machismo binds up its outside walls into hermetic chasteness so as to repress its femininity. In becoming macho a man becomes exclusively male, to the extent that penetration is usually imaged as homosexual penetration. It is to be sodomized, to get it up the rear. For this reason machismo can never reconcile itself to loss, or find a redeeming virtue in defeat. The sight of flags and banners in the dust cause only anger and resentment. Machismo never dreams that wound, scar, trauma, loss, defeat, that penetration can be fecundating, an occasion of new life. Machismo is not a virgin but a rock, a stone face, tower, island, the trance like mask of the Mafia Don.

In sharp contrast to machismo, the longer honor stays intact the more feminine it becomes. The cult of honor is often colored by hysteria, and we have already pointed out that a fixation on one's honor often heightens the womanly graces together with attention to the luster of appearances. Further honor delights in the kind of erotic camaraderie that issues in Henry's famous statement in a battle before the walls of the French town—we are a happy band of brothers. Such *preux*, such friendship is foreign to machismo which seems fated to go it alone, in what it takes to be the splendid isolation of a manly destiny. At full flush honor is not so much a tower as it is an ornate pillar, a pillar of society, bold, erect and in the company of others.

Another parody of honor occurs in the idea of a supreme "potential" just waiting for the right moment to unfold. This is the fantasy of a "gift," "talent," "power," that often exists in what Adlerians call pampered children, in what Jungians call *puer*, and in what Freudians refer to as the over appreciated child. Peter Blos here discerns the basic syndrome:

> All through childhood this child was made to feel that he was more—in some undefinable way—than he would or could validate by his performance. He was *hors concours* from the beginning. This invisible something or somebody was called the child's potential; it was constantly talked about, often in rather concrete terms, similar to a detained visitor who is about to arrive any moment.[57]

The pampered or *puer* child lives in ceaseless dialogue with his Little Prince. This potential is an angel, voice, spirit, transpersonal self who is beautiful to contemplate and yet refuses realization in the world because concrete enactment can never fulfill the grandiosity of the ideal. When potential eclipses honor, reality is experienced as a betrayal; and here lies the main difference between potential and honor: in order to retain its purity, potential must remain unrealized, whereas honor does not exist unless it is confirmed by achievement in the world. We must demonstrate it; hence the numerous rituals of feuds, tournaments, contests, matches, etc. to prove that it exists. Unlike honor which is willing to submit to the arbitrations and judgment of the world, the man who is catering to his potential will always believe that the world misunderstands him, probably because its stupid ranks are filled with barbarians incapable of such a serene, cerebral act. Potential keeps us locked within a glass cocoon, which we may intellectualize or inflate or romanticize as a subtle body or transpersonal self, etc., from which we will never awaken save to shyly flutter here and there in acts of ephemeral attainments. To sum up then, through a life of honor we build a *name* rather than a stone wall or a subtle body. This name constitutes the beauty of our soul. In Aristotle's beautiful and haunting phrase it is our means of "taking possession of the beautiful." We may imagine it as feminine. It is our Lady, Mary, Beatrice, our Dulcinea. It is our *fama* and our *preux*, the wild deer that grazes the highlands of our soul. It is our will to power.

———

The infamous "will to power" thus belongs to a meaning complex embracing courage, valor, virtue, honor, strength, and skill. Through the coinage of this infamous idea, which many take to have laid the basis for death camps and *blitzkrieg*, Nietzsche struggled to express the perennial notion that all souls strive for honor. Honor: a sacred word. Nietzsche favored power because power enlarges virtue, stretches its long arm, converting it into a luminosity best left untrifled with. Lofty aspiration is connatural with human being; the soul dilates with every breath of flame colored lungs.

Numerous scholars have recognized this. Walter Kaufman sees one origin of the will to power in Aristotle's concept of the great soul of man.[58] After reporting the source of the idea in Nietzsche's vision of the troops marching off to war, William Barrett writes:

> But it is a mistake to locate the birth of this idea in any single experience; it was, in fact, fed by a number of tributary streams, by Nietzsche's struggle against ill health

and also by his studies in classical antiquity. Nietzsche's greatness as a classical scholar lay in his ability to see plain and simple facts that the genteel tradition among scholars had passed over.[59]

The distinguished British classicist F.M. Cornford has said of Nietzsche that he was fifty years ahead of the classical scholarship of his day; the tribute was meant to be generous, but I'm not sure that the classical scholarship of our own day has yet caught up with Nietzsche. It requires much more imagination that Nietzsche had much more of, than the classical scholars of his time. Take, for example, the obvious fact that the noble Greeks and Romans owned slaves and thought this quite natural; and that because of this they had a different orientation towards existence than did the Christian civilization that followed them. The humanistic tradition among classical scholars had idolized the ancients, and thereby, as in all idealistic views, falsified the reality. One does not need to be much of a classical specialist to know, on the first page of Julius Caesar's *Gallic Wars*, that the word *virtus*, virtue, means courage and martial valor—just the kind of thing that a military commander would most fear in the enemy and most desire in his own soldiers. (It is one of the odd developments of history—as one philosophical wag put it, making thereby a perfect Nietzschean joke—that the word "virtue," which originally meant virility in a man, came into Victorian times to mean chastity in a woman.) Nor does it recognize in the Greek word that we translate as virtue, *arete*, the clanging tone of Ares, god of battle. Classical civilizations rested on the recognition of power, and the relations of power as a natural and basic part of life.

Christopher Dawson, a traditionalist in every respect, declares—

> Whatever his weakness Frederick Nietzsche was neither a time-server nor a coward. He at least stood for the supremacy of spirit, when so many of those whose office it was to defend it had fallen asleep or gone over to

the enemy. He remained faithful to the old ideals of the Renaissance culture, the ideals of creative genius and of the self-affirmation of the free personality, and he revolted against the blasphemes of an age which degraded the personality and denied the power of the spirit in the name of humanity and liberty.[60]

Erich Heller notes—

> Rejoicing in the quiet lucidity of Claude Lorrain, or seeking the company of Goth in conversation with Eckermann, or comforted by the composure of Stifter's *Nachsommer*, a Nietzsche emerges very different from the one who used to inhabit the fancies of Teutonic school boys and alas school masters, a Nietzsche who is a traditionalist at heart...[61]

Manes Sperber transcends the confinements of the typical Adlerian view by saying—

> There is no doubt that Nietzsche thought of the will-to-power as the trait of a nobler form of man, as the means and end of overcoming humanness in favor of the superman, as a sublime quality, a new, supreme form of virtue.[62]

All souls strive for honor. So did Nietzsche strive and his quest was a physical one:

> And up again into the small, narrow, modest, coldly furnished *chambre garnie*, where innumerable notes, pages, writings, and proofs are piled up on the table, but no flower, no decoration, scarcely a book and rarely a letter. Back in a corner, a heavy and graceless wooden trunk, his only possession, with the two shirts and

the other worn suit. Otherwise only books and manu-
scripts, and on a tray innumerable bottles and jars and
potions: against the migraines, which often render him
all but senseless for hours, against his stomach cramps,
against spasmodic vomiting, against the slothful intestines, and above all the dreadful sedatives against his in-
somnia, chloral hydrate and Veronal. A frightful arsenal
of poisons and drugs, yet the only helpers in the empty
silence of this strange room in which he never rests except in brief and artificially conquered sleep. Wrapped
in his overcoat and a woolen scarf (for the wretched
stove smokes only and does not give warmth), his fin-
gers freezing, his double glasses pressed close to the paper, his hurried hand writes for hours—words the dim
eyes can hardly decipher. For hours he sits like this and
writes until his eyes burn.[63]

There are many ways to read this passage, this evocation of a
strange room. But in the isolation, the sense of physical trial, the
moral stamina which conquers illness, I hear a clash of arms, the
distant echo of knight-errantry, the roll of an agnostic drum. Bereft
of possessions and driven by what strange motive I do not know, Nietzsche turned his life into a battlefield. He attained a moral knighthood. He bit the bullet. Will triumphed over agony. Speaking with
another goal in mind, William James has captured the code by which
he lived:

> This ideal of the well-born man without possessions
> was embodied in knight errantry and templardom…
> We glorify the soldier as the man absolutely unencum-
> bered. Owning nothing but his bare life, and willing to
> toss that up at any moment when the cause commands
> him, he is the representative of unhampered freedom in
> ideal directions.[64]

The extent of Nietzsche's suffering and struggle, together with his commitment to a soldierly ethos, must be reckoned as organic to his vision; otherwise, the true nature of that vision will continue to elude us.

Is it any wonder really that Nietzsche, as master classicist, should have glimpsed the spring of human action in a manner that tallies with Aristotle: "...men seem to pursue honor to assure themselves of their own worth; at any rate, they seek to be honored by sensible men and by those who know them, and they want to be honored on the basis of their virtue or excellence." (*Nicomachean Ethics I*, 1095b, 27-29) Aristotle played tutor to a king of kings. From his master, the student Alexander imbibed the iron colored nutrient of mind whose sub-distinctions split the Gordian knot and carried Greece to the shores of the Ganges. In view of such accomplishment, who can doubt the quickening stimulus of a concern for honor? Honor, *virtu*, power, pomp, the splendor of breath taking shape like a frosty helmet: these things also recollect the Middle Ages when Chastellain, scribe and witness for the barbarian splendor of the House of Burgundy, declared "Honour urges every noble nature To love all that is noble in being. Nobility also adds its uprightness to it."[65]

The Renaissance was also rife with such conceptions. Burckhardt touches on both the shadow and the splendor, when he explains that the sentiment of honor "is compatible with many vices and susceptible to extravagant delusions; nevertheless, all that has remained pure and noble in many may find support in it and draw new strength from it." Nietzsche belongs to this company. When playing with the kindling sticks of power, he lit the torch of *virtu, arete, preux* and honor. His line reaches back to gaudy Renaissance *magnifico*, continues on to chivalry, and then to Aristotle, master of those who know. Far from being a nihilist, the witty slayer of the godspell for metaphysics, Nietzsche was in fact a friend of tradition, of "our dear West," insofar as that tradition wills to be itself. Like Froissart and the other custodians of chivalry he dreamt of sublime deeds. That he got the Prussians instead of *preux* stigmatizes us, not Nietzsche. Nietzsche was out of step with modernity because modernity is out step with the past. Nietzsche knew that while human motivations may seem multiform all the roots eventually reach down into the heart, where repose virtue, reserves of decency, and the will to power. The archaic notion that a hairy heart symbolizes courage, cunning, subtlety and craft, together with a host of other virtues, may very well spell out intuitively that the roots of all good things extend into the heart, the seat of motivation. Nietzsche's heart, I am sure, was matted with a comely foliage.

Until now we have focused on the gist of Nietzsche's thinking so as to document his loyalty to the creative springs of tradition. But let us shift attention now to the riddle of his style.

In matters of style Nietzsche often seems jejune, especially to a mind accustomed to philosophical civilities and to the relaxed sententiousness of geometric prose. In contrast to a Hegel or a Leibniz, who fashioned their metaphysics as an architect constructs a vault, Nietzsche seems a bull let loose in a china shop. He seems to have relished conflict far too much, so that difference obsessively spills over into insult. Instead of building a system whose premise could suavely modulate into a massive truth, Nietzsche vented spleen and vital substances covering his page. Although he may have honored the rules of war; nonetheless he gloried in the clash—

> My practice of war can be summed up in four propositions. First: I only attack causes that are victorious; I may even wait until they become victorious. Second: I only attack causes against which I would not find allies, so that I stand alone…Third: I never attack persons; I merely avail myself of the person as of a strong magnifying glass that allows one to make visible a general but creeping and elusive calamity. Thus I attacked David Strauss…Thus I attacked Wagner…Fourth: I only attack things when every personal quarrel is excluded, when any background of bad experiences is lacking…On the

contrary, attack is in my case a proof of good will, sometimes even of gratitude.[66]

Self-display, polemics, ludic feints, the knock-out-blow, sedition
against stupidity, these are the termini of Nietzsche's vision. When
he wrote, he crammed his wisdom into points and parables destined
to dispatch a rival. Truth, for Nietzsche, was a woman, a scarf to
decorate his lance. Philosophy was a game to be won.

As a stylistic buccaneer, whose métier is brash polemics, Nietzsche again shows surprising continuity with that tradition to
which he is supposed to have dealt a death blow. For that tradition
comes down to his house in images of struggle. Riddles, matches,
contests, bouts; the Western mind lights up with these, mainly se-
lecting agonistic structures for the expression of its genius. Near the
fire source of this tradition one may espy the features of a sophist, the
shaman's son about whom Huizinga comments—

> He may be regarded as an extension of the central fig-
> ure in archaic cultural life who appeared before us suc-
> cessively as the prophet, medicine man, seer, *thauma-
> turge* and poet and whose best designation is *vates*. The
> sophist has two important functions in common with
> the more ancient type of cultural rector: his business is
> to exhibit his amazing knowledge, the mysteries of his
> craft, and at the same time to defeat his rival in public
> contest. Thus the two main factors of social play in ar-
> chaic society are present in him: glorious exhibitionism
> and agonistic aspiration.[67]

When the sophist came to town it was a grand event, an exhibition, *epideixis*. The crowds came thronging, willing to lay down
considerable sums of money—Prodicus, for example, charged fifty
drachma for his lectures—to witness incredible feats of memory,
magic disquisitions or simply to stare at men like Hippias Polyhistor,
"the man of a thousand arts, the mnemotechnician, the economic

autarch whose boast it is that he has made everything he wears..."
Minstrel, troubadour, *polytropos*, genius without portfolio: to the
crowds such a man must have seemed a miraculous being on equal
footing with the gods. Perhaps Gorgias dreamed it so in that he became so rich from the practice of his art that he was able to dedicate
a statue of himself to the god at Delphi, made of solid gold.

The crowning achievement of the sophist was his skill at verbal combat. "[I]n short, the profession of sophist was quite on a par
with sport."[68] The sophist delighted in the fray coming to town to
defeat and dispatch all comers. Mantled in fantastic garb spilling the
treasures of his memory, tossing off glittering asides, ad libs well-
rehearsed, the sophist dispatched his rival with the slings and arrows
of an outrageous and silver tongue. "The spectators applauded and
laughed at every well-aimed crack. It was pure play, catching your
opponent in a net of argument or giving him a knock-out blow." [69]
What the winner took all of was both money and praise and a piece
of his adversaries' pride and hide.

Have Adlerians misunderstood Nietzsche, ascribing to him
views he never held or at least failing to comprehend the prismatic
complexity of his genius? In as much as they tend to perceive in his
work a prolonged exaltation of a primitive power instinct at war
with civilization, the answer must be a definitive *yes*. Nietzsche was
no power-monger, no votary of Wotan, the Berserk, who nightly
swooned to the runic music of the Valkyries. Instead he wed tradition, both in regard to the substance of his thought, which consisted
of a sustained defense of those ancient virtues which once warmed
the Western soul into its manhood; and in his style, which exhumed
sophistry, with all its pugnacity and glitter. Was not this Nietzsche,
the evocation of his name continues to send shudders cascading
down the spine of pious folk, less a brutal anti-Christ than a small
boy dreaming of magic and swords. Nietzsche retained the dream of
chivalry when the reality seemed lost.

He swam in a dazzling current that had slipped underground
while rationalist foot trod heavy up above. Nietzsche was neither
humanist nor magi; instead we must take him at his word: he was

a warrior, a philosopher of *thymos*. But we must not misread *thymos*, to make of it something at odds with the dignity and bloom of our corporate past. The West arose from *thymos*: "Sing, Muse, of the wrath of Achilles." The richest parts of our collective image stem from its cultivation. Nietzsche would have been at home trading barbs with the dazzling tongue of Antiphon: blue robed Charlemagne would have welcomed him to the ferment of his court; the cobbled streets and smoky torches of a medieval college town where syllogistic points were sometimes scored with daggers—that would have suited him entirely. Perhaps the best summation of Nietzsche's work is to say that while encased within his glacial room, he strove to halt the tailspin of the old tradition. He sank so low sometimes perhaps to reclaim roots.

In light of the vitality of the Nietzschean texts—their store of richness and metabolizing power—we must begin to wonder about the strange Adlerian amnesia in regards to Nietzsche; an amnesia that at times appears to have afflicted Adler himself. Why have Adlerians not scaled the Nietzschean heights in order to extend their clinical and conceptual horizons? Why have Adlerians, with few exceptions, shied back from Nietzsche or at the very minimum, radically underplayed, to the point of undermining the Adlerian-Nietzschean golden thread. There are two reasons.

First, because they fear the Nazi stigma. They don't want swastikas painted on their walls. If Nietzsche foreshadowed Hitler and his gang of cutthroats then nothing good can come from admitting to a Nietzschean paternity. But Nietzsche didn't father Fascism. As nearly every reputable Nietzschean scholar has declared, the ostensible affinity is bogus, a mockery of scholarship and understanding. By denying their Nietzschean antecedents, then, or by trying to conceal them, Adlerians merely reveal their incomprehension. Second, Adlerians shun Nietzsche because to acknowledge Nietzsche's overwhelming influence on Adler might very well seem to lessen Adler's reputation, to dim his genius. And yet if Nietzsche was authentically traditionalist then perhaps only Adlerians can truly understand him, for Adler is the psychologist of tradition.

Adler's amity with tradition can be demonstrated according to a fourfold way: it is evident in his view of *gemeinschaftsgefuhl* as honor within the metaphor of contest; it is visible in his choice of themes: city, courage, common sense; it is illustrated by Adler's own sense of tradition which is always focused by the great works of the high traditionalist—

Our knowledge of man as an individual has existed from time immemorial. To give only a single instance, the historical and personal narratives of ancient peoples—the Bible, Homer, Plutarch, and all the Greek and Roman poets, sagas, fairy-tales, fables, and myths—show a brilliant understanding of the human personality.[70]

And it receives final confirmation in Adler's personal choice of living spots. The spirit of this place was linked to Adler's mind with his independence from Freud and the discovery of his own definitive vision. It is perhaps the key to the riddle of the man. Here in beautiful, astonishing language Adler's biographer evokes that place.

The year 1910 was Adler's launch into freedom. The work of his mind was his own and could freely bear his name.

He now gave up his general practice to devote himself entirely to psychiatry; and the whole household moved from Czerningasse to a roomy flat in the heart of the city close to the old University, No. 10 Dominikanerbastei.

Adler loved this spot best in Vienna. The Dominikanerbastei was once manned against the Turks, and had held the city—with its freedom and its learning—safe from barbaric hordes.

No one who before the 11th of March 1938, strolled through those courtyards and sheltered alleys, under trellis-covered cafés, will ever forget its freedom and light-heartedness. Here on long summer evenings, hatless, coatless people sat in old doorways, or in the open-air cafés, greeting each other with kindly eyes. Tourists passed through these alleys sometimes but did not linger. There was no traffic and the rich never entered them.

The very houses leaned forward as if to greet each other; the wind of time had shifted the cooked roofs; forgotten trees bloomed in the corners of cobbled-stoned courtyards. Here and there through a break in the houses flashed the shining roof of the Stephansdom.

Medieval signs still swung in front of tradesmen's shops, an Eye of God above a chemist's, or a cheerful reminder of the Holy Ghost. Many of these old doorways were graced by a statue of Saint Florian flaunting his rickety water-can in one hand, apparently sure that its playful trickle was enough to deal with the sheeted flame attacking his toy church in the other. Lamps still burned before age-old madonnas in dark stone niches.

The old University opposite the post office, had long been out of use, but its ghost still seemed a part of the moonlight lingering upon its cobbled square and in the shelter of its ancient walls.[71]

Not once but twice Adler elected to make his home at a precise spot where Europe had been saved by chivalrous, sword repulsing, Saracen scimitar.

Against the advice of all his business friends and relatives, Adler bought a big house and garden, an hour's run from the Stephan's Platz, at Salmannsdorf, a little village in the Wienerwald. Once more Adler founded his home upon the exact spot that marked a decisive victory for European culture, over the barbarian hordes that attacked Vienna under Suleiman the Turk.[72]

This choice of living spots is more indicative of the direction and wealth of Adler's teaching than any thought he ever put to paper on any of the sparkling gibes that lightened café life among his friends in Old Vienna.

Further, just as Adlerians are the only ones who can understand Nietzsche, so the Nietzschean connection—Crookshank's golden threat—enriches Adler by forestalling the etiolation of his "traditionalism" into a bloodless coda devoid of flesh and fire. If Individual Psychology belongs to the party of tradition, it is because tradition gives us power. Nietzsche reminds us that tradition is strength, or as Harold Bloom has put it, "Out of the strong comes forth strength, even if not sweetness, and when strength has imposed itself long enough, then we learn to call it tradition, whether we like it or not."[73] And to the question of the worth of tradition Bloom responds? "it is valuable precisely because it partly blocks, because it stifles the weak, because it represses even the strong."[74] Power requires something to be resisted, grappled with, some mass of material to be moved. Where there is no sense of tradition; where there is no sense of the overwhelming grandeur of the past; there can be no power. We all know this with a knowledge carried to our hearts and that it is precisely those men and works who seem possessed by the past—its magnitude and wonder, who understand as Faulkner says, that memory believes before knowing remembers; who commune with the glamorous and old disastrous things—who radiate the keener sense of power, charisma, strength. Is not Nietzsche's thought more powerful because he communed with tradition and Adler's because he anchored his imagination in the thought of the past? As Adlerians, in the light of Nietzsche, we prize the dead freight of the past because it gives us something to resist and in resisting, love, because it is the deep, resonant, enraged engagement with this material that allows us to fulfill our destiny as the being whose being is determined by the will to power.

———

We now must look at the other side of the coin. We now must frame a paradox. If in part Adlerians have mistaken Nietzsche, they have also understood him very clearly, perhaps more so than any comparable body of interpreters. If Nietzsche at his best emerges as a champion of the West, who presents a spirited defense of *arete* and valor, which is in turn illuminated by a complex phenomenology; at his worst he is something else entirely: a corruptor of that notion. If Nietzsche reached for chivalry, he reached too high; if the arrow flew towards heraldry, it overshot the mark. Nietzsche's defense of the ground and high pitch of Western chivalry is marred by a fatal error—not an unattractive error but a fatal one. He viewed tradition through a flawed and fatal lens; and it is this which Adlerians have objected to, doing so, I think, with an instinctive grasp of the issues involved.

When Nietzsche reclaimed chivalry, he resurrected it to the image of the Knights Templars. It is the spirit of the temple that animates his work. Formed during the crusades to be the sword of the church, the Knights Templars were begun in 1119 when a band of eight knights united to defend the temple and the road to Jerusalem. Sworn to remain chaste and celibate and to be constantly in prayer, the Templars were monk-knights, who were dedicated to the noble task of conquering all the enemies of the Faith.

Their symbol was the sacred red cross which they wore on the breast of their armor. Although intended to be a monastic order of knighthood, each of whose members were bound by a vow of poverty, the knights of the temple amassed incredible riches. Corrupted by the rich sensations of the flesh available in an Oriental land far away from the cold vigor of the North, the Templars succumbed to the Eastern passion for secret power wielded by great wealth. Tax exempt from the start, and acting as bankers for the Pope, the Templars acquired a sinister reputation as money lenders at rates much lower than the Jews or Lombards who competed with them. Unlike the knights of St. John, they supported no hospitals: charity was not a part of their mission. Further they were widely suspected of witchcraft and the use of the black arts. It was said that they approached heresy, worshipping a Dionysian Christ with mystical and gnostic overtones. For two centuries they thrived. Their monasteries and temples spread out all over Europe, so that by the beginning of the fourteenth century they claimed thousands of members—two thousand in France alone. They existed almost as a law unto themselves, completely independent from the normal channels of power. To some they seemed a dagger pointed at the heart of Christendom.

Since our interest is in the Templars as a symbol rather than a historical reality, let me amplify this picture by borrowing from Walter Scott, whose Brian de Bois-Guilbert is the most famous and familiar Templar in the Western psyche. Breathes there a boy with soul so dead, that never to himself hath said: I must read *Ivanhoe*? The Templar first appears in the thick white dust of the evening riding in the company of horsemen. He is "thin, strong, tall, and muscular"; he appears to have "sustained a thousand toils, and [was] ready to dare a thousand more." He wears a scarlet cap and a scarlet monastic mantle. On the mantle there is "cut, in white cloth, a cross of peculiar form." One squire leads his war-horse; while a second squire holds aloft a lance "from the extremity of which fluttered a small banderole, or streamer, bearing a cross of the same form with that embroidered upon his cloak." His shield is covered with scarlet cloth. Then come two Saracen attendants. "The whole appearance of this warrior and his retinue was wild and outlandish; the dress of his squires was gorgeous, and his Eastern attendants wore silver collars round their throats, and bracelets of the same metal...Silk and embroidery distinguished their dresses, and marked the wealth and importance of their master; forming, at the same time, a striking contrast with the martial simplicity of his own attire." The horses too are Saracen, Arabian steeds that "might have passed for a personification of substance and of shadow."[75] Scott captures here that mix of restraint and passion, humility and splendor that characterized the Templars, fierce monks who praised war.

I hold that Zarathustra is a Templar. Is not that strange and curious creature who appeared to Nietzsche bearing a Dionysian message for the world in fact a votary of the strange rituals of the Temple? It is against the background of the Templar that we may understand Zarathustra's fierce, cold, warrior's ethic which finds in the class of swords a divine elixir for the soul; the emphasis on valor, pride, *esprit* and honor here too makes sense; so too the stress on grace, style, light, the *cortesia* that greeted Lady Lou with the handsome comment: "What star has brought you here, Dear Lady." Is this not the Templar's ethic: "*The good four. Honest* with ourselves and with whatever is friend to us; *courageous* toward the enemy; *generous* toward the vanquished; *polite*—always: that is how the four cardinal virtues want us."[76] This is the fierce honesty of the desert; the courage of the sword matched to nervous scimitar; the generosity of *Coeur de Lion* and Saladin; the *cortesia* of the Frankish kingdoms in the East. Is this not the Templar's soul in the shade and cool of his Oriental palace: "O my soul, over rich and heavy stand there, live a vine with swelling udders and crowded brown gold-grapes— crowded and pressed by your happiness, waiting in your superabundance and still bashful about waiting." Nietzsche's heraldry is Templar like: the lion, eagle and the snake. And his reflection on mystical techniques of chastity, his erotic physiology, probably have a background in the Templar cult. The entire action of the final book of Zarathustra: the inverted mass, the Ass Festival, the golden ball, the sweet lyre and fragrance deeper than day has been aware, and of course the ecstatic praise of Dionysus, may very well unconsciously rehearse Templar ritual.

As a religious order, the Templars were founded at the beginning of the twelfth century. During this century there took place what Denis de Rougemont has called, "a complete revolution in the western *psyche*." It was a time when the dark, secret, colorful flame of gnosis blazed over the West to cripple and finally destroy the High Middle Ages. To de Rougemont gnosis represents "the reappearance in Western man of a symbolical East."[77] It vitalized the Cathars, the Elect, or Pure, who made the light-grazed Montségur their religious stronghold.

> The pure or Cathars were affiliated with the great Gnostic streams that flowed across the first millenary of Christianity...The Cathars therefore rejected the dogma

of the Incarnation, and *a fortiori* its Roman translation in the sacrament of the mass. They replaced it with a supper of brotherhood which symbolized purely spiritual events. They also rejected baptism by water, and recognized only baptism by the consolatory Spirit: the *consolamentum* was the major rite of their Church.[78]

The Cathars veered away from the body and the blood, the bread and wine, the cool, bright chill of water. Gnosis also generated the warbling clarities of the Troubadours says de Rougemont. We need to remember here that it was the troubadour knights that Nietzsche admired above all others. It also corrupted the Templars.

What is *gnosis*? Eric Voegelin described it as a substitution of a "super-celestial dream world" for the gritty actualities of existence. Gnosis spurns life on what Adler called "this poor crust of a planet." For our purposes, let us define gnosis as a form of the imagination that flees from the imperfections of existence to take refuge in distant, starry zones, where it may dwell in complete unification with the one. "The fundamental dogma," according to de Rougemont, "of all Manichaean sects is that the soul is divine or angelic, and is *imprisoned* in created forms—in terrestrial matter, which is Night."[79] The soul is luminous aspiration, divine force, pure energy, cosmic pulse. In comparison to the beauty and superiority of the soul, all mortal existence is inferior: the body is "mud," "tomb," "dungeon," "grave," "pit of everlasting perdition"; history is a "lie," "deceit," "web of Maya," a nightmare from which we are trying to awaken; others are isolated, solitary selves caught up in the fruitless trivia of existence, impaled upon a bed of slumber. It is especially in regard to others that gnosis brims with arrogance. One text sums up the vision of terrestrial existence in language reminiscent of Prometheus' famous speech about what men were before he, the master spirit, conferred upon them the gift of fire.

...Ignorance inspired them with terror and confusion, and left them unstable, torn and divided, there were many illusions by which they were haunted, and empty fictions, as if they were sunk in sleep and as if they found themselves prey to troubled dreams. Either they are fleeing somewhere, or are driven ineffectually to pursue others; or they find themselves involved in brawls, giving blows or receiving blows; or they are falling from great heights...[etc., etc.]: until the moment when those who are passing through all these things, wake up. Then, those who have been experiencing all these confusions, suddenly see nothing. For they are nothing—namely, phantasmagoria of this kind.[80]

In gnosis that is what the world amounts to: nothing, phantasmagoria of this kind. Observing the terms of its imprisonment the soul recoils in sharp disgust and this disgust itself comprises an ecstatic illumination. Its soul flames directly upward, passing through the realms of various daimons, fictions, thrones, all of which try to ensnare the soul and block its rise, but if the soul persists it will finally reach the eternal object of its desire, which in gnosis is often imaged as a woman—*Wisdom, Anima, Sophia, Shakti*—with whom it merges in complete absorption. This is the shaman scrambling up the world tree, the Mithraic votary god climbing up the second ladder, the Neo-Platonist on his voyage to the dark side of the moon, the alchemist on his journey through the planetary houses. But if the soul persists, all tatters in his mortal dress are burned and purged away. All identity, differentiation, uniqueness, disappears. Another name for this experience is death. To be agnostic is to be half in love with easeful death, to give Eros a torch pointing downward.

Two points here for clarification, the first of them being that the gnostic flight to the Beyond is not necessarily identical with the Platonic ascent to the realm of forms. Though gnosis can't be saved for Individual Psychology, Platonism can. This includes the Plato of the *symposium* and the *Phaedrus* where the philosopher presents an almost mystical vision of the ascent, suitably offered through the mouth of the oracular priestess Diotima. According to the teaching in these texts and others, the philosopher attains to a vision of the forms through a kind of divine delirium, enthusiasm, mania and various stages of transport. But we must be careful here in that the weight of Plato's teaching is to interdict the idea that this ascent is a solitary quest, as it is in gnosis. Instead, the ascent is fundamentally dependent upon community. In the Seventh Letter, for example, Plato described the path of knowledge as "a fire" that "is kindled in the soul," "transmitted from one to the other." Friedlander comments that without the participation in community the philosopher will never attain the full ecstasy of ascent.[81] The gulf between Plato and gnosis is further widened by Plato's sense of what this ecstasy entails. The condition of ecstasy is both a condition and a product of the vision of forms. In a state of ecstasy the philosopher beholds the prototype of beauty. Having caught a fiery vision of the truth, his wings begin to grow and he once again finds life worth living. But at no time during this vision, as is always the case with gnosis, does the philosopher lose his individual identity or the structure of his soul. The goal of the Platonic life is not the gnostic one of absorption, but vision, and the consequence of vision is not an abolition of the self but an accentuation of its forms, a heightening of its virtue. The soul advances in knowledge, order and virtue, not ecstasy. Subsequent to his vision, that is, after he settles back to earth, which again departs from gnosis, the philosopher should dwell upon his reminiscences, which may cause others, who are blind to his ecstasy, to consider him mad. But this madness does not equate with isolation, and is thus not true madness at all, not, at least, in the Adlerian sense, since the heightened virtue of the philosopher aides the community. In this sense Plato almost corresponds to Confucius who maintained that the vital order of the community rests upon a prior establishment of a vital order in the soul. And Adler has been called, both by Maret and Lewis Way, the Western Confucius.

An additional point. *The Adlerian description of neurosis curiously approximates the traditional picture of gnosis.* It is as if in describing the neurotic, Adler had Manes, Basilides, Valentinus or even Plotinus in mind. The same emphasis on inferiority appears. For Adler, the neurotic is he who cannot bear being bound in a body, a mere, imperfect sack of flesh and bones. Unable to accept the insult of an ordinary fate, the neurotic takes wing in what Adler in one place calls "the flight from the dark feeling of one's inferiority".[82] And in another place "frequently this 'will to be up' is expressed in a strongly figurative manner especially in dreams, but also in symptoms, and takes the symbolic form of a race, soaring, of climbing mountains, etc."[83] Soaring upward the neurotic enters into what Adler calls the sphere of fiction, and these fictions are frequently personified as thrones, powers, daimons, etc. "Sometimes in a situation of uncertainty the personified, deified guiding idea is met with as a second self, as an inner voice like the daimon..."[84] The neurotic totally identifies with these fictions, that is, he ascribes to them reality; and in time, in the farther reaches of psychosis, he becomes a god, a luminous flame, a divine point, with little or no connection to the cosmological traffic of the earth. Adler's name for this divinity is the hermaphrodite, a frequent aspiration of the gnostic; or narcissus, the gnostic hero. Neurosis is vanity, said Adler in one of his most paradigmatic sayings. Lewis Way beautifully sums up the Adlerian doctrine—

> The neurotic lifestyle, though a reciprocal totality in all its stages, tends all the time to become more accentuated and characteristic. It evolves by the dynamism contained in its contradiction, which is that of seeking to evade all tests of life while maintaining the prestige of personality...Hence he seems to advance up what Adler called the narrowing path. At the end of this subjective vista stands his goal in the shape of his own Ego, the focal point and incarnation of perfect security and absolute power. Elevated and isolated above the world, he hangs like a star untrammeled in space to guide his footsteps.[85]

Neurosis reprises the old gnostic credo that the true souls will become a star at death, perhaps the death-in-life that neurosis comprises. The neurotic with his cult of daimons corresponds to the ancient gnostic whose ascent up the starry ladder is in essence a vindictive, symbolical obliteration of the entire earth. *For Adler, then, gnosis is neurosis.* Gnosis cannot be rehabilitated. Sanity requires that it be rooted out.

Gaston Bachelard, whose keenness in these matters is unexcelled and perhaps unrivalled, has demonstrated that Nietzsche's imagination is fundamentally gnostic in nature. Its colorations are always of the air, never earth; never water, never fire. "Hail to me...my abyss speaks...I have turned my ultimate depth inside out!" Thus cries the gnostic soul in a shrill voice reminiscent of various gnostic prayers. In matters of the earth Bachelard avers: "Nietzsche is not a poet of the *earth.* Humus, clay, open and plowed field do not supply him with images.[86] By estranging himself from the earth, Nietzsche renounces all that is incarnate: things, body, history; and with the rewards and continuities that embodiment proves. Without earth we have no boundaries, limits, shapes, uniqueness or identities. We bid farewell to the nourishment of realism. In regard to waters, Bachelard opines: "Nietzsche is not a poet of *water...*Water is too servile: it cannot be a true obstacle, a true adversary for Nietzsche's struggling hero." By rejecting water Nietzsche loses connection with the womb, breasts, rain, from all that is deep flowing and eternal, from the springs of poetry, from the Lethean-like consolation of forgetting; from what David Jones has called "The Lady of the Pool." Without still waters our souls can never be restored. With respect to fire, Bachelard admits that "Demonstrating that Nietzsche is not a *poet of fire* is a more delicate task." And yet "it is not the *substance* which imbues and tones Nietzsche's...imagination."[87] By spurning fire, Nietzsche forfeits inspiration by the inner seer who stays in connection with the earth, leaving the earth to sustain its fierce and luminous intensity. Paul the tentmaker; Rilke cleaning house; St. Theresa sweeping. After all of these elements have been purged, all that remains is air, shrill, alien, isolated, cold. The gnostic imagination par excellence.

Now when a gnostic imagination struggles with the materials of Western history, as did Nietzsche; when a gnostic imagination grapples with the perennial themes of honor, valor, courage, *preux*, as did Nietzsche; when a gnostic imagination strives to overcome its weakness, inferiority and identification with the feminine, as did Nietzsche's; when a gnostic imagination reaches toward chivalry through the intermediary of the East, as did Nietzsche, *then the Templar will materialize. This is the Templar complex.* The Knights Templars seized the imagination of Nietzsche; it was the Knights Templars who provided at least in part the imaginal soil for the creation of the idea of the will to power. It was neither Wotan nor Dionysus, but rather the complex arrangement between the two that the Templar instills.

The Templar complex is curiously bound up with fascism, especially in its most virulent form, which is Nazism. We need to make this observation because the "traditionalist perspective," which we are defending here, is often charged with being crypto-Fascist. Nothing could be farther from the truth. Tradition reflects the Knight. Fascism corresponds to the Templar. Hitler was quoted by Rauschning, the *Gauleiter* of Danzig, as having said:

> You ought to understand Parzifal differently from the way it is generally interpreted. Behind the trivial Christian dressing of the external story, with its Good Friday magic, this profound drama has quite a different content. It is not a Christian, Schopenhauerian religion of compassion, but the pure and aristocratic blood that is glorified. To guard and glorify this is the task for which the brotherhood of initiates has gathered itself together. There the king suffers the incurable sickness of corrupted blood. There the ignorant yet pure man is led into the temptation of yielding to the guile and ecstasy of a corrupt civilization in Klingsor's magic garden, or else he may choose to join the knight elect who guard the secret of life: the pure blood. We, all of us, suffer from that sickness of contaminated mixed blood. How can we purify ourselves and atone? Take heed: the com-

passion which leads to knowing is only for the inwardly corrupt one, for him who is split in himself. And this compassion knows only one course of action: to let the sick one die. The eternal life which is the gift of the Grail is only for the truly pure and noble...How is one to stop racial decay? Politically we have acted: no equality no democracy. But what about the masses of the people? Should one let them go their way, or should one stop them? Should we form an elect group of real initiates? An order, the fraternity of templars around the Grail of pure blood?[88]

In commenting on this passage Whitmont declares:

Hitler eventually answered this question in the affirmative: the *Ordensburgen* of the S.S. were formed as Grail castles for the purpose of cultivating a pure race for the *perfecti* in a holy marriage of the racially select. Hitler's extermination of minorities, notably Jews, may well have been intended as a ritual offering; the *holocaust*, the burned sacrifice to the Holy of Holies. His mode of operation unleashed gruesome Dionysian orgies of destruction. A myth disregarded, forgotten, and repressed, erupted and immersed the world in a cataclysm of destruction.[89]

Whitmont assumes here, as do all votaries of Dionysus, all advocates of a revived Templardom as the agency of psychological renewal, that the terrors of the Nazis, and of Fascisms generally, may be ascribed to repression of the powerful "instinct" in the psyche that is depicted in the splendor of the antique Dionysian ritual, and in its medieval counterpart in the cult of the Temple and the Grail. Repression, it is said, distorts this instinct and bestializes it, so that it returns with a knife that is soaked in blood. Where Dionysus is not repressed, his nature, it is assumed, is almost calm and pacific.

...the enthusiast is...full of god, the Maenad takes to herself the very name of the god. Also the "enthusiast" possesses for the time the power and the character of the deity, as Plato tells us in the *Phaedrus*. The Maenads bring milk and honey from river and rock, the daughters of Anios can turn everything they touch into wine. And there is method in the madness for the wild movements of the Bacchai, the whirling dance and the tossing of the head, the frantic clamor and the music of the wind-instruments and tambourine, the waving of the torches in the darkness, the drinking of certain narcotics or stimulants, are recognized hypnotic methods for producing mental seizure or trance, and the drinking of the blood and eating the raw flesh of an animal that incarnates the gods is also a known form of divine communion. And what are we to say of the silence of the Bacchai, alluded to in the strangest of Green proverbs? It is the exhaustion that follows upon over-exaltation, or is it the very zenith reached by the flight of the spirit, when voices and sounds are hushed, and in the rapt silence the soul feels closest to God." [90]

All milk and honey: thus the Maenad appears in nature, away from the city, enveloped by the cult. If instead of repressing Dionysus, if instead of detaching ourselves from the temple, gnosis, polytheism, animism, etc., we instead gave them homage, affirmation and tried to integrate the instinct as a vital part of consciousness, then the terrors associated with the Fascist and Nazis could be averted. So ends the argument.

Now the problem here, as William Lynch has shrewdly observed, is that Dionysus does not confine his ecstasies to the mountains; but instead invades the city and in nearly every case dismantles all its structures. At the conclusion of the *Bacchae* the entire city lies in smoking ruins, while the god looks on, smiling, up above. Lynch examines and then rejects the idea that all the destruction is caused by the prior denial of Dionysus' divinity, and then goes on to label Fascism as the consequence not of the repression of Dionysus but of his true Epiphany. Lynch explains that violence occurs so often in the myths of Dionysus that it seems dishonest to call them overlays or accidents brought on by human *hubris*.[91] When Dionysus comes to Thrace, King Lycurgus resists him. The king is subsequently torn apart by wild horses after first mistaking his son for a vine bush and cutting him down with an ax. In Orchomenus he bitterly transforms three sisters into beasts; while in Argos he drove all the women mad so that they kill and then devour their children. The god seems fond of violence and vengeance, the credo of any eye for an eye, or rather a death for a death. Even Cadmus, who welcomed Dionysus into Thebes at the end of the play reproves him for his bloodthirstiness. What seems to enrage Dionysus is the attempt to maintain distinctions: distinctions between divinity and humanity, *polis* and nature, male and female, etc. It is always in response to some human attempt to maintain distinction that he works his darkest, bloodiest, direst magic. "The clue to understanding the spirit of Dionysus is the brilliance and magnificence of its love and its hate, its capacity for both enthusiasm and destruction, together with its total ambiguity, its inability to keep these two forces together. It is always one or the other."[92] One or the other. Or both and beyond. Gnosis also features this all or nothing complex. It cannot tolerate difference or abide distinctions, but instead, in de Rougemont's words, "requires union—that is, the complete absorption of the essence of individuals into the god. The existence of distinct individuals is considered to be a grievous error."[93] A gnostic ethics saturates the Dionysian cult. Thus we must reject the assumption that the horror of the Nazis was a consequence of the repression of Dionysus. Indeed, in Adlerian fashion, we must spurn the very notion of an overpowering, unconscious content. Adler spoke of misunderstanding, not repression, not because he wanted to deny that every consciousness is married by shadow, but because he wanted to rule out the idea of a *deus machina* inside us who mechanically overpowers consciousness with "repressed" contents. It was the repression of Dionysus that caused

Fascism; rather it was the failure to repress him, to turn him into a unicorn who could be disciplined by the virgin, the cult of honor. Fascism is simply Dionysus without Christ, the Templar without the knight, instinct without honor.

Psychologically Fascism expresses the Templar complex. Fascism is the ideology of the Templar. Indeed Fascism may be defined as the ideology that results whenever the gnostic imagination takes hold of the traditional themes of Western culture. The "heroes" of Fascism will always present themselves as champions of orders much as the Templars presented themselves as defenders of the faith. Historically this holds true from D'Annunzio, to Juan Perón, from the exotic wave of Hitler's rhetoric to Mussolini's strut. Democracy, they charge, is a weak and fragile aberration from all that once gave the Western soul its fire and steel. And this argument is not a complete distortion of the truth. Neither Plato nor Aristotle was a friend to democracy, nor Vico or St. Thomas. All have tended to favor what was called a mixed regime. On the surface at least Fascism may seem a chivalrous rage for order: it exerts an aesthetic appeal; invokes loyalty to a chosen leader; invites a feeling of tribal unity. As Susan Sontag observes:

> ...it is generally thought that National Socialism stands only for brutishness and terror. But this is not true. National Socialism—more broadly, Fascism—also stands for an ideal or rather ideals that are persistent today under other banners: the ideal of life as art, the cult of beauty, the fetishism of courage, the dissolution of alienation in ecstatic feelings of community, the repudiation of the intellect, the family of man...[94]

And this is always the case with Fascism; on the surface the pose of Fascist leaders will seem justified especially when brown shirts are compared with the red flag of revolution which would spell the total death of chivalry, the death that Burke foresaw in the business of the guillotine. But in being partly right, the Fascists were completely wrong. The presence of the Templar complex, the presence of gnosis, vitiates and in time totally negates the traditional values that Fascism purports to defend. At first it is usually a matter of degree, proportion, even taste: instead of the gracious gesture, we get the *Sieg Heil* or the gross esthetic of Mussolini's Roman salute, which had its roots in the fact the Mussolini didn't like to be touched. We get a machine in the library as at the Vittoriale, D'Annunzio's famous shrine of Fascist taste, with its pink candles, porcelain dogs and ladies, its beads and goblets, where the rugs he chose to highlight his armors could be not washed. Vulgarity overwhelmed the incense. Historians often mention an initial apprehension or dislike among aristocrats for Fascist crudity. When they are insensitive to the psychological realities of Fascism, they mutter this almost disapprovingly, as if it were a mere symptom of class prejudice rather than an aesthetic grasp of the truth. But was it not Baron von Stauffenberg, the scion of an illustrious family whose line ran back into the mists of the Middle Ages, the soldier who put his life and reputation on the line by placing the bomb under Hitler's table at the Wolf's Nest. But if taste is what you need initially, two eyes will do in time. For eventually the great beast of gnosis will spread its wings as Fascist crudity spills over into a parody, an aping and finally complete viscous subversion and inversion of all the West holds dear. The traditional values are all corrupted: purity becomes a racial notice instead of moral one; chivalry gives way to strong arm squads; blitzkrieg and the murdering of civilians, even genocide; Shakespeare's sacred band of brothers becomes the all-powerful, monolithic state; the beauty and solemnity of sacred liturgy is superseded by the rally and the mechanical cathedral of lights; the realities of the body are replaced by the idealization of a sexless, androgynous human form; and finally in place of the compassion and sanities of Christ we meet the deliberate regressions of a bloody Dionysus. Insofar as the Templar complex infringed upon Nietzsche's vision, that vision approximated Fascism. It is the Templar's nature to awaken Fascism, prompting it like dark storm clouds that flare across a tranquil sea. And as we have tried to demonstrate, the Templar complex is present in Nietzsche's work, especially the spectacular and lyrical lights of Zarathustra. But does this negate our earliest point? Have we not depicted Nietzsche as working in high continuity with the best traditions of the West? Feverish, shattered, almost sightless, sinking into madness, ensconced in a strange room: was this not the Nietzsche whom we presented as engaged in the noble task of recovering timeless rights of honor? Are we not now, therefore, prosecuting an entirely different point?

Instead of contradiction we have uncovered conflict. On the one hand—and we have the considerable weight of even Christopher Dawson's testimony to press the point—Nietzsche was representative of our tradition. On the level of mind, desire, intention, will, he was one with the traditions of chivalry. He is defender, luminary, exemplar. On the level of imagination, however, Nietzsche was heretical: he succumbed to gnosis. He fell victim to the Templar complex. In was because of the pain this conflict generated, that Nietzsche was so attracted to the Dionysus *mythos*. He sensed the correspondence of the mythos with his private travail. But it was not the blood violence that exerted an appeal: instead it was the agony of a dismembered god; the divine and helpless child who is torn to pieces by forces he cannot understand. "I saw a staring virgin stand / Where holy Dionysus died, / And tear the heart out of his side." As Jan Kott comments:

> The basic Dionysian myth, present most strongly in the Orphic tradition, tells about the passion, death and resurrection of the divine child. The newly born son of Zeus, called Dionysus, or in other records Zagreus, was kidnapped by the Titans. He tried to escape or confuse his captors by taking in turn the shape of goat, lion, snake, tiger and bull. While he was in this last disguise, the Titans tore him to pieces and consumed his raw flesh. Zeus killed the Titans with a flash of lightening, and of the soot that remained of the fire that had burned them, men were created. Dionysus' head was saved by Athene or Rhea; his dismembered fragments, the *disiec-*

ta membra were miraculously joined together; Dionysus was resurrected.[95]

What this episode seems to promise is the possibility of a res-urrected, re-ordered imagination that is born from the body of the community in the same way as Dionysus is reborn from the body of Zeus. Nietzsche perhaps dreamt of such a transformation and there-fore recognized a kinship with the god. And yet the violence and ambivalence of the god precludes real transformation. In the myth the coming of Dionysus foretells the destruction of the community instead of its rebirth. Destroying the temple, he does not bother to rebuild it. But Nietzsche could never shake off the dream of Dio-nysus; never free himself from the magic shackles of the Templar complex; never re-order himself from the image of the West. In the depths of his soul, the Knight and the Templar continue to struggle for ascendancy, with each at times attaining to a triumph.

An early dream which Nietzsche recorded while still a school boy of fifteen, exposes this conflict. In the dream it is night. The dreamer wanders in the Wood. From a nearby lunatic asylum (how close is madness in this dream!) there emanates a terrifying shriek. The soul still wanders until it meets with a hunter whose features are "wild and uncanny." The hunter (who is surely Wotan) lifts a power-ful whistle to his lips and blows "a shrill note" that robs the sleeper of his sleep. Wotan, surely. But while the classical interpretation of this dream marks it as Nietzsche's first encounter with the arche-typal complex of Dionysus—Wotan which was to haunt him all his life; what I find of greater interest is the fact that this dream begins with Nietzsche on his way to *Eisleben*, Luther's town, but the encoun-ter with the hunter seems to shift the dream in the direction of the gloomy undergrowth of the *Teutschenthal*, which means, German Valley. Nietzsche's dream thus pits the old high medieval civilization of Luther against the magical, Germanic past. Further, according to Paul Tillich, this Lutheran civilization finds its most beautiful and typical expression in Dürer's famous symbol of the knight: "It has rightly been said that Albrecht Dürer's engraving, "Knight, Death, and the Devil," is a classic expression of the spirit of the Lutheran Reformation and—it might be added—of Luther's courage of confidence, of his form of the courage to be. A knight in full armor is riding through a valley, accompanied by the figure of death on one side, the devil on the other. Fearlessly, concentrated, confident, he looks ahead. In Nietzsche's dream this knight is almost conquered. Against him there stands the dark arms of the Templar. Against Luther's courage stands the ruins of Wotan. Against the *chevalier* is arrayed the Templar. The dream pits civilization against gnostic culture, with no resolution except the message to the dreamer to "wake up" to the dilemma that was threatening to impale him. In later life, as Nietzsche's stars set into the turmoil of his madness, this conflict was against rehearsed. Although the symbol of Dionysus has possessed him intellectually, to the point that in *Ecco Homo,* Nietzsche actually assumes the mask of the god; but in the end, during the final stages of his madness, it was Christ who came to him, so that his final act of individuation was to sign his letters, "the Crucified One." Nietzsche's life and work is paradigmatic because he enacted the basic conflict that has riven Western culture; the battle between the knight and gnosis. While entirely loyal to the West and its tradition of chivalry, personal honor, loyalty, and a political order erected on the base of a community of well-ordered magnanimous souls and eloquent imaginations; his efforts at personal integration were derailed by the wild flux of gnosis that came to him in the guise of the Templar complex. These two streams of chivalry and gnosis course throughout his work, clashing, dividing and joining, creating the perilous beauty that has prompted so many outlandish explanations. There was no resolution for Nietzsche except the one that existed in his madness.

In the early fourteenth century the Templars were suppressed. In one of the most extraordinary episodes in all of European history, Phillip the Fair destroyed them. He stunned them with his boldness. During the reaches of a single night, in 1307, French troops loyal to the king, seized the temple headquarters in Paris and arrested every Templar living in the kingdom. The trials were sensational. The Templars stood accused of various counts of heresy. It was said that witchcraft, sorcery and magic played a part in their secret rituals; while it was supposed the worship of Christ had given way to adoration of idols, especially of curious Oriental gods much like Dionysus. Trial followed trial throughout the whole of Europe, until the Templar order, together with its branches in England, Scotland, Aragorn, Castile, Germany and Naples were abolished by the Council of Vienne in 1312. The final end came in 1314 when Jacques de Molay, the Grand Master of the Order, was burned at the stake, and as the faggots flamed and the smoke engulfed him, the Grand Master called down a curse upon the Pope and king who had condemned him. In his last words, muttered in his agony, he summoned both king and Pope to meet him before God's throne before a year was done. Within a month the Pope was dead, to be followed by Philip seven months later, cut down at 46, sans visible accident or illness. Even in his death cry the Grand Master turned the mind of Europe to a belief in his exalted magic, as if he, not Gabriel, would blow the final horn. The curse lives on, however, subsisting in the Western imagination as a perennial temptation to adopt the path of gnosis. Forty years ago, Rudolf Allers, the Catholic Adlerian, linked psychoanalysis with the troubadour chivalry that invaded the West in the twelfth century and which was exemplified in the Templar. Allers grasped that it was the fundamental work of Adlerian psychology to combat this alien form of chivalry that now came from Vienna as it once drifted along the trade routes and the refulgent gardens of Granada. But today it is not psychoanalysis that houses the ancient threat. Today the gnostic inspiration has passed to other schools of psychology and culture that march forth as loyal troops or allies under the Templar's wind-tossed banner. And thus the real battle today is between traditionalist and gnostic, between two forms of chivalry, between two ways of serving the imagination, between two ways of ministering to the soul. Long before the word became a rallying cry for contemporary gnosis, Ansbacher spoke of Adlerian psychology as being a psychology of soul. Today Adler must cross swords with Jung. The central dilemma of psychology, and ultimately for contemporary man, is: are we to form our souls in the image of the knight or the Templar?

Is our imagination to be symbolic or angelic? Is our psychology to be exoteric or esoteric? World-inspired or a mystical retreat? Are we to speak of the will to power or of the gnostic soul? Though Nietzsche has delivered us this question, he provides no answer.

CHAPTER FOUR

―――――

It seems that resistance, as the contrary to the exertion to power, makes power possible.

— James Hillman, *Four Kinds of Power*

A desire sprang up in the hearts of the youths to find out which one of them could be king at Rome. From the depths of the cavern this answer, they say, was returned. "The highest power at Rome shall be his, young men, who shall be first among you to kiss his mother." The two sons Tarquin gave orders that the incident should be kept strictly secret, and, as between themselves, they cast lots to determine which should be the first, upon their returns to Rome to give their mother a kiss. The Liberator thought the Pythian utterance had another meaning: pretending to stumble, he fell and touched his lips to the earth, regarding her as the common mother of all mortals.

— Livy, I, 56

We close the circle now with power, coming back to where we started in order to address directly Adler's consideration of the will to power. Lewis Way, an authoritative Adlerian, differentiates between two species of the will to power. In a consideration of Adler's debt to Nietzsche's instinctualist view of power, Way opines:

> Power is not considered by Adler in these instinctivist terms. In contrast to Nietzsche, he believes that the

striving for power derives from the necessity for self-preservation, that is an over compensation for insecurity, in fact, it arises, not from a feeling of strength, but a feeling of weakness. Where there exists that overflow of pure strength described by Nietzsche it does not take the socially hostile form of aggression or domination, but is coupled with a feeling of joyousness which is creative and co-operative. I believe that Nietzsche himself perfectly understood this, for he speaks often and very beautifully in his work of creative joy. Yet he failed to draw the right conclusion from this experience, which is that there are two directions of the striving for power. The one has its origin in the feeling of weakness and inferiority, and makes for the goal of socially hostile aggression; the other springs from the spiritual abundance he describes and proceeds towards the overcoming of natural obstacles and hindrances.[1]

In Way's view, power is not so much an inherent evil opposed to the striving for significance; rather power is a power word, a comprehensive concept, the unitary reality of which both superiority and significance are faces. The question is not "to will or not to will," instead we are always willing an increase of our power, so the only dilemma is how to strive for power in a way consistent with *gemeinschaftsgefuhl*. By looking momentarily through a Nietzschean lens, Way discovers an Adler unknown to many of his followers, an Adler who emerges as a supreme phenomenologist of power who grasped the difference between power as superiority and power as *gemeinschaftsgefuhl*.

Although the distinction between superiority and significance may appear to be a rule of thumb, derived solely from clinical experience, it is in fact packed with immense philosophical sophistication. Because Adler excelled as a clinician, we too often gloss over his metaphysical acumen. But Adler was a philosopher, although, a philosopher who refuses to close himself off in his study away from the commotion of the street. As he himself declares quite openly.

I must admit that those who find a piece of metaphysics in Individual Psychology are right. Some praise this, other criticize it...I see no reason to be afraid of metaphysics; it has had a very great influence on human life and development. We are not blessed with the possession of the absolute truth, and on that account we are compelled to form theories...[2]

Clearly, Adler was a philosopher, but what distinguishes his thought is that it was bred from the material of experience rather than out of the scrutiny of classical texts. And yet, by probing the materials of experience, Adler repeated much of the classical inquiry into power. Initially defining his problem in a manner that was typical of the Greeks and Romans, Adler arrived at the same impasse, which he then transcended. He did this largely on Augustinian lines, though Adler's solution was unique.

Adler's first approach to the riddle of power was via his discovery of the mechanism of *compensation*, which discovery still merits him a place in the freshmen text. *Power is a compensation for inferiority.* Except for its foreshadowing in various authors—Hobbes, Stendahl, Nietzsche, of whom Brachfeld ticks off a list[3]—this appears to be a novel thesis, at least for modernity. And it surfaces already in Adler's first book, of which I now propose to dash off a terse deconstructive reading. In his book on the organs Adler overturns the common place which assumes that power is an overflow of vital, irresistible charisma, so as to conceive of power as a lack, the awareness of a lack, which we then clarify, differentiate and bring into connection with the world. Is not a corollary assumption, then that without a lived awareness of our inferiorities, a continuous engagement with the necessary angel of incompetence, we can never be authentically powerful? May we not assume that where there is no power, it is because there has been a psychological massacre of our wounds? On the basis of his organ book, we may say that Adler first detected compensation working in the dark material of the cells. Inferiority grips the nerve tract of the organs.

The inferiority to which I refer applies to an organ which is developmentally retarded, which has been inhibited in its growth or altered, in whole or in parts. These inferior organs may include the sense organs, the digestive apparatus, the respiratory tracts, the genito-urinary apparatus, the circulatory organs, and the nervous system.[4]

The roots of power then extend into a kind of unconscious Kundalini, a mysterious Taoist exercise, where the organs, the lotuses, become the focus of a radiant concentration that senses their inner light. Initially compensation has the charter of a kind of sensuous, magical, autoeros. It begins as the psyche's "special interest" in the spirit of an organ.

In Taoism every organ has a consciousness. He meditates on them so as to find and awaken their soul. Adler depicts this same kind of process occurring organically. To obtain power we must first sink into the rank, dewy, subterranean reaches of the body. When the body first feels the moist breath of the spirit, that is Adler's "special interest," it begins to stir with life. These first stirrings are drowsy and heavy with sleep. They are also frankly sensual, with the body becoming a deep lagoon where exotic creatures frolic. It is the body where "Intolerable music falls / Foul goat-head, brutal arm appear, / Belly, shoulder, bum, / Flash fishlike; nymphs and satyrs / Copulate in the foam." Here the body blooms with polymorphous perversity. I call this moment the Weimar complex where each organ becomes a cabaret. The air is thick with smoke and the smell of sex. The wine flows freely. Nudity, homosexuality, transvestitism is the rule instead of the exception. *Schonheiststanze* is the rage. Every organ is an erotic dancer like Anita Berber or Josephine Baker. In *Death in Venice*, Thomas Mann describes such an autoerotic awakening in the character of Aschenbach, who falls in love with Adzio, a beautiful young Polish boy. Each day Aschenbach goes to the beach in order to contemplate his "naked god with cheeks aflame" as he walks along the burning beaches. Aschenbach, an artist whose life has been a stint of service to sublime ideals, awakens. He brightens his appearance with colored ties, handkerchiefs, jewelry, perfume. But even this is not enough, so he submits to the ministrations of a barber. The barber works his magic and from a mix of creams and perfumes a new being is born. Gazing into the mirror, Aschenbach divines—

> A delicate carmine glowed on his cheeks where the skin had been so brown and leathery. The dry, anæmic lips grew full, they turned the colour of ripe strawberries, the lines round the eyes and mouth were treated with facial cream and gave place to youthful bloom. It was a young man who looked back at him from the glass...[5]

What this autoerotic awakening reveals is the autoeros of the organs. It is as if the hero, the compensation complex, the complex that produces power must first become a woman, as Alcibiades dreamed it doing on the night before he died, and as Herakles actually did when he went among the Amazons, in order to discover his narcissistic inferiority, the womanly parts of himself. Adler's definition of the inferior organ is the autoerotic organ, the organ that seeks its own pleasure outside of culturally sanctioned channels.

> Thus the superior psychic realm is forced to do certain tasks, which in the beginning are not easy, but which on the average undoubtedly succeed by reason of the heightening of the functional capability. In the case of the inferiority of the organ, however, and the corresponding insufficiency of the related portions of the nervous system, the participation of the organ and its activity in the demands of culture remain behind. The function then does not follow the required cultural paths but is predominantly engaged with seeking pleasure...the organ has become accustomed to wanton activity...[6]

In order to realize power, the erotic organ must be awakened, awakened with a burning kiss, seduced by some internal oratory—

to once again engage the world. Narcissus must be civilized and enter the gates of the city. The organ must be attuned to the other. Now on the one hand this attachment simply means adjustment, the betterment of one's material lot, in which case power equates with adjustment. But on another level, compensation may produce something grander.

> In favorable cases of compensation, the inferior organ has the better developed and psychologically more potent superstructure. The psychological manifestations of such an organ may be more plentiful and better developed as far as drive, sensitivity, attention, memory, apperception, empathy, and consciousness are concerned.[7]

To shift these abstract words into a more sensuous rhetoric, we may say that compensation sometimes generates virtue, excellence, high renown. Indeed this first book swarms with illustrious names, especially those of rhetoric and music—Democritus, Mozart, Beethoven, etc., as if Adler were struggling to voice the old idea that the pen is mightier than the sword, the mightiest pen the one whose lyrical sounds and rhythms skillfully modulated by a practiced voice are those that approach the condition of pure rhythm.

Adler's first excursion into power is thus marked by two assumptions, the first of which is that power is the result of compensation, that is, a way of knowing and living with our wounds; and, second, that power may mean either material adjustment or else superior abilities, *virtu*, excellence, even *preux*.

What are we to make of the fact that Adler initially images compensation as a kind of biological craft, a work of organic industry, occurring without the contribution of consciousness? If we take this as a piece of biological theory we might find some vindication for it in contemporary speculations. Thus Ansbacher compares Adler's compensation theory to Walter B. Cannon's idea of homeostasis.[8] But on these grounds it is a relatively simple task to discredit Adler by faulting his theory for its lack of empirical content. Paul Stepansky leveled such a charge.[9] But this is much too simple and in Stepansky's case pedestrian, as if it were cricket to read a psychological text as an essay in biology. When Adler speaks of compensation occurring on an organic level, we must read him as a cosmological thinker, that is, he was reaching for a norm of power that would ground it in a cosmic principle. He is already thinking of our power as somehow a creation of the earth, a participation in some cosmic reality by virtue of which participation we are empowered. To really get a fix on the Adlerian idea of power, we must reach back to the ancients who also endeavored to root their ideas of power in an elegantly realized conception of the cosmos.

Like Adler, the Greeks and Romans were connoisseurs of power, so that Cochrane sums up the history of classical philosophy as a millennium-long reflection upon power. "[T]he vision of Hellas resolved itself into a vision of power."[10] When classical antiquity thought of power it imagined the barbarian who in the first place was the embodiment of power as in Persian kings or in flamed-core, bronzed-hair, Germanic chieftains. The barbarians meant fleets, wealth, manpower, armies like insects swarming in the dusk. "And golden Babylon / Pours forth her crowds— / Borne by their ships— / Who in drawing the bow / Rely on their boldness. / And the tribes from all Asia / Who carry the sword / Follow beneath the / Awesome parade of their king. / …And the furious leader the herd / Of populous Asia he drives, / Wonderful over the earth, / And admirals stern and rough / Marshals of men he trusts: / Gold his descent from Perseus, / He is the equal of god."[11] Although we usually think of the myth of Nordic superiority as being born in Germany, in fact it sprang to life in Rome, where it surfaces in the strange eulogies of Tacitus.[12] But in the second place, contrasting wholly with the first, the barbarian was deemed to be an inferior creature, a crude example of the demiurgic cunning that first breathed spirit into dust. The barbarian was barbarous, outsider, alien, a tongueless beast. In literary convention which dates back at least to Herodotus and which soon came to govern philosophic discourse, civilization was deemed as a triumph over the barbarian. For all the noble souls of classical antiquity, the symbol of civilization was the triumph, the public exhibition of the barbarian bound in golden chains.

But while the Greeks and Romans were proud souls full of ostentatious sparkle, they were not naïve enough to assume that the barbarian was a wholly external foe; instead they recognized the barbarian within. Insofar as the barbarian symbolized naked force and power, this implies that classical antiquity was aware of its own power, which is a commonplace; but since the barbarian also symbolizes inferiority, this suggests that the Greeks and Romans were also sobered by a proud sense of their own inferiority. This is not so obvious. The Golden Age, perhaps was also the Age of Anxiety (Dodds) instead of the second following on the deterioration of the first. Indeed the Greeks and Romans seemed to have an especially keen sense of their own inferiority. The Homeric fables are as much tales of failure as success. In the *Iliad* a thousand ships set sail, crammed thick with spears, shields and booty hungry men, but after ten years, this great power has accomplished nothing. The ships set idly by while the Lords of the Earth bicker over trivia. The *Odyssey* relates the story of a man who fails to find his way home until aided by divinity. Romulus was an orphan, suckled by a she wolf; Aeneas, a defeated soldier, an exile far from home. In an essay called "The Failure of Aeneas," M. Owen Lee sums up the Virgilian world view which gave its stamp to Rome:

> It may then be possible to state Virgil's notion of tragedy in such terms as these: the world is a tragic place because, in a cosmic scheme wherein constructive and destructive forces are struggling to achieve their ends through human agents, good men are powerless to prevent evil. Even the man who is pious and does no evil is powerless to prevent suffering, and may be called on by his very pietas to inflict it.[13]

The *Aenead* concludes with an image of savage, darkened, confused agony—the hero tormented by the sky god's furies. By imagining the barbarian as both powerful and inferior, classical antiquity recognizes the power of inferiority to stimulate the soul to grand, novel, permanent achievement. The Greeks, together with the Romans, grasp clearly the Adlerian insight that "culture is based upon a feeling of inferiority." Aware perhaps of their moral inferiority, the renegade schizoid aspect of the psyche, the Greeks and Romans invented universal law; realizing their lack of military gifts, which were common in the North and East, they devised the phalanx and the short sword which made them the terror of their enemies; sensing the absurdity of the cosmos, which the Greeks named Ananke and the Romans Fortuna, they elaborated forms, stability, and the radiant order; feeling their own powerlessness, they constructed cities, eternal cities which made them masters of the earth. All the grandeur and the glory confirmed the Adlerian notion that it is precisely those achievements to which our inferiority impels us that have the greatest longevity and ardor.

As urban men the Greeks and Romans grasped power. By looking at their image of the city, by looking through the agora and forum, we may screen out the classical conception of power. In working out the classical definition of power in this way, that is by looking at what the Greeks did, build cities, rather than what they said through the mouths of their philosophers, we are embodying Adler's injunction to look at what people do rather than what they say. We are elaborating a psychology of things rather than a psychology of reflection. In the ancient world the city was power, the visible archetype, the concrete source. As Lewis Mumford says, "To exert power in every form was the essence of civilization..."[14] Divinely sanctioned through its genealogy of heroes, enshrined in statuary and eternal architectures; bodied forth in myths and the lofty diction of the tragedies; Athens was the power that destroyed the Persian kings—

> Athens hateful to her foes
> Recall how many
> Persians widowed vain
> And mothers losing sons....

Armies, navies,
Lazuli-eyed,
Warship led
O woe,
Warships armed destructively
By grecian arms.[15]

Divinely clad, Rome was the power that stepped forth in history to subdue the proud. Participation in the life of the city meant participation in the life of power, so that St. Paul, hustling round the Mediterranean, could unnerve his interlocutors by simply uttering *civis Romanus sum*, words which come down to us mantled with the air of complete authority. In legal fact Roman citizenship was the power to escape the bite of the whip. Outside the city, there was not power. In worshiping the *polis*, which was the object of a cult, the ancients worshipped power, the power within themselves to impress the world with their image.

The classical conception of the city, and hence, the classical definition of power was double edged, both sides of which appear in Adler's preliminary formulations. The Greeks understood power as both adjustment and *virtu*. Although the Greeks were never fond of money-changers, they afforded them a haven in the agora, which was the nucleus of urban life, and where merchants sold everything from garlic to shoes. A poet writes "You will find everything sold together in the same place at Athens: figs, witnesses to summon, bunches of grapes, turnips, pears, apples, givers of evidence, roses, meddlers, porridge, honeycombs, chick-peas, law suits...allotment machines, irises, lamps, water clocks, laws, indictments." "There," continues Mumford, "a temple or shrine would hold its place in a huddle of workshops, and the peasant with his donkey might jostle a philosopher pausing, as Plato must have paused, to watch a potter or a carpenter at work before his open shop."[16] By centering the life of the city in a place which was also the nucleus of commerce, the ancients made the simple acknowledgement that the purpose of the city is also to address man's material needs, so that—

> To the great majority of Greeks the *polis* must have
> commended itself, as it did to Pindar, as on the whole
> the most eligible state for the man of middling circum-
> stances. To such a man it offered the best prospect of ob-
> taining what he really wanted—security from external
> danger and the promise of material well-being. Histori-
> cally speaking *polis* was a middle-class solution to the
> problem of power...[17]

In that the city offers a solution to the dilemmas of power, we
may say that one classical conception of power consists of adjustment. Power is functioning, the power to function well enough to
obtain satisfaction from material needs.

Let us call this imagining of power in which adjustment is the
goal, power of the bourgeois complex. The terrible bourgeois—Nietzsche's herd, masked men, Plato's bassanios, etc. And yet there was
a kind of discreet charm attached to the bourgeoisie, in that many of
the images that cluster around this complex indeed emit a kind of
glow, a luster of contentment—the contentment of the shopkeeper,
round and portly, as he putters around his dry goods and tobaccos;
the contentment of suburbanite as he barbecues in his backyard version of Versailles; the contentment of the solid citizen, the Rotarian
or the Elk. What finally condemns this attitude, however, is that all
too often it degenerates into a terrible small mindedness—the small
mindedness that finally destroyed Greece and rendered it defenseless against Philip and the Macedonians. The modern version of the
bourgeois is the small mindedness that ultimately becomes a feck-
less insularity that confuses humility with cowardice and security
with virtue. Whenever we refuse a risk or gamble in order to hang
on to our security; whenever we confuse cowardice with caution; we
are succumbing to the bourgeois complex. Our inner merchant has
bought our soul.

And yet there were those who ached to drive the money-changers out, to shut down the entrepreneurial stalls. These were the
sublimer spirits who in lieu of a city devoted to material securities

demanded a city consecrated to virtue and human excellence. In a profound sense, the materialistic view of the city, revolted these proud spirits. They found it repugnant, for power to them meant virtue not adjustment—

> Thus envisaged, the *polis* constitutes a response to the specifically human demand for a specifically human order. In this sense it may properly be described as "natural." But its "naturalness" is in no sense a spontaneous growth. On the contrary, it is that of an institution designed, within limits conditioned by the potentialities of the material, to secure mankind from "accident" or "spontaneity"…thereby making possible the attainment of his proper *telos*. From this standpoint the order embodied in the *polis* is profoundly unhistorical. What it promises, indeed, is immunity from the "flux" which is all that idealism discerns in mere movement.[18]

Here is the second formulation of power: of virtue as power, the power to rise above the flux. We obtain power through transcendence. Through cultivation of the divine scintilla in us, we pass beyond the confines of all that is mutable, rising like Parmenides on the chariot of truth, in order to dwell in a divine permanence removed from matter, change, motion, the commotion of the *inferiores*. Power is here refusal to take our form from any bodily thing. This is power conceived on the Platonic model, but on this point Aristotle is in complete agreement, for he too exalts form over matter, the type over the individual, the universal over the particular. For both Plato and Aristotle, who philosophically grasped the style of life already enacted in the *polis*, power is abstraction, the power to abstract ourselves from outward circumstance in order to internally commune with eternal truth.

But something mars the classical ideal of power in that it approaches what Adler calls the masculine protest, a concept that marks a second great contribution to the psychology of power. Adler defines power as the desire to be virtuous, noble, strong, which is the universal goal of human kind, but in the masculine protest, nobility with inferiority. Here the heavy bear that goes with us becomes a she bear, a gargantuan hulk, who threatens to engulf us, to mire us in the sad waste of human imperfection. Like Hamlet we look upon our apportionment of dust to find that we dislike it—

> What a piece of work is man! How noble in reason! How infinite in faculties! In form and moving, how express and admirable! In action how like an angel! In apprehension, how like a god! The beauty of the world! The paragon of animals! And yet, to me, what is this quintessence of dust? Man delights not me.[19]

In this masculine protest, we purchase power by identifying with the "masculine," with the supreme reality of act, form, energy, dynamism, and rejecting everything "feminine," that is, fate, chance, motion, matter, all the inferiors.

> It is a question of what the neurotic understands by "masculine" and "feminine." It runs out that by "feminine" he understands almost everything that is bad, certainly anything inferior...Everything that is active is regarded as being masculine, everything passive is "feminine."
>
> The effort to get rid of these "feminine" traits is experienced as "masculine"...in neurotics the masculine protest, this protest of masculinity can always be shown to be present.[20]

The masculine protest is the attempt to acquire power by identifying power as transcendence of the limitations of the flesh. But, says Adler, this is illicit and self-destructive because it splits humanity, harms the self, throws the first stone against the part of us that dares to have intercourse with matter. When we ascend by virtue of the masculine protest, we do not really ascend but only levitate, removing ourselves from the plane of humanity without really going any place at all. The masculine protest is no real transcendence, it is fake transcendence and as such composes Adler's definition of neurosis; it is the *primum movens* of unsuccess. Instead of being compensation, the masculine protest is overcompensation.

In order to rhetorically enrich this point let us call this form of power the power of the fakir. Masculine protest corresponds to the fakir complex. In his own eyes the fakir appears pure, remote, detached, his mind fixed on verities as he mumbles sacred words and spells or stirs strange retorts. He believes his own imagination and reality to be superior to those of others. He knows while others can only believe. He abides within a cave, a tower, a temple, a monkish cell. He is Spengler's Pythagoras, Nietzsche's Christian saint. But to others and to the world itself he appears withdrawn, preoccupied, inaccessible, unavailable. His purity and prayers are self-exalting; his magic a form of defense. His religion a means by which he keeps the world at bay. Whenever we feel superior to the world and others; whenever we feel blessed, while the world seems damned, the fakir is working his false enchantments.

The masculine protest carried Adler beyond the classical paradigm. He began to curve away with his clinically hard won realization that the ache for transcendence, and all the pretty talk about the divine scintilla, could mask a hatred for reality. The Greeks were afraid of matter, for which they had almost a physical revulsion. As E.R. Dodds has recognized, asceticism was born in Greece, in the school of golden-thighed Pythagoras, who burdened his acolytes with exotic rules pertaining to the flesh. Abstinence is the lesson Pythagoras imparted to his followers—an abstinence from anything that would plunge the spirit back into the flesh. Even his famous injunction against beans may be understood as an attempt to suppress the anarchic, subterranean voice of the body, the dove in the belly, the spirit in the gut. When these prescriptions are internalized they scar the mind with a paranoia of the body. Even Plato was not wholly exempt from this charge, although he, like Yeats, his greatest modern counterpart, balances his distaste with a determination to return to the foul ragged bone shop of the heart. Nevertheless, Plato often imagines enlightenment as a liberation from the coffin of the body. In the ascent to the forms, the place of origin is always presented through the imagery of darkness: it is a grim and lifeless place where the eyes are full of darkness (Republic, 518A, 516E, 517D); where the mind's eye is buried in the mud (533D); where the imagination is entrapped in the hollows of a cave (Phaedo 11C). In the Phaedo's concluding myth the enlightened souls "are liberated, as from prisons, so that they may rise to a purer habitation above the truth earth." (Phaedo 114B) In addition to the body, the Greeks rejected anything even linked with matter. Because history is involved in the study of concrete particulars, they rated history even below poetry, while both, of course, fell below the standard of philosophy. In the *Poetics*, Aristotle writes, "Poetry is something more philosophic and of graver import than history, since its statements are of the nature of universals, whereas those of history are singulars." Women also suffered by association. The true philosopher ignored her because of her anti-logical corruption. In curtly dismissing Xanthippe, his wife, from his prison cell, so as to make way for the male friends who were his companions in philosophy, Socrates sums up the classical attitude toward women which is that they are a piece of property, sans virtue, to which the true philosopher is required to be indifferent. Boys, not Beatrice, set Socrates aflame. The lot of women did not measurably improve until the rise of the Christian emperors—Constantine and especially Theodosius, the model of Augustine's Christian prince—whose legislative edicts reorganized the family, undermining the despotic sway of the *pater familias*, revoking the savage laws that allowed fathers to prostitute their daughters or female slaves or repudiate a wife on the grounds of mere incompatibility and therefore pauperize her since the family's wealth belonged to him alone. Under the sovereignty of the Christian princes, fathers who attempted to sell their daughters instantly forfeited all rights over them, while divorce instigated by a husband obliged him to remit his wedding gifts and to return the dowry, at the same time surrendering his right to remarry, whereas the wife could remarry after a lapse of a year. When feminists today return to Greece to embark on pagan meditations in an attempt to find a new more confident ground for reimagining the psychology of women, they actually identify with the aggressor, incorporating into their own imagination a wealth of misogynist assumptions. They identify with an incorporeal reason, an anti-matter rage. Even at their best, the Romans too inclined toward priggishness. So when philosophy assumed the purple, as it did with Julian, the Apostate, the consequence was an abstract spirit running wild. Like all Platonists, Julian held a special horror of the body, with the result that to him the Christian cult, wherein the body was an object of grace and veneration and finally redemption, represented complete absurdity. Pickled heads and moldy bones, these become the new gods of the Roman people, said his friend Eunapius, in a sentiment that Julian entirely shared. To Julian the body appeared a trap designed to impale his spirit, blocking transcendence and getting him with King Helios, the sun god. According to Julian and to the reformed *Romanitas* that he tried to impose on the Roman people, truth was accessible only to the pure in heart, which meant of course the pure in body. In his numerous philosophical tracts in Platonist inquiries, Julian emphasized—

> ...the importance of asceticism, and life resolves itself into a continuous effort of purgation. Accordingly, while [*sophrosyne*] σωφροσύνη, the classical principle of self-control, still remains, it yields primacy in the hierarchy of virtues to piety or holiness...One result of this is to enhance the desire for personal chastity as a precondition of fulfillment.[21]

Chastity; reform; purgation; these were Julian's watchwords as they were also the assumptions which under various names had been codified into the classical spirit. The absurd assumption that a wise man could be happy even while being roasted alive and turning on a slowly turning spit, represents another manifestation of the same spirit, as if pain were nothing but an insubstantial, flitting phantom instead of being a powerful evidence of the body's indissoluble union with the soul.

The classical disposition to shrink back in terror from the body is captured with all its significant undertones, in a series of medieval woodcuts which show the aging Aristotle, bent on all fours, with a naked courtesan riding on his unclothed back. With a whip she drives him on, savagely controlling him with a bridle attached to a bit between his teeth, teeth through which Aristotle discoursed with the divine Plato and taught his letters to a King of kings. Having rejected the horse, the Mediterranean horse of commonsense, about which D.H. Lawrence speaks,[22] the common sense that reminds us that we are spirits anchored in the flesh, in sexuality, in the earth it-self, Aristotle has now become a horse, a hapless gelding instead of a stallion of the sun. Wanting power through transcendence, philoso-phy has been reduced to an abject powerlessness. In the woodcut, philosophy is only the power that the courtesan, the woman, elects to give it. Tradition has ascribed the name of Phyllis to the courtesan who symbolizes the sensual eros of the earth and all the human fea-tures banned from the classical paradigm.

When we identify power with transcendence, we are on our way to a superiority complex. This is another of Adler's presents to the psychology of power: power is superiority in a unique com-bination of transcendence with titanism. Superiority is Plato with muscles; the saint with a sword; the redeemer as imperator. As with the masculine protest, superiority is very much a fakir's trick, a rec-ipe designed to yield transcendence, so that in a superiority com-plex we lead the life of the spirit, focusing on high ideals, inhabit-ing the vertical dimension, abstaining from the leavening richness of social forms. Superiority is characterized by abruptness, lack of tact, aversion of conviviality, although it can imitate these things, and does, when it suits its overall design. We stay uninvolved, re-moved, distant, unapproachable, unavailable right now, always in the office, writing, working, in a meeting, working out. By stay-ing uninvolved we stay unimpeachable, everything correct, lords of decorum, proper, in Derrida's sense. The superiority complex is all peak and sky, complete transcendence, invisible presence, not expected today, but perhaps tomorrow. In a superiority complex we are as gods.

We should not attempt to formulate too easily any particular superiority striving; but we can find in all goals one common factor—a striving to be godlike.[23]

At the same time this is transcendence with a curve in that superiority does not simply transcend the earth, it also struggles to control it, to make it fruitful and conform to an image of perfection. Whereas the masculine protest denies the earth, superiority defies it. The first is flight, the second fight. One attempts a passive mastery—be quiet and it will go away, while the other strives for active control, man the torpedoes, fight on. One is Greek, the other Roman. The first is Cathar, the second Calvin. But both masculine protest and superiority are defined by their refusal to accept the vital fact of human embodiment in a world to which it owes its loyalty. In a superiority complex we become Titans, fireballs or energy, conquering imperators, superhuman heroes, or what Adler calls "power-and-property Philistine[s]."[24] Here, sans any consciousness of our decision, the decision being purposely misunderstood, we adopt the Titan's ethic of might makes right, of winning through intimidation, or complete assertion, of testing ourselves, of leaping at every chance to prove ourselves the better man, of striving for whatever will give us the competitive edge, for whatever will enhance prestige, whether it be a degree, fine house, fine wife, large salary. We want to be the strongest, brightest, toughest, smartest. This titanism will also include an element of cunning, of cruel, cold, careful calculation. We are always thinking, measuring the odds, trying to move up to our place in the sun, always trying to stay in control. That all this "body" is ultimately a defense against the body is confined by the "superior" man's oversensitivity about which Adler writes, "The neurotic psyche discloses itself most readily in oversensitivity," and then offers a complete phenomenology showing that such persons—

...cannot get over a painful impression and are unable to free themselves from a lack of satisfaction. They are unable to reconcile themselves with life and its institutions, that is, with other people. They give the impression of stubborn, defiant individuals, unable to create a substitute satisfaction through "culturally directed aggression," but insisting rigidly and firmly on "having it their way." They show this tendency in every situation and throughout their lives.[25]

As we did with the masculine protest let us personify this form of power as the strong man complex. Striving for superiority enacts its views. We might call him Caesar or conquistador and envision him as bestride the world, a magnificent colossus who comes, who sees, who conquers. He is always on the march, atop a chariot, astride a horse, at the head of a column of invincible troops whose shields and lances flash invincibly in the golden noonday sun. Whenever we become unconscious advocates of total war, of doing anything and everything, in the name of what we consider the good, the just and righteous cause, we enslave ourselves to the vision of the strong man. We are on our way to a festival of cruelty.

If in superiority we are both transcendent and engaged, mind and matter, angel and Titan, then in superiority we are a house divided against itself. Behind every superiority complex is a piece of inferiority, said Adler, which means that when power is objectified as superiority we have divided our firmaments from our depths. In superiority we split ourselves, so that the spirit becomes all spirit, all serene, invisible presence, all innocent Ariel; while the body inflates into a force of nature, all Caliban, all meat. But by no means is the body symbolically abolished as in the masculine protest. Rather it has become all body, deprived of spirit.

The key to the superiority complex may be in the recognition that in order to become pure spirit, a celestial citizen in the commonwealth of forms, we must also be pure body, pure Titanic body, body as a force of nature, who can perform the task of controlling matter, of shielding the divine and innocent precincts of the soul from the sordid encroachments of an incriminating matter. How else to do this, other than by becoming palpable giants who get the job done? Thus the superiority complex does not exclude a certain grandeur. It is glory touched. We can't help but admire the titanic energy that manically accomplishes so much, beats the odds, stays in complete control of the fluctuating circumstances that defeat other mortals. This is Melville's Ahab, Faulkner's Thomas Sutpen, Shakespeare's Coriolanus. Often it exudes a kind of awesome strength which pits itself against the most intractable of tasks and conquers; but this strength is flawed by its confusion with contemptuous resistance to the opposition of the *externalia* of resistance. This strength recalls the machismo we spoke of earlier, which never allows itself to be penetrated. True strength is not mere resistance, not mere counter-force to force, nor is it the simple passion for visible success that is bodied forth in objects. Rather, I should be inclined, with Allers, to put the situation this way:

> If a man possesses a sufficient depth of insight into the
> objective orders of value, which he has made his own in
> a vital sense, that "strength," in the sense of an effort to
> realize these values and reject their opposites will de-
> velop more or less automatically.[26]

While the superiority complex may possess valor and strength, it lacks the pity and honor which characterize genuine power. The phenomenology of superiority reveals angelic pretense and high ideals coupled with a certain coarseness. Since it has wings, it can abide the mud. All the titanic strength accomplishes is the building of a grand wall which has the purpose of protecting the transcendence of the spirit. Success is its wall, the guarantee that it has been chosen. Superiority is the religion of success and unless we grasp the religious roots of superiority we will never be able to understand phenomena as diverse as clinical neurosis, the will to empire, Calvinism, capitalism, etc.

Although the complex may fight battles, it does so only to keep its honor clean and innocent. This innocence I find to be the most salient clinical feature of power when it is conceived of as superiority. Superiority always seems so innocent, guileless, so completely unaware of how it uses and exploits others, how it hurts and damages feelings, how it walks right over people, brutally, when the occasion demands it, but usually more politely with the civilized language of nod, slight, failure to acknowledge or remember, cold rebuff, unanswered question. When confronted with the tragic consequences, the dark and crimson fruit, to which its passion for transcendence inevitably gives rise, it tends to assume it has only made a mistake which can be corrected once its cause is found. Because of its chronic innocence (which others sense as unrelatedness), the innocence that is always consubstantial with abandoning the earth, the superiority complex is never touched by wisdom; it never learns but remains indomitable, fierce and uncomprehending to the end. Part spirit, part body; part redeemer, part Titan; it is the Titan as redeemer; it is Prometheus.

For an ancient image of superiority, we may turn to Prometheus, who is both God and Titan. On the one hand, he is a saint, holy man, revolutionary of the spirit; on the other, he is a Titan, Giant, a civilizing genius that transforms matter into form. But what does Prometheus do to the cosmos? What does the superiority complex do to Zeus, who ought to be the ordering principle of the psyche? In other words what does the superiority complex do to the psyche? Prometheus creates a cosmos, where below, on the rocks, where he is agonizing, everything is reduced to power, to Kratos and Bia, who are the physical agents of Zeus; who are Zeus become all body, Zeus become a Titan; whereas Zeus as spirit remains invisible, an omniscient eye ensconced in a starry roost.

> Number one is not seen but his physical presence can be felt from the opening to the last. Every word spoken on the lonely rock is reported back to the Father, every word listened to. Above successive tyrants assume pow-

er in their turn and the tie of "unlimited torture" continues uninterrupted. Below the ants have learned to cook, write and count, build houses, send ships out on to the water, melt metals. In this rough anthropology, politics and *techne*—the history of power and history of material culture—are rigidly separated from each other.[27]

Rigid separation: this is the key to the superiority complex. The Promethean act is an act of self-division that sunders being, that upsets the *kalos kagathon*. Zeus, who in most tales is a great lover of the earth, a fecund, brilliant, showering genius, here becomes both invisible spirit—he is never glimpsed in the play—and Kratos and Bia, both beautiful and brutish, both fantasy and fist, that is, he becomes all fantasy by becoming all fist. So long as Force and Might complete his work, he will never appear among us. Superiority is a combination of spirit and sting. The spirit develops a stinger in order to retain his wings.

This is power as command, which Canetti takes to be the quintessence of power.

> Every command consists of momentum and sting. The momentum forces the recipient to act, and to act in accordance with the content of the command; the sting remains behind in him. When a command functions normally and as one expects there is nothing to be seen of the sting; it is shielded and unsuspected.[28]

I would correct Canetti here to say that it is not the sting that remains invisible but rather the source of the sting that escapes detection. The source is Zeus as number one, invisibly aloft. To wield power as superiority requires the removal of the self from its expression. It is power wielded through the intermediary, flunky, messenger, thug. The thug may be one's own body. This means the power will remain wholly visible, smashing into its object with dull thud or pop-crack lash; and yet, simultaneously, power as superiority always remains removed, with the result that the violence will seem arbitrary, sudden, inexplicable. It appears both without cause and sans logic. From the outside Zeus' actions appear irrational, as do the bully boy manners of Prince Stavrogin, another symbol of superiority, a fatal aesthete nourished on the doctrine of transcendence, a dreamer of beautiful dreams, of azure waves and magic panoramas, who nonetheless is—

> Suddenly, apropos of nothing...guilty of incredible outrages upon various persons and, what was most striking, these outrages were utterly unheard of, quite inconceivable, unlike anything commonly done, utterly silly and mischievous, quite unprovoked...[29]

So irrational are the outrages of superiority that they verge on the absurd. So irrational is the torture of Prometheus that one legend accounts for its denouement by claiming that the whole ritual had become absurd. As Kafka says, the gods grew weary; the eagles grew weary; the wounds closed wearily.

And yet what appears to be a snake in paradise, a bizarre, repulsive act by a beautiful soul, is required by the logic of self-unity which is impaired in the superiority complex. Whereas the masculine protest acquires self-unity by conceptually abolishing the body—though this abolition be illusory—superiority must come to terms with a body whose reality it has confirmed in its attempt to turn animated flesh into mere muscle and meat. The logic of self-unity requires some kind of reconciliation. When superiority dominates the psyche, we achieve this by converting embodiment into a spectacle so interesting, so magically perverse, that it captures the spirit's attention. Further, since the spirit tends to wander, its essence being a migratory wing, we may assume that over time these spectacles will become increasingly bizarre, shocking, morbid, in a desperate attempt to coerce the spirit to attend. And inasmuch as Adler associates superiority with violence, especially in his summary recollections from which we have been drawing, we may speculate a special appetite for spectacles of cruelty. With the superiority complex, already we stand in the shadow of the Divine Marquis. At first, we will enjoy the spectacle of others suffering so that we become what one romantic writer called amateurs of suffering.

> It is actually possible to become amateurs in suffering. I have heard of men who have traveled into countries where horrible executions were to be daily witnessed, for the sake of that excitement which the sight of suffering never fails to give, from the spectacle of a tragedy, or an auto-da-fé, down to the writings of the meanest reptiles on whom you can inflict torture, and feel that torture is the result of your own power. It is a species of feeling of which we can never divest ourselves—a triumph over those whose sufferings have placed them below us, and no wonder—suffering is always an indication of weakness—we glory in our impenetrability...you will call this cruelty, I call it curiosity—that curiosity that brings thousands to witness a tragedy, and makes the most delicate female feast on groans and agonies.[30]

Although formulated in less poetic vein, this is what Adler calls depreciation:

> In this depreciation tendency of the neurotic, which cannot be overrated, we find the origin of the important reinforcement of certain character traits representing further readiness intended to injure other persons, such as sadism, hatred, always wanting to have the last word, intolerance, and envy. Active homosexuality, perversions which disparage the partner, and sex murder also follow from the depreciation tendency, as concretized symbolism of conquest according to the schema of the sexual superiority of the male. In brief, the neurotic may enhance his self-esteem by disparaging the other

211

person, in the most serious cases becoming lord over life and death[31]

But in time, however, superiority requires that we make a spectacle of ourselves, and incur the spirit's affection that way.

> The superiority complex, as I have described it, appears usually clearly characterized in the bearing, the character traits, and the opinion of one's own superhuman gifts and capacities. It can also become visible in the exaggerated demands one makes on oneself and on other persons. Disdain; vanity in connection with personal appearance, whether in the way of elegance or neglect; an unfashionable mode of attire...arrogance; exuberant emotion; snobbishness; boastfulness; a tyrannical nature; nagging; a tendency to depreciate...[32]

In the end we go down like Caligula to join the races, or like Thomas Sutpen, Faulkner's case study of superiority, to trade mutilating licks in the gladiatorial bouts of slaves. Cleaving to what Faulkner calls in another novel "the ultimate root of things." The superiority psyche, the complex of superiority, lounges in complete degenerate, rapturous thrill as it gazes upon its own body engaged in some savage act of bone crushing activity. In its most satanic instance of pathology, the superiority complex appears in the bizarre phenomenon of the rape and torture crime, which strings out into two successive horrid moments what is psychologically co-present in the inner enactment. In the actual commission of the crime, the murderer is a savage piece of titanic bestiality and then later a serene and quiet presence who lounges with beer and cigarettes to watch the whole thing played on tape. The superiority complex attains psychological equilibrium through the continual exhibition of brutal behaviors in which the spirit seems to have no part, but it is there, watching, observing, entirely engrossed.

Superiority thus differs from masculine protest in that it is not entirely ready to dispose of its attachment to the earth because it has discovered the necessity of controlling the earth in order to guarantee transcendence. I suspect it also derives some pleasure from the sensation of embodiment, the all consuming passion of the creature-glow, which is why, in therapy, moving from Achilles to Heracles, from Caesar to significance is not nearly so different as shaking Socrates awake from his lucid rapture with transcendence in order to re-involve him with the earth. Inasmuch as Adler occasionally speaks approvingly of the superiority complex, as for instance in this passage where he says—

> It is the striving for superiority which is behind every human creation and it is the source of all contributions which are made to our culture.[33]

We must mark it as a genuine advance over the masculine protest, over the equation of power with transcendence. Since the difference between the two conceptions revolves around the body and the contribution of the body to empowerment, we may say that Adler was here reaching for a definition of power that would be ground in the body and in the earth.

The formula of power as superiority would make tragedians of us all, or rather, witnesses to tragedy, who continually feast their eyes upon fresh articulations of human torment. But this formula soon shatters when a stranger appears upon the stage. The stranger may be death, absurdity, contingency; it may be the coffin of a child or an athlete dying young; but the message is the same: reality cannot be controlled, not even by the strongest. The formula of power as superiority shatters against the reality of *ananke*, Fortuna, evil. This could mean rebirth, were superiority to yield, but unable to surrender its perfection, its flawless surround of limpid concentration, instead it submits to a steady diminution of its being. It shrinks, contracts, undergoes a shrinkage of horizons until it loses touch with reality. It takes recourse in what Adler calls safeguards, to one of three basic styles of life which he here enumerates—

> The first type includes persons in whom the intellectual sphere dominates the expressive forms. The second type is marked by an exuberant growth of the emotional and instinctive life. A third type develops rather along the line of activity.[34]

Finally, superiority sacrifices body in order to cling to the fantasy of transcendence. It continues, however to contrast the masculine protests in that it experiences its reduction of power as isolation instead of pure transcendence. Tortured by the distinct sensation that its sorry state arises from a loss of nerve, it suffers rather than enthuses. It ends with melancholy instead of mania. It ends in Rome instead of Greece.

In antiquity the equivalence of the superiority complex was the phenomenon of emperor worship, the deification of dead kings. The Caesar cult represents classical antiquity's final attempt to come to terms with power. It did this by shifting from a paradigm of power as transcendence to power as superior. Antiquity embraced the Caesar cult in a last gambit to remain empowered in a world where the uncontrollable mysteries of the bestial floor had shot to pieces the old ideal of power as transcendence. After five centuries of hard experience, antiquity discovered that we cannot preserve the purity of the spirit through rites of purification only. Matter is not nearly so submissive; instead it is resistant, a tremendous rival, a call of the wild that spills out from the latencies of muscle, emitting a call of nature, NOW. If we are to flame upward in a state of perfect purity, then we must either civilize matter wholly, stamping it with a sign of civilization, molding it into an image of formal perfection, or else we must build a wall, trench, ditch, indestructible city, over which Fortuna has no sway. We must become Titans to achieve transcendence; we must bruise the body to pleasure the soul. And so the Romans commenced to seek out Titans who could wield a sword or build a wall;

they turned to power as superiority, to the superior man of "surpass-
ing excellence, goodness of a heroic or divine order," (Aristotle) who
possessed "a degree of right reason and constancy which must be
deemed superhuman and attributed to a god" (Cicero) who through
a supreme act of statecraft imposes a permanent order on the flux.

As Caesar said, the Romans were a fanatic people who never
shrank from the adaptation of whatever novel expedient could get
the job done. What they saw, they conquered. From the Etruscans
they adapted fresh notions of industry, commerce, building and also
their techniques of divination; from the Greeks they derived the
framework of their constitution and the inspiration for a universal
law; from the Samnites they took the spirit of the legionary organi-
zation with which they crushed the armies of Hannibal; from the
Carthaginians came the model for their war-galleys. But where did
all this energy derive, if not from a spiritual commitment, a religious
vocation? We err in attributing to the Greeks a spiritual genius, while
extending to the Romans the prize of practicality. The Romans were
not practical out of simple dullness. Marcus was not Mussolini. Instead, they were a brilliantly spiritual people, who perhaps carried a
spirit more deadly, more holy, more freighted with a blazing weight
than anything the Greeks imagined. One symbol of the Roman spirit
was the virgin, the college of the vestals who were charged with the
tending of the city's sacred flame. The vestals were accorded a very
high social status; they were, for instance, the only women who could
ride through the city in a *carpentum*, a two-wheeled wagon, the use
of which was confined to tribunes, senators, magistrates and con-
suls. Another less symbolic example (the Woman in the Wagon is
one of the most ancient images of the goddess): when other women
were relegated to the top tiers at theatre or games, the vestals seated
themselves in the imperial box. The Romans privileged the vestals
in sundry other ways as well, so that in some sense, I supposed, they
were emancipated women; and yet they had betrayed their vow of
chastity, the penalty being burial while still alive. The high status of
the vestals reflects a corporate attachment to the realities of the spirit; the horror of defloration reveals the Romans to be purists in all

215

matters of the spirit, believers that the truest spirit is the purest one, the one least entoiled with matter; and the history of Rome records how they sought to save their spirits: through the iron surface of muscular accomplishment in battle, architecture, engineering, law. The Roman Empire was in some sense a mystic empire, a condition of spiritual enlightenment.

> The Romans first came here nineteen hundred years ago—the other day...Light came out of this river since— you say Knights? Yes...We live in the flicker—may it last as long as the old earth keeps rolling! [As for the empire, it] is not a pretty thing when you look into it too much. What redeems it is the idea only...not a sentimental pre- tence, but an idea: an unselfish belief in the idea—some- thing you can set up, and bow down before, and offer a sacrifice to.[35]

By subduing the dark sublunary realm, the Romans demonstrat- ed their spiritual ascendancy. Anything that challenged empire must be rooted out. "It's not the brotherhood of the fields or the Lares of a remembered hearth, or the consecrated wands bending in the fertile light to transubstantiate for child-man the material vents and flows of nature into the breasts and mind of the goddess. / Such- like bumpkin sacraments / are for the young times / for the dream watches / now we serve contemporary fact. / It's the world bounds / we're detailed to beat / to discipline the world-floor / to a common level."[36] If we're to call the Romans anything let us call them earnest and reserve that word for any attempt to raise the spirit by empower- ing the body so that bodily we may subdue all bodies and so defend the spirit from any return of the repressed.

The career of the Emperor Julian furnishes the perfect symbol of the Roman solution to the problem posed by power. In Julian we find the spiritual solution to the problem posed by power. In Julian we find the spiritual ambition coupled with a Titanic zeal. Julian was attached to the spirit, and the Roman attachment to spirit, which he perfects, is nowhere more beautifully expressed than in his account of his conversion experience in the old City of Troy—

> When I was summoned to headquarters by the blessed Constantius…getting up one morning at first light I reached Ilium from Troas about midmorning. And [Bishop Pegasios] came to meet me and (as I wanted to explore the city—this being my excuse for visiting the temples) to act as my guide, showing me all that there was to be seen. But now—listen to what he said and did! There was a heroön of Hector with a bronze statue set up in a tiny shrine. Standing opposite it, they have a great Achilles in an open court…And I found fires—I might almost say great beacons—burning on the altars and the statue of Hector had been anointed until it glistened. I looked at Pegasios. "What's this" I said, cautiously testing him to see how he himself thought, "Do the Ilians sacrifice?"
>
> "Is it at all out of place that they should worship a good man, their fellow citizens, as we [Christians] do the martyr's?" he said.
>
> Now the analogy was not quite sound, but for the times his attitude was commendable. But, look what came next! "Let us go over to the shrine of Athena of Ilium," he said, and led me there with great enthusiasm, to open the temple…[37]

Athena's Temple. The beacons. The shining fires. The glistening torso of a hero. A noble heart that is driven wild. Later, in the mysteries of Ephesus, Julian was to experience divine communion with the Sun, where-after he emerged on fire with divinity, avowed to live a life of self-purgation that would instill in him the purity of heart required for reunion with the spirit. And yet, Julian was a Roman, not a Greek, that is, his dedication to the ideal of transcendence did not occasion him to forsake the world, to seek out self-salvation in the quietest groves of some Platonic academe; rather—and here he shows his Roman stuff—it enthused him with a nervous, fiery energy to civilize the world, or to recivilize it, insofar as Christianity had spread its stain. Julian was not only a philosopher, he was also the type of the superior man, the hero with a nimbus playing about his head.

> He was a remarkable man and would have ruled the empire with honour if the fates had but permitted it. He was eminent in the liberal arts, but much the better read in the literature of the Hellenes, so much so indeed that his Latin learning was by no means comparable to his Greek. He spoke very freely and skillfully and had the most tenacious memory. He was in some respects more a philosopher than a prince...However, he was a great lover of glory and demonstrated a longing for it verging on intemperance. He was a persecutor of the Christian religion, but one who held back from shedding blood. He was not unlike Marcus Aurelius, whom in fact he did study to emulate.[38]

Julian was a tireless worker, a feverish student, a brilliant general and administrator who secured the Rhine; cut taxes by three quarters; refilled the granaries; rebuilt the ravaged cities of the North; won the respect and allegiance of the armies. As one admirer put it: "Such was the prince who rebuilt the temples, the author of deeds stronger than oblivion, himself more powerful than oblivion."[39]

Now it has been said that the Caesar cult was an alien Oriental graft upon the occidental Roman spirit. It Orientalized good Roman stock turning the Tiber into the Nile, Rome into Egypt, the emperor into a sacred king. To be sure, emperor worship was bathed in Asiatic splendor: the panegyrics of philosophers gone off their heads, such as Seneca in his *De Clementia*; well organized court factions arrayed against each other on every point; brood of sycophants—

"How quickly they turn from the setting to the rising sun" said a bitter, dying Tiberius; the emperor's likeness everywhere, lining shops and streets; imperial statues, objects, amulets, to which the populace must do homage; the sacred status of members of the imperial household, so that not only the emperor but his consort was divinized as well; the gigantic pomp of games and circus; the solemn rituals of approach to a being who was addressed as *domus divina*, "my lord and god." But though the trappings were Asiatic, the cult of emperor worship was in many ways homegrown, the culmination of trends already present in the golden days of the democratic *polis*. The idea of power as superiority was foreshadowed by earlier myths of the *polis* which ascribed its founding to the strength and wisdom of strong men such as Lycurgus and Theseus; and also by Plato's dream of a "dictatorship of the intelligence" whereby the sword would pass to the philosopher who could enforce goodness by subduing anything that conflicts with it. But it was really Alexander who embodied the shift away from transcendence to superiority. Having the advantage of the best education available in his day—Aristotle tutored him—Alexander viewed himself as a philosopher whose duty is the cultivation of the divine spark within and then the communication of that wisdom to others, so that they, too, may know the god within and ascend to the forms. Alexander's political program deliberately set out to revolutionize human affairs. When the martial fires faded, a new age would begin, with the ideal of a universal brotherhood supplanting the bitter blood feuds of the *polis*, their pompous, acrimonious disputes.

> ...above all...Alexander professed to be a philosopher. It was, as such, that he is said to have discovered a formula of relationship with his subjects in the concept of philanthropy (φιλανθρωπία), that love for the weak and helpless which inspires the man of divine attributes (θεῖος) to extend to them his protective care. In this sense the role of the sovereign was, so to speak, extra-political. Towards members of the cosmopolis he stood in the re-

lation of Savior and Benefactor (Σωτὴρ καὶ Εὐεπγέτης), a kind of "intermediate being" occupying the somewhat vague borderland which divides God from men...[40]

Like all philosophers, Alexander dreamt the dream of Plato, hungering for the rapture of liberation from the earth, but he differed from his precursors in that he understood that such a divine state could be realized only through "the disciplining of the world-floor to a common level." He thus hit upon the formula of superiority, which is that we escape the world by mastery, attaining transcendence through control. Precisely this, this king of kings aspired to: he matured as both philosopher and leader, an invincible radius of energy shouldering the task of an earthly providence. For Alexander to even sit upon a riverbank or at the edges of the Macedonian camp, was to be seized by an indescribable, overpowering ache to push on further, to extend his empire's reaches into the exotic spice lands of the East; but not so as to feast upon the glittering spoils of plunder, but with a metaphysical intention, a wish to usher in a universal order that would make a philosopher of every man. This dream very nearly materialized, so that—

> The mere fact of Macedonian ascendancy meant that the language of Homer came to be the *lingua franca* of the dominant classes from Egypt to the Caspian, and from the Danube to the Persian Gulf. Within this immense area, metropolitan centres were established at points of strategic and commercial importance along the great trunk-roads, and Greeks were encouraged to emigrate to these new *foci* of "civilized" life. The king himself embraced and recommended to his followers a policy of racial assimilation through intermarriage with natives of the East. Perhaps the most startling development was the institution of military schools in which Greeks and Iranians competed on equal terms for posts in the imperial service.[41]

The universal state, Greek speaking, civilized, where even the division of the races would be overcome, would open to the radiant universe of transcendence. Alexander came within an ace of establishing Plato's republic here on earth. He almost crowned himself a philosophic king of kings.

Alexander's eyes glittered through the divine masks of the Caesars. Like him, they answered the ancient riddle of "What is power?" with the response, "Power is superiority," superiority to the eachness of each thing and circumstance. Power is the ability to become a god, a golden glow of spirit, all flaming *numen* of the head, by becoming master of the earth. Power is the Titan who tames the earth. Power is to become a god. And gods they were, first in the afterlife though the deification of dead emperors and then through their deification while they still were living.

In becoming gods, the Romans shed the flesh, which maybe the psychological datum enshrined in Gregory's account of the Emperor Julian:

> His character was revealed to some by personal experience and to all by his coming to the throne...[I have known it] ever since I lived with him at Athens...There was a double reason for this journey, the hypocritical public one of acquainting himself with Greece and that country's schools, and the more secret one, communicated only to a few, of consulting the sacrifices and oracles there upon matters relating to himself. So far back in time did his paganism extend! At that time, I remember, I became not at all a bad judge of his character, though I am far from being very clever in that way. What gave me true insight was the inconsistency of his behavior and his extreme excitability...his neck unsteady...his shoulders going up and down like scales...his eye rolling...his feet restless...his nostrils....his laughter bursting out unrestrainedly...his head nodding...his speech stuttering, broken up by his irregular breathing...As soon as I

saw these signs, I exclaimed, "What an evil the Roman world is breeding!"[42]

Although usually dismissed as a conventional piece of Christian animus directed against an apostate, I wonder if Gregory was not here creating a symbolical case history designed to reveal the flaw in Julian's conception of the heroic life, which was its theoretical scorn for the realities of the body. In this image Julian's body appears as it did to Julian himself, as an errant piece of anarchic materiality. What finally aborts the Roman project of power as superiority is the presence in the soul of a drive towards unity which cannot tolerate the exclusion of the body from any definition of the good life. When power is conceived of superiority over what the existentialist calls "situatedness" and what Adler refers to as "the iron logic of communal living," the abandoned body will try to restore lost unity with whatever means lie at its disposal. As we have said, it will become an object for the spirit's voyeuristic pleasure; *physics* humiliates itself in order to seduce the *nous*. Thus arises the Roman appetite for spectacle and cruelty, which when it inflamed the soul of his friend, Alypis, horrified St. Augustine, who in his horror describes the passion, as it seized a reluctant votary:

> So they came to the arena and took the seats which they could find. The whole place was seething with savage enthusiasm, but he shut the doors of his eyes and forbade his soul to go out into a scene of such evil. If only he could have blocked up his ears too! For in the course of the fight some man fell; there was a great roar from the whole mass of spectators which fell upon his ears; he was overcome by curiosity and opened his eyes, feeling perfectly prepared to treat whatever he might see with scorn and to rise above it... He saw the blood and he gulped down savagery. Far from turning away, he fixed his eyes on it. Without knowing what was happening, he drank in madness, he was delighted with the guilty contest, drunk with the lust of blood.[43]

The Roman passion for cruelty almost defies description, save in the most indignant prose—

> Rome had become the arena of arenas, where the usual activities of a city were subordinated to the mass production of violent sensations derived from lust, torture and murder...In Rome, tragic death....turned into mass murder, spewing unlimited terror without a saving touch of pity...in the Roman spectacle, even honest animal impulses were deformed and defiled.[44]

At first the emperors held themselves aloof from these sordid entertainments, retiring to the imperial podium from whence they ruled on life and death, but as the empire deteriorated, the emperor himself became the spectacle, entering into the fray as did Caligula, who made himself the hero of staged chariot races, mock naval battles and gladiatorial matches, where the blood spilled, gushing from pulsing veins. For Caligula, deification and bestialization went hand in hand, bound by psychological necessity.

The emperor cult transformed the empire into theater, the body politic into a stage. The mob became a glittering throng and every barbarian an aspirant to the imperial purple. With Claudius, the idiot became a god. But death appeared to close the show. Alexander, the universal monarch, who promised to usher in a new *aeon* and upon whose shoulders fell the Herculean task of imposing form on the restlessness of matter, met death like any other mortal, where after the Platonic cosmopolis dissolved into the watchful, competing empires of the Seleucids, Antogonids and Ptolomies. Augustus, the Virgilian prince, a colossus straddling the world, died from eating poisoned figs; Tiberius was smothered; Caligula cut down by assassins at the games; Claudius was poisoned. Julian, the noblest Roman of them all, took a spear thrust in the side while battling the Persians and dreaming of Plato and conquest. He spent his last night coaxing truth from arcane speculations.

The hero fell...and so he is carried back to his tent, to the black bed, the lion-skin, the paillasse which is all his bed consists of. The surgeon says there is no hope. The army...groans...and when all around him have fallen to weeping, not even the sophists present being able to control their feelings, he rebukes them all, but the sophists more than the rest, because "the life he has led till now is about to bring him to the Islands of the Blessed, but they are weeping as though he had so lived as to deserve Tartarus." The scene was like that in Socrates' prison cell: those there were like those with the philosopher; the wound was equivalent to the cup of poison; the words, to his words...but when his friends urged him to name a successor...he referred the election to the army.[45]

Libanius imagined the earth grieving at Julian's passing, "shearing itself of its curls;" but more likely the grief antedated the emperor's death, going back perhaps to that moment, shrouded in the mists of his biography, when he first absolved himself of attachment to the earth.

Although menaced by the specter of death, the empire tried to preserve its sanity in the manner common to every superiority complex; that is, it resorted to the three styles of life which Adler found to be characteristic of this condition. First, there was the steely, dour, intense, abstract conservatism of Cato, Livy and cohorts who commanded men to conform to established norms no matter what the price and thus extended to the dead the right to govern the living. The *toga senilis* despised the wisdom of the street. Such views vowed hatred of every social change; it squashed revolt; damped down every flare of ecstasy; condemned the Scipios; cast down the Gracchi; murdered Caesar; destroyed Marc Antony. Second, there were the emotional convulsions of the mystery cults, of Isis and the golden ass, with their spookery, theurgy, magic recipes, their zodiacs and star drunk mumbo jumbo. This was the Rome of Apuleius, promiscuous celebrant of every cult, ass-eared angel bearing the vessel of the goddess. Third, there was the feverish, restless activity of the libertine. This was the Rome of the *vomitorium*. It is the Rome brilliantly captured by Fellini in his *Satyricon* and clumsily exploited by Guccione in his *Caligula*. Though our fantasies compound the sensual excess of Caesar, they nonetheless lodge in psychic truth.

Whatever name we call them—whether it be bourgeois, fakir, or the strongman, the wages of these misconceptions of power are death. Having cut itself off from history, the classical world was left behind by history and by a fresh world view which valued history as an instrument of the divine will; having heaped abuse on matter as the prison of the soul, the classical world found it didn't matter anymore to a populace who hungered for the mystery of fish and loaves; having banned the feminine, it found itself unable to enchant, attract and inspire fantasy and then to contain and nurse it; so that the old altars were abandoned. Because it would not come to terms with power, classical antiquity faded, becoming silent as the Delphic oracle to whom Julian sent for news. As Cochrane observes: "... the error of Classicism may be summarily described as a failure to identify the true source of power and, therewith, its true character and condition."[46] Just as the emperors did, beginning with Tiberius, power in the end deserted Rome to take up residence in a magic villa where tired old men of state, astrologers and boys convened to dream a dream of power whose features bore little resemblance to the actualities of earth. Tiberius was all these things at once: conservative man of state; superstitious astrologer; erotic deviant. After Tiberius, Caligula. "After me, the deluge," said Tiberius. Mere anarchy was loosed upon the world.

So the classical world perished on the shoals of power. And so Adler would have perished at least in the sense that his thought would have rigidified into a banal authoritarianism that characterized the latter days of Rome. In time Adler might have veered back into Platonism or Epicureanism. But Adler advanced beyond the ancients by making what we might call the Augustinian turn, that is, he formulated a fresh idea of power that avoided the impasses that ultimately unnerved the ancient world.

With a thunderous brilliance, St. Augustine rose up out of the deserts of Africa to savagely denounce the intellectual foundations of the ancient world. Augustine was the scourge of classicism. His god cooked fish for men rather than dissolving them into the primordial mists of divinity.

Restless, educated, rhetorically inspired, the discoverer of *memoria*, saved in a garden by a child's voice rather than by flashing visions atop a mountain, Augustine was the first true psychologist in Western history. As such, he reflected upon power as the goal of human life. In *De Civitas Dei*—especially the magnificent chapters 22, 23, 24—Augustine sharply rejects the flabby sentimentalism that opposes power to benevolence. Although the will to power can easily be perverted, on its own it simply represents the natural human impulse to affirm himself in the face of danger and destruction. Augustine further recognizes that the error afflicting the great classical philosophers in their effort to articulate a psychology of power was the incredible assumption that the sensate object world was somehow an illusion, an amorphous mass metaphysically impoverished. Having deprived the concrete world of its intrinsic goodness, they had no choice but to conceive a power as transcendence or superiority, which is a corruption of power. But the Christian philosopher cannot accept this, or the abuses to which it gives rise, because his faith commits him to a belief that the world is a divine gift from the creator, a treasure to be preserved. Hence any reformulation of power that will respond to the legitimate human desire for it, must somehow reconcile power to the splendor of the world, for it is the failure to be so reconciled that crippled classical philosophy. This splendor, maintains Augustine, would be self-evident were it not for the willful, perverse blindness of mankind. Here enters the psychology of conversion which was completely unknown in the classical world, where virtue was achieved either through intense cultivation of the speculative faculty, (Plato) or habituation (Aristotle). What conversion reveals is that all power emanates from God.

If God is the kingdom and the power forever, then to participate through grace in the life of God is to participate in power. The real antithesis in human life is thus between the love of power, which alienates us from God and thus negates our power, and the power of love, which reawakens our relation to God and to the object world of which he is the author. If all power comes from God, then power will manifest itself in a renewed relationship to the things of God including the material things of flesh, body, society and others. Conversion brings with it the power to make all things new; it brings with it the power to renew "a rotting and disintegrating world." Grace confers "...strength rather than weakness, not the vain dream of a Herculean or superhuman strength, but the substantial strength which flows from dependence upon the true source of illumination and power."[47] Rather than superiority, Augustine defines power as *gemeinschaftsgefuhl* derived from participation in the power of God, a participation won through the divine overflow of grace, a participation that renews our relation to the sensate joys of life in a material world. In the Augustinian conception, power is not transcendental; it is *gemeinschaftsgefuhl*, the formula for the regeneration of a dying world.

Like Augustine, Adler accepts the will to power as a natural impulse, even as the definition of man. Like Augustine, Adler realizes that power cannot be identified with transcendence of circumstance. This is power as the masculine protest, power as the superiority complex which is the nucleus of all neurosis. Further, like Augustine, Adler affirms that the only solutions to the abuses to which power gives rise is by asking what the world wants, as Adler did in 1914 with his introduction of *gemeinschaftsgefuhl*. And like Augustine, Adler recognizes that this turn requires a kind of conversion which Adler calls *insight*. Adler here condenses his view of insight, refuting, by the way, all those who reject insight for behavior therapy, by simply noting that insight that doesn't lead to chance is simply not true insight at all.

> One often encounters the following objection: "What do you do when the individual has recognized his error and doesn't correct it?" If he actually recognizes this error—if he understands the connection and persists in

his attitude despite the harmfulness involved—we can only say that he has really not understood everything. I have not yet seen a case of this kind. *Really* to recognize an error and then not to modify it runs counter to human nature; for it is opposed to the principle of the preservation of life. The objection concerns a pseudo-recognition of errors. It is not a fundamental recognition until the social connection is actually realized.[48]

Adler differs from Augustine, however, in that in Adler's case what the insight or conversion reveals is that the world is the source of power. In order to fully grasp the nature of power, we must incorporate the idea of resistance because power always requires something to oppose or struggle against. Progressive resistance increases power—something every power lifter knows; so, too every athlete; so, too, every poet battling with what Harold Bloom calls the "Anxiety of Influence." It is what Jacob realized with the Angel. Recall our original definition of the will to power: 1) the Will to Power is the determining drive in human nature. It is the basic need and the final goal. Power is the ability to affect a goal through the exertion of strength. The increase of power means the increase of strength, might, command, control, suasion or influence. Whether it is Life over Death (survival); Mind over Matter (security); for Love or Money (success); or Good over Evil (*virtu* or significance), all human beings strive to maximize their power. Now we add that if: 1) The will to power, the striving for superiority, provides the basic drive of human nature; and 2) progressive resistance increases power; then, 3) perfection of our nature depends upon resistance. Love your fate, said Nietzsche in, perhaps, his profoundest statement. Adler seconds this: Love the limits set by fate, nature, time and space, "the iron logic of communal life," its standards and traditions. Love your enemy. This is social interest. This is *gemeinschaftsgefuhl.* Sartre said, "My hell is other men." Adler counters, "No, not my hell, my ladder to heaven." No Hector, no Troy burning; no madness; no History as nightmare from which to awaken; no Fate with which to grapple; no

Ted Williams, no Larry Byrd, no Joe Frazier; then no Achilles, no Homer, no Nietzsche, no van Gogh, no Joyce, no DiMaggio, no Ali. Love your fate. Love your enemy. Love the earth *because* it resists the spirit's flight. Because of that resistance the baby walks, the spirit gains the power to stand erect as man. The earth empowers man to be the spiritual creature that he is. How can we not love that through which we become ourselves?

What is missing in any definition of power that equates power with transcendence is the outstanding fact that transcendence is intelligible only in terms of the material realities of the earth. By offering us a place to stand and to stand against, the world itself, like some great generous beast, confers upon the possibility of transcendence, the possibility of power, and in this manner must be named as the source of power. The world is the source of our human power because it allows us to stand up, to assume the upright posture, to ascend into the vertical dimension, into the life of the soul. Insofar as we believe the earth to be the handiwork of a divine artisan, the Adlerian psychological conception of power is compatible with the Augustinian theological notion in that both redefine power so as to require engagement with the world. Nonetheless they are not identical.

If all power comes from the world, then the more we participate in the life of the world, through whatever medium, the more we participate in the life of power. By drawing near to the world by attitude or through ritual gesture, concrete sacrifice, or material engagement we draw near to the source of power, aligning ourselves with its invincible design. By returning to the things themselves we return to the source of power. Finally the world empowers us; our empowerment comes from the world. This was Adler's great discovery in his final reformulation of power as *gemeinschaftsgefuhl*, here evoked in austere and majestic language. *Gemeinschaftsgefuhl* is

> ...The feeling of belonging together, the social feeling extends in favorable cases not only to family members, but also the clan, the people, all of humanity. It may even....

extend to animals, plants and inanimate objects, ultimately to the cosmos at large.[49]

This is power as cosmic feeling, power as the natural piety, with
which we hope our days to be bound each to each; it is the power to
be enchanted by the miraculous generosity of the real. It is the power
to marvel at the simplest things: the ardent, crushed, low glow of a
stove, the generous curve of a drinking cup; the frail and gallant optimism of a window. Without such presences, without the nourishment of concrete things, we would not have power, we could not be
men or women, could not truly be ourselves.

Rather than being a transcendental wish that propels us into
a beyond, where every wish is satisfied, power is engagement,
utter, complete engagement with the dense compactness of concrete things. The man of power is not some gargantuan ape with
bulging muscles nor is he the mystic or the shopkeeper; instead
the man of power is the man of the world, the man of power is
perhaps urban man, the hero, for whom the city and civilization
is itself a natural place. Insofar as we are all determined by our
will to power, aching for what we take to be its magical distinctions, then it is the renewal of our kinship with the earth, with
body, things and others that becomes the inexpungable condition
of human integration.

Again we come back to the hero, for knights and soldiers have
always somehow known this, perhaps because their lives depend
upon their mastery of all the rites and lore of power. In all the mystical arts of combat, whether deriving from East or West, from *Bushido* or chivalry, there has always been available the knowledge that
all power finally derives from the generosity of the earth. It is only
the earth who can give us an existential leg to stand on. The swords-
man or the open handed warrior who embarks upon long journey
and ordeal which in the end will yield the acquisition of true power
must first learn that all true power comes from the earth. In grueling exercise after exercise, through sword play and in struggle, he

must persist until in an exercise or drill he suddenly feels the current flowing upward into the body so that his wrist becomes a kind of bow string radiating throughout his body and into the air until one's movement becomes a graceful whirl of movement around the axis of the spine. The spine becomes the very center of the cosmos, the connecting link between the polar star and the Southern Cross. At such an instance, the warrior feels true *thymos*, the surging of the heart; in being wholly rooted it becomes an invincible, pure force that sweeps across a battlefield with the same gentle, invincible grace as a fan sweeps through the air.

Mink Snopes was such a hero. In the last few pages of his novel *The Mansion*, William Faulkner poetically sums up all the themes that we've extracted here. He tells us of the end of a man of honor, a man of power, who at last makes his peace with earth.

> And in fact, as soon as he thought that, it seemed to him he could feel the Mink Snopes that had had to spend so much of his life just having unnecessary bother and trouble, beginning to creep, seep, flow easy as sleeping; he could almost watch it, following all the little grass blades and tiny roots, the little holes the worms made, down and down into the ground already full of the folks that had the trouble but were free now, so that it was just the ground and the dirt that had to bother and worry and anguish with the passions and hopes and skeers, the justice and the injustice and the griefs, leaving the folks themselves easy now, all mixed and jumbled up comfortable and easy so wouldn't nobody even know or even care who was which any more, himself among them, equal to any, good as any, brave as any, being inextricable from, anonymous with all of them: the beautiful, the splendid, the proud and the brave, right on up to the very top itself among the shining phantoms and dreams which are the milestones of the long human

recording—Helen and the bishops, the kings and the unhomed angels, the scornful and graceless seraphim.[50]

CONCLUSION

Today, the heroic challenge forces a confrontation with heroism itself. Heroism is asked to face its own myth, thereby
releasing the imagination to find other ways to think about
power which has been defined for so long by heroic notions.
— James Hillman, *Four Kinds of Power*

The firedrake is an evocation to the hero.
— Albert Murray, *The Hero and the Blues*

Bachelard once wrote that he would never be anything but a
psychologist of books. With this he implied that every text has a
psyche. Now, by psyche I do not mean anything so simple as the
writer's conscious intention; but, rather, the guiding fiction of a text,
the symbolic urgency that is its root and crown, as well as its *principle of unity*. That is to say, my sense of the psyche is Adlerian, in that
it was Adler who first equated the psyche with the invisible, fluid,
dynamic principle that structures human life into unity. The psyche
is the harmony, the pulse, the fire. It is the elusive "something" that
remains after we have analytically subtracted every essence. The
psyche is the agency of synthesis. Perhaps because he disliked the
tint of gnostic colorations; or perhaps because he anticipated the
purchase of the word by a professional class of mandarins, Adler
seldom spoke of psyche. Instead, he hammered out his own vocab-
ulary, various times speaking of "guiding image," "life form," "life
plan," "life line," "line of movement," "personality," "whole individ-

ual," and "psyche," until finally settling on the term *life-style* which expresses the idea that—

> [T]he never resting creative mind...remains pressed into the path of the...style of life, as does everything that has a name in the various schools of psychology, such as instincts, impulses, feeling, thinking, acting, attitude to pleasure and displeasure, and finally self-love and social interest. The style of life commands all forms of expression; the whole commands the parts.[1]

By substituting text for mind and psyche for life-style we lay the groundwork for an Adlerian hermeneutics. The work is psycho-centric rather than logo-centric. If it extols the breath, it is because the breath is anima, *ruah*, soul. We imagine the psyche as the erotic glue that holds the world of the text together. It joins, orchestrates, synthesizes, binds. Further, since Adler maintains that only imagination can grasp a life-style, we may assume that the soul of the text is most liable to yield her guarded lore to an approach that is simultaneously imaginative, spirited, fantastic. What image controls the Adlerian text—text meaning here the accumulated deposits of his work including writings, gossip, *personalia*, collected lore. For me it is Alcibiades; for me, it is the hero. It is Constantine and Charlemagne, Hotspur and young Prince Harry. It is Hopkins chevalier "Brute beauty and valor and act, oh, air, pride, plume, here / Buckle! And the fire that breaks from thee than a billion / Times told lovelier, more dangerous, Oh my chevalier!" In my mind's eye I see Drake and his mystic queen in whose eyes the Jesuit said one could see the devil, and I see the ocean chivalry of the conquistadors, stallion stances and poise. I see the *condotierre* and the bonny prince in his blue cockade. I see Napoleon's marshal, Murat—

> He was brave only in the presence of the enemy; in that case the bravest man in the world. His impetuous courage carried him into the midst of danger. Then he was

decked out in gold and feathers that rose above his head like a church tower. He escaped continually, as by a miracle, for he was easily recognized by his dress. He was a regular target for the enemy, and the Cossacks used to admire him on account of his astonishing bravery.[2]

And Faulkner's General Stewart, "his plumed hat in his hand and his long tawny locks, tossing to the rhythm of his speed, appeared as gallant flames smoking with the wild and self-consuming splendor of his daring." I see the Southern armies in the field.

Now on the psychological level the hero represents the splendor of personal integration, which is not very much in vogue now, though it is very much the goal of the Adlerian tradition. For Adler unity is a *perspective*—and the perspectival character of my approach is something I do not wish to gloss over, for to do so is to forfeit psychological integrity—and so Adler was always intrigued by the logic of the whole, which he distinguished from logic of the heart and head. The way things hang together, the way they are *arranged*, stimulated his attentions. And yet unity cannot be confined to a mere perspective, for it is also the goal of all authentic psychological work. We all ache for unity. Psychosynthesis is a sublimely and noble task which we all must undertake if we are to individuate, that is, to scale the cosmic ladder in a way that leads to the enrichment and subtilization of the community. I speak of subtilization in order to indicate that communities are psychological as well as material realities. The Holy Roman Empire, the Stuart dynasty, or even the antebellum South are examples of subtle communities, in that while they existed only for a specific duration in time, they nonetheless continue to affect the imagination. Their symbolic permanence confirms the presence of a *gemeinschaftsgefuhl* that is absent in more materially successful cultures.

In this sense they are true places, though they are no longer found on any map. "True places never are," said Melville. The various hero myths confabulate the process so that we may glimpse its central features, which are misidentification and engagement with

the materials of our own mind. The materials may be called complexes, attitudes, structures, sub-personalities, etc. The hero's quest
will always include an encounter with all of them. The hero's quest
will always include an encounter with the *Magician* who spirits us
away into the enchanted forest or the Big Woods, where we undergo
a kind of vision in which we glimpse the radiant, eternal, unchanging truths of human nature. Odysseus and Aeneas descend into the
underworld; Achilles and Hercules are taught by Chiron whose cave
is atop a snow peaked mountain; Perseus journeys to the cave of the
Medusas; Bellerophon scales Heaven atop an aerial mount; Christ
goes into the wilderness; Arthur into the enchanted forest; Lancelot and Trystan into a hermit seclusion; Ike McCaslin into the Big
Woods; Ishmael takes to the sea. Here there is an existence where
the very snakes are grandfathers. In addition to the Magician, we
must also meet the *Sage*, who symbolizes doings of the household
gods and the traditions of the race. The Sage teaches us to build a
fire, the Magician to peer into it. We must also engage the *Seeress*
who is simultaneously seductress and unravished bride. She is fantasy incarnate, the factor of symbolization. And we must also cross
paths with the *Eternal Youth*, the spirit of romance and adventure
whose flashing eyes and flowing locks are ablaze with aspiration and
with purity. The psychoanalysts have described these meetings as
developmental stages: to fully individuate we must first be animistic
infants whose realities are wholly governed by the eternal forms of
primary process (the Magician); next a superego develops (the Sage)
then comes latency where the developmental task is symbolization
(the Seeress); which is then followed by adolescence where the ego
must fashion an ego ideal (the idealism of the Eternal Youth). And
while, of course, these stages are literally enacted in succession and
so account for psychological development, they are never really resolved, that is they survive in the adult mind which must continue
to dis-identify and engage them. Instead of thinking of an ego, however, I prefer to imagine the hero because the hero is usually a tragic
figure unless he overcomes his pride, his belief that he must stand
against the world—both inner and outer—instead of standing with

it. The fact that nearly every hero comes to grief—Herakles agonizing in the fire; Arthur impaled by Mordred—does not imply, however, that his quest for unity is illusory. It says only that the goal if fictional which psychologically suggests that we attain to unity through fiction, through the imagination, as if the goal of the heroic quest were not exactly individual wholeness but a *vision of the whole*, of *gemeinschaftsgefuhl*, of the love that moves the spheres. This vision makes us whole rather than we achieving it on the merit of our own decisions. But make us whole it does.

The hero also has a cultural significance; but in order to grasp its specific function we must first hazard a definition of culture, which we must do, of course, in the shadows cast by Spengler, who both liberated and throttled thought with his famous distinction between culture and civilization. Our first clue though comes from Cicero who identified culture as the unique habitation of human being. Culture is our element; we are culture making animals; without it we become like Nebuchadnezzar, metaphorically dropping on all fours to live like beasts. Now there are many ways to define man, but his most overpowering enigma is that the man is a mind encased in matter, a spirit betrothed inseparably from pounds of the flesh, which argues that culture must be that medium whereby the abstract universals corresponding to the spirit are wed to the concrete particularities of the flesh. Since human culture is neither mind nor flesh, neither idea or percept, we must assume that culture is an image, or a set of images, that somehow reconcile the different and often clashing strands of our material and spiritual natures. If culture is the form and substance of the imagination, then work on the imagination equates with work on culture. And the reverse is true as well: great cultural events shape the imagination. The artists and the hero work hand in hand together. A culture becomes more cosmopolitan to the degree that its images are comprehensive enough to embrace and order the full range of our humanity. These images flower in a host of festivals, rites, observances; they are often solemnly articulated in philosophy and creeds; they are enshrined in objects; enforced in law; and bodied fourth in poetry. In a particular place, in a particular time they change life with an indefinable excitement, rhythm, air that permeates the very streets. This is culture.

The hero is an image common to almost every culture. *But it is not just any image; instead it is the image that transforms culture into civilization.* Without the sense of mission that the hero brings, without his nerve and torch, culture decomposes. It turns incestuous, feeding on its own vitals like one of Hemingway's hyenas, eating its remains, becoming uroboric, a convoluted compost heap without civilizing function. When the hero lays down his sword the symbol loses its point, its ability to change a life. For this reason some of the most valiant spirits of our time recoil from the very word culture. Thus Miguel de Unamuno:

> ...Culture—oh, this culture!—which is primarily the work of philosophers and men of science, is a thing which neither heroes nor saints have had any share in the making of. For saints have concerned themselves very little with the progress of human culture; they have concerned themselves rather with the salvation of the individual souls of those amongst whom they lived. Of what account in the history of human culture is our San Juan de la Cruz, for example—that fiery little monk, as culture, in perhaps somewhat uncultured phase, has called him—compared with Descartes.[3]

It is not that when culture is deprived of its heroes, it turns ugly, because the reverse is often true: its isolation becomes a cult of splendor where every task is charged with deep symbolical significance and where magic reigns. To employ a literary image, we might say, that *culture becomes like Prospero's Isle, where the very air is enchanted with wondrous noises.* But though entirely beautiful, culture alone remains infertile. When the hero is absent, the soul—let us imagine her as Prospero's daughter Miranda—finds only the shallow compensation of spiritual inflation (we may imagine this as incestuous identification with Prospero) or bestial regression (greeting Caliban with open arms). Into this magical security of Prospero's Isle there came a ship bearing a potential hero, a message from the world, and it is this which redeemed the soul from its barrenness. The play maps the passage from the "rough magic" of culture to what Frank Kermode calls "the magic of nobility."[4] At the end of the play the magic isle is still a dukedom, now under Caliban's new rule, but the duke and his daughter are no longer islands to themselves.

Instead they return to the community as a result of the influx of the world as theme, dominant, lure. Further, Prospero has felt the world's attraction by constellating the hero in himself. It is his power, we should remember, that calls up the storm that brings new heroic inspiration to the isle. Of all the determinants that make up the composition of culture, it is only the hero who is attuned to the world—attuned in the sense that his destiny requires engagement with the world. In glorifying the *übermensche* and the will to power, Nietzsche and Adler were striving to keep culture fertile by adding to it the ecstatic thrust of civilization. Only the hero can save culture from a stagnant, perfumed, rich decay. It is not that the hero is anti-culture, anti-dream; rather, the hero is the medium through which the dream affects the world, the means by which the roots of the heavenly tree of culture branch out into a high civilization.

To speak for a moment to a provincial issue: I fear that depth psychology—and here I'm using the term in a generic sense to apply to Adlerian, Freudian, Jungian, Assagiolian, Lacanisan and Hillmanian psychologies—is on the brink of becoming nothing but a culture. I fear that we are losing our extraversion, our civilizing impulse, which during the formative years of our discipline was very much alive. From the very start of his project Freud imagined himself as a conquistador admitting that he was "not really a man of science, not an observer, not an experimenter, and not a thinker. I am nothing by temperament but a *conquistador*—an adventurer, if you want to translate the word—with the curiosity, the boldness, and the tenacity that belongs to that type of being."[5] In a famous letter to Groddeck, Freud describes psychoanalysis as a "Wild Hunt": and when, following the defection of Adler and Jung, Freud's most loyal supporters traded secret rings and formed the Association, which was designed to protect Freud and insure purity of doctrine, they saw themselves on the model of Charlemagne's paladins.[6] Even as Freud's life wound down and he was forced to contemplate the approach of death, he was still fascinated by "that magnificent rascal Napoleon, who remained fixated on his puberty fantasies, was blessed with incredible good luck, inhibited by no ties apart from his family, and made his way through life like a sleepwalker, until finally shipwrecked by his *folie de grandeur*. There scarcely ever was a genius so totally lacking in distinction, an absolute classic anti-gentleman, but he was cut on the grand scale." Depth psychology really did once flash with a heroic spirit. We have already mentioned Jung's dream of the Templar. As more evidence of the heroic impulse, there is Assagioli's restoration of the motto, the hero and the code of honor as an indispensable technique in psychotherapy; we might also mention his recommendation of the study of the heroic lives in his method of the ideal type; Lacan's view of neurosis as a false heraldry; and Hillman's celebration of the martial archetype.

And yet after a century of biographies, which tell us all about Freud's fainting spells and colon troubles, Jung's silly excuses for his philandering, and literally thousands of debunking excursions into the privacies of the giants of our field, it is difficult to affirm the heroic grandeur of our quest. What we have been trying to do throughout this work is to restore the hero to depth psychology, to restore the sense that every depth psychologist is engaged in a noble task of immense significance to the fate of what the poet calls "our dear West," and of what Heidegger refers to as the "Land of Evening." Psychotherapy really is involved in the fate of civilization. We have been listening to Adler precisely because so few have listened, so few have credited him with the genius that was really his. We are trusting in him precisely because he has been shipwrecked in Ortega's sense—"I no longer believe in any ideas except the ideas of shipwrecked men. We must call the classics before a court of shipwrecked men to answer certain preemptory questions with reference to real life." We have been listening to the shipwrecked man because he also was a hero.

Adler: as there are many Nietzsches, so there are so many Adlers. In a chalk drawing once in the keeping of Mrs. Cornelia Michael and reproduced in Ellenberger's *The Discovery of the Unconscious*, the artist Horowicz caught the spirit of the Adler who has captivated me. The drawing depicts him only from the chest up. A face, hand, perhaps a heart is visible. The broad, trunk like chest dominates the drawing covering the entire bottom half. Adler rests his head upon one hand, leaning into it, the back of the open hand pressing into the check. The shadow of an angle forms there in an otherwise round face. Disheveled hair sweeps over a massive forehead. No doubt it has been brushed away an instant before. The tie is askew. The clothes are rumpled and look slept in. The lips are thick, full, the nose is flat. The master wears a mustache. Dark hooded eyes brood and gaze raptly at some unknown friend or patient. In the drawing Adler looks weary but resigned, dreamy but attentive. He seems a massive presence, kind, composed, entirely available. By some miraculous fusion of art and circumstance the artist has touched on Adler's soul, which was based entirely in the chest, in the vision that streams forth from the chambers of the heart, blood, breath, *thymos*. Clearly here is a *coeur de lion*, the soul of a hero.

The hero is at the root of Western consciousness; he grounds what Derrida has called the White Mythology. The myth is a fabulous scene "which reassembles and reflects the culture of the West: the white man takes his own mythology, Indo-European mythology, his own *logos*, that is the *mythos* of his idiom, for the universal form of that he must still wish to call Reason."[7] Now Derrida is well advised that in knowing we can't help but know ourselves, that is now the world according to the frames, paradigms, structures, and attitudes that we have elected to identify with; but he thinks the White Mythology to be an especially poisonous frame of reference because it has been constructed for the purpose of repressing what Jung once called the abysmal side of bodily man. The White Mythology, that is, the mythology that enthrones a hero, is a kind of thought imperialism that obtains order out of chaos by labeling everything it fears as chaos which it then expels to the margins of consciousness. Writing, passion, matter, the Other, *différance*, the feminine, the Unconscious, psyche, eros, especially homoeros—all these are merely marginal entities with no legitimate claim either on philosophy or life. The main culprit here, according to Derrida, is "phonocentrism:" the privileging of the voice, which merges—

> ...with the determination through history of the meaning of being in general as *presence*, with all the sub-determinations that depend on this general form and organize it within it their system and their historical linkage (present of the object sign is *eidos*, presence as substance / essence / existence (*ousia*), temporal presence as the point (*stigma*) of the now or the instant (*nun*), self-preserve of the cogito, consciousness, subjectivity, co-presence of the self and the other, inter-subjectivity as an intentional phenomenon of the ego, etc. Logo centrism would thus be bound up in the determination of the beginning of the existence as presence.[8]

The White Mythology is logo centric. The hero is defined as he who speaks and who believes that in speaking he is fully present to himself. The hero is the orator. Logo centric thought maintains its domination via the manufacture of apparently "self-evident" oppositions which have the effect of subtly elevating one term while debasing the other. Opposition becomes the means by which the White Mythology subdues the world. In other words it is the hero's sword. In order to disarm the hero, Derrida staged a series of dazzling obliterations of these hierarchies which have been intended not so much to liberate the repressed term, for that would be to merely invert the hierarchy and therefore to leave the hero with the sword, but to unstitch the very opposition, to open up a breach through which a new term might emerge, an anti-concept, an undecidable, for which we have no term in conventional psychology. Although Derrida has considerably toned down his rhetoric since 1967, when in an influential lecture delivered at Yale, he hailed this unthought concept as a kind of Yeatsian rough beast, it is clear that he aspires to nothing less than a complete reorganization of Western consciousness. Though he would spurn the identification of the undecideables with myth, Derrida is elaborating a new mythology that unseats the hero to replace him with the *pharmakon*. And like the Greeks holed up outside Troy, his ranks have been swollen with countless allied isms: feminism, projectivism, structuralism, archetyplism, which avidly await the lighting of the hero's pyre.

The assault academic exercise has naturally provoked a counter-reaction. Although it hasn't found its voice in the arts, though that too is surely coming, this counter reaction has seized the cinematic, political and religious imaginations. The pendulum is swinging, or better said, it swung. The sword of the hero is still very much with us.

Now there is a difference between Roland and Rambo, between Perseus, Theseus and Bellerophon and their ostensible modern counterparts, between honor and machismo; and yet in asserting the splendor of integration, Adler is very much out of step with the contemporary tends of deconstructionism. Is there not a third way between the One and the Many, a *tertium quid* that would celebrate the hero while also keeping him in touch with the magical multiplicities of the self? I think most definitely there is, and so I want to conclude this book by first allying Adler with a trinity of spirits who took the hero very seriously indeed, and then to address the hero myth directly, hoping to show that all the gore that we tend to associate with the hero is more a consequence of our misreading than it is an integral dimension of the myth.

The luminaries with whom I would like to unite Adler are Bacon, Vico and Coleridge. In a succinct little essay, to which the next few pages are much indebted, Elizabeth Sewell establishes the affinity of these three thinkers on the basis of their shared fascination with the idea of the *heroic*. Throughout their collected pages the word occurs continually. For example, in the introduction to the standard English edition of his works, Bacon is compared with Columbus, for *"Like Columbus, he was the hero of an Idea: and like so many heroes of fabulous quests, he bore a magic sword, to whit, his unrivalled power of speech.*"[9] In the *Novum organum*, Bacon himself makes the identical comparison, writing that—

> ...it is fit that I publish and set forth these conjectures of mine which make hope in this matter reasonable; just as Columbus did, before that wonderful voyage of his across the Atlantic, when he gave the reasons for his conviction that new lands and continents might be discovered besides those which were known before.[10]

As "a hero of the moral world," is how Vico steps forth from the prose of his editor who also informs us that Vico found the term particularly delightful.[11] In his famous orations, each one of which was a tremendous burst of eloquence, such as *De mente heroica* delivered in 1732 at the University of Naples, Vico often equated the hero with the divinity lodged in one's own mind, the cultivation of which is the role of education. Vico exhorted his auditors to impress their minds with the images of the great heroes from antiquity and also from the more recent past. When thinking, the student ought to remember Alexander, who journeyed to the edges of the world, and also the sublime Columbus. Coleridge also conceived of his work as a voyage of discovery, a heroic quest into the depths of the mind.

After noting the oddity of the usage in the context of strictly intellectual labor—

> To most people, who do not write books, there is nothing heroic about being a writer, or even a thinker, however speculative and original; nor do the lives of these three men exhibit anything of the heroic as we ordinarily conceive of it. Rather, we see in each case a melancholy human spectacle of disappointment, weakness, even failure. *Hero* is an odd word to find here.[12]

Sewell goes on to muse on what could justify the use of the "noblest, most ancient, bravest, and loneliest of human metaphors."[13]

The reason, she explains, is that all three were engaged in the investigation and extension of a method of discovery, which she calls the Poetic Method. In some this method requires the "expurgation of the intellect," the casting aside of "the idols of the mind," so as to recover the wild, savage, elemental power of the mind, which is then remade so as to stimulate individual and collective transformation. The method coheres as—

> a continual, profound, and lonely struggle to unmake and remake the deeps of the human mine (one's own first, then the minds of others—hence, in part at least, the concern with education), moving away from the null and dead habit, besetting distortions, and native disorder and toward a creative order, out of which grow the human self and our own lives and thoughts, our civic institutions in their (and our) ongoing history, and our discoveries in science.[14]

Because it is perhaps unavoidable to imagine this elemental making place as "the depth," it is permissible to imagine the hero as he who descends to the depth—*Vico, infernal shades, grandeur, the gold bough*, wrote Michelet the year he encountered Vico—for the sake of cultural renewal; but the curious turn in this version of the *nekyia* is that instead of emerging from the depths, a Viconian hero apparently elects to dwell there, engaging in a daring, miraculous and ongoing exercise of making. Rather than an image of descent and then ascent, which typifies the conventional view, this is an image of making and remaking as if the hero himself were a kind of imagination, a distinct symbolic form, who is continually reforming the imagination so as to keep it connected to the world.

A pertinent value, then, of Ms. Sewell's article is its lively subversion of the idea that the hero's sword is somehow bloodied on the soul, that the hero disputes imaginal autonomy which it tries to supersede by will, force, power and coercion. Instead, the hero is himself a symbolic form who differs from other imaginal realities only in

245

its degree of attachment to the world. The hero is very much attached to earth, to a world for which he recklessly pours out his substance. And his attachment to the earth bewitches him with power, for, as we have seen, all power, all mortal power, descends ultimately from the generosity of the earth. The hero thus emerges as the most powerful form of the imagination, the way that the imagination imagines its own power, the way the imagination empowers itself. On this basis it is easy to grasp the sense of Blake's strange statement that "Jesus is the imagination," for, psychologically, Jesus is the imagination, the heroic imagination who pours out his vital substance for the good of the world. If the ego is the psychological equivalent of the hero, then Adlerian psychology is an ego-psychology; but to conclude by virtue of this fact that it is somehow superficial is to display a superficial understanding of the hero. Full confirmation of this view requires an analysis of the hero myth.

Because the variations on this fundament are almost infinite, I want to focus on the myth as a whole, in terms of its overall design, rather than focusing on a single story, where one or another ingredient may be emphasized due to local conditions. The story unlikely involves four main characters: a dragon, an aging king, his daughter, and the hero, although often the king's wife will play an important role. The basic plot is rather simple. The drama occurs in a kingdom, long ago and far away, which seems beset by disorder. The discontent may be a result of ambition, jealousy, misplaced eros, etc. The disorder seems to constellate a dragon, calling him up from the fiery depths. During the day the dragon lives in a lair which reeks with snapped bones and decomposed flesh. Sometimes there is a treasure. But periodically the dragon takes flight across the countryside which he devastates, consuming stored up victuals, scorching the earth, befouling the radiance of the air. The people turn to the king who summons his magicians, wise men, lords requiring of them a solution to the dilemma. Some will usually sally forth to battle with the beast, but they do not return, at least not in one piece. On the whole, however, the wizards have no answer and so the king decides to consult an oracle. As the devastation continues, they wait expectantly, but when the messenger returns he bears the chilling news that only virgin flesh will appease the dragon, and not just any virgin, but the king's own daughter. The daughter is always beautiful, the apple of her father's eye. She is bright, submissive, curvy, obedient, unstained. She will do her father's will. Although the king balks at first, eventually he yields and dispatches his daughter to a place apart where she is chained to a post, cave, altar, to await the dragon. The dragon sweeps down on her, covering her with shadows of barbarian tumescence, but at the last moment the hero appears. Spun out of the union of heavenly lust and forced mortal compliance, he is lion-skinned, broad torsoed, and with a club, magic ship, or flying pony. He is often immature but always celibate. Like Achilles he may have a spot of vulnerability, but mostly he is unafraid. He strides forth to joust and slay the dragon. He rescues the princess whom he takes as wife. In time they ascend the throne together and renew the spirit of the kingdom.

We commence by noting that the king is identical with the kingdom, for as Ernst Kantorowicz has noted in his brilliant *The King's Two Bodies*, the traditional idea maintains that the two are inseparably fused. While, before the eyes of God, the king is accepted as an immortal soul harnessed to a few frail yards of flesh, he also is the body politic incarnate. He is the body politic: existentially he weds the individual with the corporate essence. In this sense, every monarch is a Grail King whose ailing body is both a private affliction and a plague on the land. Inasmuch as the hero myth theme is a tale of a king and his kingdom, let us speculate that it presents the dynamics of a single psyche, but a psyche that cannot be understood apart from its relation to community. The psyche, then, that we shall be studying, the perspective, that is, that we are going to be taking on is fundamentally Adlerian. Here "Individual Psychology is social psychology." In considering the hero myth, we shall be approaching the psyche as if it were a royal creature, a kingly host who has been charged with the redemption of the community. The question is how can the community be redeemed, and who is the hero such that he can accomplish such a task.

Next, the dragon. Since in all the tales awakening of the dragon coincides with the decline of the old king's powers, which have veered off into senescence or evil, I wonder if a secret league does not exist between them. As the kingdom withers, the dragon stirs, which suggests that the king's malfeasance not only provokes the dragon but actually produces it, *as if the dragon were nothing but the coagulation of a disordered imagination*. We might say that the dragon objectifies an autonomous superiority complex, a complex become autonomous through its fantasy of superiority to the world. The dragon bodies forth superiority in all its grandiosity. As Adler says:

> Where it succeeds, it naturally strengthens the masculine tendencies enormously, posits for itself the highest and often unattainable goals, develops a craving for satisfaction and triumph, intensifies all abilities and egotistical drives, increases envy, avarice, and ambition, and brings about an inner restlessness which makes any external compulsion, lack of satisfaction, disparagement, and injury unbearable. Defiance, vengeance, and resentment are its steady accompaniments.[15]

Clearly Adler was skilled in dragon lore. As this superiority fantasy autonomously intensifies, it condenses. It acquires a body whose consistency and depth competes with anything in nature, indeed overwhelming nature as if things and others did not count. Imagination affects the world, in this case as a dragon that comes to exist independently, as a great beast who consumes the world. It is a superiority fantasy that has come to exist independently of inferiority.

As far as the daughter is concerned, she is obviously the king's fantasy, since it is through her that he is connected to the future. She is airy hope and hoped for circumstance. She is manners, grace, his soul, his civility and gentleness. In her presence his desires are internalized. She serves him and is his hostess. She teaches him the lore of flowers. And yet, the myth reveals her to be a power also, in that the maiden represents the king's one chance to slay the dragon and restore his kingdom. Because the dragon covets her, he will be slain. Therefore it is through her magic, the magic of her appeal, that the king has power over the dragon, the power to defeat him. The king's daughter is fantasy become a sword. But not only fantasy, not only power, for the maiden is also the psyche's vulnerability. She is the part of the psyche that is weak, untutored, inexperienced. She is the king's one spot of vulnerability, the single flaw in his massive defense of knights and wizards who congregate about him. These "powers"— the knights and wizards—may be imagined as what Adler calls "safeguards"; but, as the story indicates, they alone cannot deliver him from this plight. For such deliverance he must seek a deeper wisdom which is her, commemorated as an oracle. What the oracle reveals is the king's inferiority. Because of his daughter he is suddenly made vulnerable. As we have said, she represents the part of the king that is weak. But there is a braveness here, a commitment to community. Since the daughter shows a willingness to be sacrificed for the sake of the corporate good, we may in addition see her as the king's and thus the psyche's innate, but undeveloped, social interest.

Now, let us stir the brew, let us make psychodynamics out of psychic aspects. Let us say that the maiden is the psyche's fantasy, the king's own soul; and let us say that this fantasy is potentially a power, a power strong and splendid enough to eventually conquer the dragon. Further let us speculate that in being both inferior and socially minded the maiden is that complex in the mind that opens onto the community through her wounds. If misery loves company, then true company, true community is at least in part a product of the psyche's inferiority, of inferiorities shared and publicly admitted. "Inferiority is the source of culture," says Adler. The king's daughter thus becomes the symbol of a style of fantasy that joins to others through an admission of its own wounds.

The hero is clearly a younger version of the king. He is the king once again in *potentia*, ready for chance, hoisted up in the air on winged sandals or a sky horse. He is the potential redeemer of the community, the potential ordering factor of a psyche connected to the world. By shifting emphasis away from what is lost in the story—

the dragon—to what is gained, we can surmise how this transformation is accomplished. When the hero comes upon the scene, the soul, that is the maiden, has been reduced to nothing but inferiority. There she stands: a virginal white apparition staked out to a post, rock, the borders of a wasteland, where she stands exposed in all her naked frailties. At the same time, the soul has been inflated into nothing but superiority—every superiority complex is also an inferiority complex, says Adler. It is all dragon, force, power, meat. It is a presence that consumes the world. At the hero's coming these complexes manifest themselves in their starkest form and so we may guess that the hero's sword is first and foremost the sword of separation. Here, the hero is like the Adlerian therapist whose initial task is the arduous work of distinguishing between inferiority and superiority. How do we feel inferiority? Where and in what precise way? And how do we take flight from these wounds? How do we conceal these wounds? How do we gobble them up as would a dragon? In killing the dragon, the hero averts a premature conjunction that would restimulate the cycle of inferiority-superiority, depression-grandiosity, which would culminate finally with the re-entrenchment of a superiority complex. The dragon would ascend to the throne. The secret identity of inferiority and superiority is imaged by the dragon's desire for the maiden. She herself is evidently a kind of dragon, an object of his desire. He recognizes something familiar and intensely attractive in her.

The hero is the dragon slayer, but he is something more as well. *As Nietzsche says, he would slay the dragon,* must become the dragon, which means that the hero does not so much destroy the dragon as take his place. He is simply a dragon without the wings, he is a superiority complex that has shifted into a striving for significance, a desire for *gemeinschaftsgefuhl.* In rescuing the maiden he rescues fantasy as well, rescues a style of fantasy that embraces its inferiority, that finds its soul in its symptom and through its symptom connects to the world. When the hero marries the maiden, he marries an aspect of himself as well, he marries his own imagination. The hero is thus the psychic dominant whose imagination redeems the world. The kingdom comes to him through her, her vision, her history, her

soul, and it will always be through her that he connects to the kingdom. More than dragon killer, more than brutal, bloody murderer
of beast, the hero is simply the worldly style of the imagination; the
psychic complex that connects to the world through imagination.

But what about the blood and guts which seem so integral to the
hero myth? To what are we to chalk up these more violent aspects?
Although we can't explain the violence away, we can explain it by
looking at the preliminaries of the episode. Upon the first encounter with the danger that will in time assume the proportions of the
dragon, the hero is often beaten and has to flee for help, which he
does by moving vertically, from the known to the unknown. He may
ascend with magic shoes, or winged pony, or he may descend with
golden bough in hand, or at the chest of some dark Sibyl. He descends into what we call the depths—referring to psychological reality rather than geographical space—where he may drift for a while
or consort with nymphs, mentors, monsters, shades. What happens
here, psychologically, is that imagination takes over, either in literal
life, so that, like Aeneas he is visited by a vision of the future, or
metaphorically, so that he is given a divinatory eye, magic cape, pair
of sandals, winged pony.

Down in these dread caves, the elemental making places of
the mind, the hero discovers his inferiority. Like the maiden, he
feels alone, exposed, afraid, and so we may assume that what happens in the depths is that the hero constellates the maiden himself.
He learns that he is not all solar brightness. Down below he often
cheats, steals, murders, lies awake and lies straight faced, so that
here, in these precincts, the hero does not glow so much, but rather
emerges as a darker being with a dirty nimbus. Perhaps the best
way to put it is that the hero realizes he is one of us. Imagination
takes over to renew inferiority and through inferiority to connect
him to the world. If he would slay the dragon, he must become the
dragon, then he who would rather not yield to the blood lust, must
constellate the dragon in himself, the fictitious animal who may
symbolize a superiority complex, when it is isolated from inferiority, or significance when it has the courage to accept inferiority. In

the second case, the dragon may become the symbol of the community as it was for the Byzantine emperors and the British kings. It may become a shining exhalation instead of a scourge. This is what the hero learns in these early episodes: he learns the courage to be imperfect and thus enter into a community that can be symbolized by the dragon.

Further, as we compare the two stories, we are forced to the conclusion that the first one counts for the most, since the myth usually depicts the "great" battle with the dragon as bordering on an accident. The hero almost stumbles on it. Bound for home, he comes across a scene of terrible devastation: a princess lashed to a dragon tree, awaiting her doom surrounded by amulets and torches. Naturally he intervenes and brains the dragon and marries the intended victim. But the accidental, almost incidental flavor of these scenes suggest that the dragon killing amounts only to a flourish, the myth theme playing itself out so as to impress a truth.

With one critical difference: repetition seems to up the level of violence, while also posing what were initially the level of violence, while also posing what were initially ambiguities more in terms of black and white. It is as if the myth dreams itself onward becoming increasingly violent in the process. It seems to simplify and exaggerate itself in order to incur out interest. It forces us to heed its depths. Therapy often presents us with an analogous scenario: a shunned piece of fantasy becomes an inflation which, when left unattended to, is bodily enacted on the street. And perhaps this is culturally where we are right now: entoiled in a massive repetition compulsion, obsessively repeating the hero myth, with each enactment becoming more violent, gory, squalid. And all because we have not understood the hero myth, not quieted our minds enough to receive its strange intelligibility: the idea that the hero is itself a style of the imagination, a votary of *phantasai* whose star slung creatures guide him as he drifts in gentle solitude past northern lights and southern latitudes, riding on the tattooed backside of a mythical beast. Our violence cannot be ascribed to the hero; instead, it stems from the fact that we are not heroic enough. There is no way beyond this myth, this white mythology, but there is a way to more powerfully and more intensely live it: the way of Individual Psychology.

In sum, this entire work has been an attempt to re-imagine the hero, so as to make a place for heroic psychology in the modern world. That psychology is Adler's. He has been our torch bearer, our Perseus, our chevalier. In Greek the word *heros*, from which the word hero comes, was a chthonic term and was used, not only for the great, but for the dead as well. The cult of the hero resembled the cult of the dead. At the end of the day the sacrifice was offered, with the victim turned to the West and placed upon an altar, at the foot of which was built a blood trench to receive the hand. The cult of the hero was gloomy, dark, aware of the Furies, tied to the wisdom of the blood. The heroes themselves were often imagined as snakes; and it is this deeper, more psychic sense of the hero that Ike McCaslin learns at the conclusion of Faulkner's *The Bear*:

> ...he froze, immobile...The elevation of the head did not change as it began to glide away from him, moving erect yet off the perpendicular as if the head and that elevated third were complete and all: an entity walking on two feet and free of all laws of mass and balance and should have been because even now he could not quite believe that all that shift and flow of shadow and that walking head could have been one snake; going and then gone; he put the other foot down at last and didn't know it, standing with one hand raised as Sam had stood that afternoon six years ago when Sam had led him into the wilderness and showed him and he ceased to be a child, speaking the old tongue which Sam had spoken that day without premeditation: either "Chief," he said: "Grandfather."[16]

As Ike sees the snake, so he is granted a visitation of the ancient, weary, beautiful blood knowledge of the hero. Throughout this long excursion we have tried to bring the hero back in touch with the reminiscences of the dead, with the low torch and blood rites, while also bringing imagination back in touch with the hero, with chivalry, with pride and plume, with the three great tasks of life, with life on earth amid the company of friends. Power and imagination. Imagination and the world. Air and pride. Imagination becomes the glory of the world. Let the wolf rise gladly in the heart.

Epilogue

━━━━━━━━━

And the biggest of all collective problems, as we've discussed, is the suppression of the dead. Not hearing the voices of history. Not hearing what we've lost. And the fear of the dead, the fear of death, in our culture.

— James Hillman, *The Lament of the Dead*

In a pale sky the stars are speaking once again. The Kennedys and King died a half century ago. The twin towers fell. The worldwide financial system reeled on the brink of collapse. History has not ended. Ancient Civilizations have re-arisen in the East—Persia, China, India, and along the banks of the Amazon—Brazil. Holy Mother Russia has re-emerged from the ashes of the old Soviet empire. The "Great Game" in Afghanistan has been fought once again. Within and outside the ancient walls of Baghdad and Damascus, Sunnis war again on Shiites. Westerners know once again the fearsome threat of Jihad. We live only a hundred years from World War I when the great nations of the West blundered clumsily into their own destruction. Could it happen again?

What is to be done?—Lenin's famous question. This book answers: listen to the dead, the wise and the heroic Dead; draw upon their strength, their wisdom, their determination. In the book *Iron and Silk*, the story of a Westerner who has journeyed to China to master *wushu*, a traditional Martial Art, the sensei hands over a sword and directs his student to an ancient burial ground:

The sun had not yet gone down, and it cast a glittering reflection over the Xiang River a few miles away. The vegetable plots in all directions around us caught the light as well and glowed brightly, in sharp contrast to the deep red earth of the paths between the fields.

"Just think," he said, "under your feet is so much history! There are all sorts of treasures in this mound—probably even swords like these, only real ones that were used in ancient wars. With all this history under you, don't you feel moved? Now, practice the form, and this time don't fuss over the technique. Just enjoy it, as if this mound gave you power. This is the kind of feeling that makes wushu beautiful—it is tradition passing through you. Isn't that a kind of power?"[1]

This book has made the same type of spiritual pilgrimage, to the mounds and graves, to the Fathers and the Doctors, the Saints and Heroes, and the modern Sages of our tradition, to stand, in silence, with hat in hand, head bowed reverently at the grave of Alfred Adler, to make a stand with him, with them, in the embrace of a psychology that might be called existential spiritual—existential in its unflinching gaze at the absurdity and silliness in man, that aspect of human existence that is indeed "nasty, brutish and short," but is not dispirited nor disheartened by it, but instead, with courage, affirms the spirit, the spiritedness, the *thymos*, the eternal spirit, the upward striving, the dignity and determination, the grandeur and the greatness of our humanity.

This is in sum, at last, a fair description of the philosophy, the spiritual existentialism, the *soul* psychology, championed here, championed by Alfred Adler, the horn, so to speak, that Roland is blowing. The existential answer to the question of, "What is to be done?" is to live in continuity with the best in the Western Tradition, with the wisdom of this "spiritual existentialism," a worldly wisdom that is a force for good, "in the heart," as Hillman says in words that served to introduce this book, "as virtues of courage, nobility, honor, loyalty, steadfastness of principle, comradely love, so that war is given location not only in a class of persons but in a level of human personality organically necessary to the justice of the whole," and in heart felt solidarity with the best of all other Traditions, from the great World Religions to the sacred rituals of tribal myth, with respect, always, and ceaseless effort at understanding and reconciliation. "Peace be with you," is the ancient salutation. In union, in communion, all of us, if only for a moment, if only as a foretaste or in a fleeting glimpse of the "peace that surpasseth understanding," binding us together on this "poor crust of a planet," as Adler said, as we strive for something better. It was Adler's vision of *gemeinschaftsgefuhl*. It is neither futile hope nor forlorn dream.

Endnotes

Prologue

1. Randolph Severson, *A Catholic Soul Psychology* (Benson: Goldenstone Press, 2013), pp. 147-148.
2. James Hillman, *Animal Presences*, (Putman: Spring Publications, 2008), p. 22.
3. James Hillman, "War, Arms, Rams, Mars: On the Love of War", in *Facing Apocalypse* (Dallas, Spring Publications, 1987), p. 120.

Introduction

Epigram: D.H. Lawrence, *Movements in European History* (Oxford: Oxford University Press, 1931), p. 317.

1. T.S. Eliot, *The Complete Poems and Plays: 1909-1950* (New York: Harcourt, Brace & World, Inc., 1971), pp. 43, 48.
2. B.R. Anderson, "The Idea of Power in Javanese Culture," in *Culture and Politics in Indonesia*, ed. C. Holt (Ithaca: Cornell University Press, 1972), pp. 16-17.
3. James Lord, *Giacometti: A Biography* (New York: Farrar, Straus and Giroux, 1984), p. 15.
4. Paul Johnson, *Modern Times: The World from the Twenties to the Eighties* (New York: Harper Colophon, 1983), p. 48.
5. William Shakespeare, *Troilus and Cressida* (New Haven and London: Yale University Press, 1927), p. 28.
6. Michel Foucault, "Power and Sex," in *Telos*, 32, Summer, 1977, p. 157.

7. Michel Foucault, *Discipline and Punish: The Birth of the Prison*, trans. Alan Sheridan (New York: Vintage Books, 1979) pp. 29-30.

8. Michel Foucault, *Power / Knowledge: Selected Interviews and Other Writings 1972-1977*, ed. Colin Gordon, trans. C. Gordon, et al. (New York: Pantheon, 1980), p. 94.

9. Alfred Adler, *Minutes of the Vienna Psychoanalytic Society*, ed. H. Nunberg and E. Federn (New York: International Universities Press, 1962), p. 358.

10. Alfred Adler, *The Individual Psychology of Alfred Adler*, ed. And trans. Heinz Ansbacher and Rowena Ansbacher (New York: Harper Torchbooks, 1964), p. 111.

11. Manes Sperber, *Masks of Loneliness: Alfred Adler in Perspective*, trans. K. Winston (New York: MacMillan, 1974), p. xiv.

12. Lewis Way, *Adler's Place in Psychology* (New York: MacMillan, 1950), pp. 300-301.

13. Paul Friedlander, *Plato: An Introduction*, trans. Hans Meyerhoff (Princeton: Princeton University Press, 1958), p. 326.

14. Friedrich Nietzsche, quoted in Walter Kaufmann, *Nietzsche: Philosopher, Psychologist, Antichrist* (Princeton: Princeton University Press, 1974), p. 294.

15. Quoted in Garry Wills, *The Kennedy Imprisonment: A Meditation on Power* (Boston / Toronto: Little Brown and Company, 1981), p. ix.

16. Plutarch, *The Lives of the Noble Grecians and Romans*, trans. John Dryden (New York: Random House, undated), p. 243.

17. Plutarch, p. 234.

18. Plutarch, p. 234.

19. John Fortescue, *De Laudibus Legum Anglie*, trans. S. B. Chrimes (London: Cambridge University Press, 1949), p. 31. See also Frederick D. Wilhelmsen's brilliant discussion of these matters, on which I am much reliant, both for argument and for example of a stately and lyrical magnificence of style, in *Christianity and Political Philosophy* (Athens, GA: University of Georgia Press, 1982).

20. Sigmund Freud, *The Origins of Psycho-Analysis Letters to Wilhelm Fliess, Drafta and Notes: 1897-1902*, ed. Marie Bonaparte et al., trans. Eric Mosbacher and James Strachey (New York: Basic Books, 1954), p. 297.

Chapter One

1. John Keats, "On First Looking into Chapman's Homer," in *Romantic Poets*, ed. W.H. Auden and Norman Holmes Pearson (New York: The Viking Press, 1950), p. 377.
2. Henri Ellenberger, *The Discovery of the Unconscious* (New York: Basic Books, 1970), p. 645.
3. Oswald Spengler, *The Decline of the West*, trans. Charles Atkinson (New York: Knopf, 1956), Vol. II, pp. 234-235.
4. Alfred Adler, *The Science of Living* (Garden City: Anchor Books, 1969), p. 73.
5. Alfred Adler, *The Individual Psychology of Alfred Adler*, ed. Heinz L. Ansbacher and Rowena R. Ansbacher (New York: Basic Books, 1956), p. 182.
6. Phyllis Bottome, *Alfred Adler. A Biography* (New York: Putman, 1939), p. 14.
7. D.D. Carnicelli, "Beauty's Rose: Shakespeare and Adler on Love and Marriage," in *Alfred Adler: His Influence on Psychology Today*, ed. Harold H. Mosak (Park Ridge, New Jersey: Noyes Press, 1973), p. 293.
8. Ellenberger, p. 608.
9. D.H. Lawrence, *Movements in European History*, pp. 45-46.
10. W.H. Auden, *Collected Shorter Poems 1927-1957* (New York: Random House, 1975), p. 219.
11. D.H. Lawrence, *Movements in European History*, p. 153.
12. Johan Huizinga, *Homo Ludens: A Study of the Play-Element in Culture* (Boston: Beacon Press, 1955), p. 132.
13. Wallace Stevens, *The Palm at the End of the Mind, Selected Poems and a Play*, (New York: Random House, 1972), p. 62.
14. Ernesto Grassi, *Rhetoric as Philosophy: The Humanist Tra-*

dition (University Park: The Pennsylvania State University Press, 1980), p. 7.

15. Norman O. Brown, *Closing Time* (New York: Vintage Books, 1973), p. 55.

16. Baltasar Gracián, *The Art of Worldly Wisdom* trans. Martin Fischer (Springfield: 1942).

17. Federico García Lorca, *The Havana Lectures*, trans. Stella Rodriquez (Dallas: Kanathos, 1981), p. 63.

18. Jose Maria de Cossio, *Los Toros* (Sexta Edicion, Espasa-Calpe, 1969), p. 575, quoted in Lorca, pp. 8-9.

19. Will and Ariel Durant, *The Age of Louis XIV* (New York: Simon and Schuster, 1963), p. 14.

20. Johan Huizinga, *The Waning of the Middle Ages* (Garden City: Doubleday Anchor Books, 1954), p. 76.

21. Alfred Adler, *The Individual Psychology of Alfred Adler,* p. 343.

22. Alfred Adler, *The Individual Psychology of Alfred Adler*, p. 199.

23. Friedrich Nietzsche, *The Gay Science*, trans. Walter Kaufmann (New York: Vintage Books, 1974), p. 290.

24. Isak Dinesen, *Out of Africa* (New York: Vintage Books, 1985), p. 141.

25. Quoted in Grassi, p. 18.

26. Quoted in Grassi, pp. 18-19.

27. Marshall McLuhan, *The Interior Landscape: The Literary Criticism of Marshall McLuhan* (New York: McGraw-Hill, 1971), pp. 212-213.

28. McLuhan, p. 213.

29. Quoted in Paul Stepansky, *In Freud's Shadow: Adler in Context* (Hillsdale, New Jersey: The Analytic Press, 1983), p. 9.

30. McLuhan, pp. 214-215.

31. Frances Yates, *Giordano Bruno and the Hermetic Tradition* (New York: Vintage Books, 1969), pp. 159-160.

32. Will and Ariel Durant, *The Age of Reason Begins* (New York: Simon and Schuster, 1961), p. 51.

33. Michel de Montaigne, *Essays*, trans. J.M. Cohen (Harmondsworth: Penguin, 1958), p. 160.

34. Montaigne, p. 161.

35. Quoted in Will and Ariel Durant, *The Age of Faith* (New York: Simon and Schuster, 1950), p. 1071.

36. Alfred Adler, *Social Interest: A Challenge to Mankind*, trans. John Linton and Richard Vaughan (New York: Capricorn Books, 1964), p. 38.

37. Alfred Adler, *The Science of Living*, ed. Heinz L. Ansbacher (Garden City: Anchor Books, 1969), p. 131.

38. Alfred Adler, *What Life Should Mean to You* (New York: Capricorn Books, 1958), p. 51.

39. Adler, *The Science of Living*, p. 31.

40. Adler, *Social Interest*, p. 102.

41. Adler, *Social Interest*, p. 97.

42. Adler, *What Life Should Mean to You*, p. 55.

43. Adler, *Social Interest*, p. 96.

44. Quoted in Heinz Ansbacher, "The Development of Adler's Concept of Social Interest: A Critical Study," *Journal of Individual Psychology*, 1978, 34. p. 132.

45. Alfred Adler, *Problems of Neurosis: A Book of Case Histories* (New York: Harper & Row, 1964), p. 31.

46. Quoted in Ansbacher, "Social Interest," pp. 133-134.

47. Quoted in Ansbacher, "Social Interest," p. 134.

48. Adler, *Problems of Neurosis*, p. 79.

49. Adler, *Problems of Neurosis*, p. 53.

50. Alfred Adler, *The Education of Children* (Chicago: Regnery, 1970), pp. 10-11.

51. Quoted in Ansbacher, "Social Interest," p. 136.

52. Quoted in Ansbacher, "Social Interest," p. 136.

53. Jonathan Culler, *On Deconstruction: Theory and Criticism After Structuralism* (Ithaca: Cornell University Press, 1982), p. 150.

54. Jacques Derrida, *Writing and Difference*, trans. Alan Bass (Chicago: University of Chicago Press, 1978), p. 293.

55. Ansbacher, "Social Interest," p. 142.

56. Ansbacher, "Social Interest," p. 132.

57. Alfred Farau, "C.G. Jung: An Adlerian Appreciation," *Journal of Individual Psychology*, 1961, 17, pp. 135-141.

58. Bottome, pp. 186-187.

59. Adler, *The Individual Psychology of Alfred Adler*, p. 202.

60. Lewis Mumford, *The City in History* (New York: Harcourt, Brace & World, 1961), p. 7.

61. Robert Romanyshyn, *Psychological Life* (Austin: University of Texas Press, 1982), pp. 151-164.

62. Romanyshyn, p. 160.

63. C.G. Jung, *Memories, Dreams, Reflections*, trans. Richard and Clara Winston (New York: Vintage Books, 1961), pp. 197-198.

64. Adler, *The Individual Psychology of Alfred Adler*, pp. 169-170.

65. Adler, *The Individual Psychology of Alfred Adler*, p. 103.

66. Adler, *The Individual Psychology of Alfred Adler*, pp. 103-104.

67. Adler, *The Individual Psychology of Alfred Adler*, p. 107.

68. Adler, *The Individual Psychology of Alfred Adler*, p. 107.

69. McLuhan, p. 209.

70. Quoted in Will and Ariel Durant, *The Age of Voltaire* (New York: Simon and Schuster, 1965), p. 302.

71. Bottome, p. 20.

72. Morris W. Croll, *Style, Rhetoric and Rhythm*, ed. J. May Patrick et al. (Princeton: Princeton University Press, 1966), pp. 207-208.

73. Croll, p. 210.

74. Croll, p. 212.

75. Annabel M. Patterson, *Hermogenes and the Renaissance: Seven Ideas of Style* (Princeton: Princeton University Press, 1970), pp. 153-175.

Chapter Two

1. Sigmund Freud, *Collected Papers, III.* (London: The Hogarth Press, 1924), p. 281.

2. Adler, *The Individual Psychology of Alfred Adler*, p. 38.
3. Adler, *The Individual Psychology of Alfred Adler*, p. 38.
4. Adler, *The Individual Psychology of Alfred Adler*, p. 35.
5. Denis de Rougemont, *Love in the Western World*, trans. Montgomery Belgion (New York: Random House, 1956), p. 244.
6. Adler, *The Individual Psychology of Alfred Adler*, p. 248.
7. Huizinga, *Homo Ludens*, p. 73.
8. Friedrich Nietzsche, *The Portable Nietzsche*, trans. Walter Kaufmann (New York, Viking, 1954), p. 37.
9. Walter J. Ong, *Fighting for Life: Contest, Sexuality and Consciousness* (Ithaca: Cornell Universsity Press, 1981), p. 15.
10. Huizinga, *Homo Ludens*, p. 52.
11. Manes Sperber, p. 65.
12. Huizinga, *Homo Ludens*, p. 50.
13. Huizinga, *Homo Ludens*, p. 50.
14. Gilbert Highet, *The Art of Teaching* (New York: Vintage Books, 1959), p. 130.
15. Huizinga, *Homo Ludens*, p. 156.
16. Ong, p. 140.
17. Sigmund Freud, *A General Introduction to Psychoanalysis*, trans. Joan Riviere (New York: Pocket Books, 1953), pp. 21-22.
18. Ellenberger, p. 591.
19. Ellenberger, p. 591.
20. Adler, *The Individual Psychology of Alfred Adler*, p. 35.
21. Quoted in E. Wind, *Pagan Mysteries in the Renaissance* (New York: W.W. Norton, 1968), p. 135.
22. Huizinga, *Homo Ludens*, p. 65.
23. Adler, *The Individual Psychology of Alfred Adler*, p. 35.
24. Heinrich Zimmer, *Myth and Symbols in Indian Art and Civilization* (Princeton: Princeton University Press, 1972), pp. 212-213.
25. Adler, *The Individual Psychology of Alfred Adler*, pp. 35-36.
26. Adler, *The Individual Psychology of Alfred Adler*, p. 36.

27. Robert Baldrick, *The Duel: A History of Duelling* (London: Chapman and Hall, 1965), p. 98.

28. Huizinga, *Homo Ludens*, p. 59.

29. Huizinga, *Homo Ludens*, p. 61.

30. Alexander Neuer, *Mut and Entmutigung* (Munich: Bergman, 1926), p. 12.

31. Richard B. Onians, *The Origins of European Thought About the Body, the Mind, the Soul, the World, Time, and Fate* (Cambridge: Cambridge University Press, 1951). p. 47.

32. Onians, pp. 47-48.

33. Quoted in Richard Selzer, *Mortal Lessons* (New York and San Francisco: Harper Torchbooks, 1981), p. 81.

34. Onians, p. 13.

35. Onians, p. 169.

36. Onians, p. 170.

37. Onians, p. 171.

38. Russell Jacoby, *Social Amnesia: a Critique of Contemporary Psychology* (Boston: Beacon Press, 1975), pp. 44-45.

39. Jacoby, p. 19.

40. Onians, p. 44-45.

41. Onians, p. 50.

42. Onians, p. 53.

43. Onians, pp. 73-74.

44. Onians, p. 49.

45. Onians, pp. 49-50.

46. Adler, *The Individual Psychology of Alfred Adler*, p. 36.

47. Adler, *The Individual Psychology of Alfred Adler*, p. 227.

48. Adler, *The Individual Psychology of Alfred Adler*, p. 226.

49. William Blake, The Portable Blake (New York: Viking Press, 1974), p. 114.

50. Quoted in James Hillman, *The Thought of the Heart* (Dallas: Spring Publications, 1981), p. 25.

51. David Jones, *The Dying Gaul* (London: Faber and Faber, 1978), p. 127.

52. de Rougemont, *Love in the Western World*, p. 251.

53. Quoted in de Rougemont, *Love in the Western World*, pp. 251-252.

54. John Keegan, *The Face of Battle* (New York: Viking Press, 1976), pp. 25-26.

55. E. Kretschmer, *Physique and Character* (New York: Harcourt, Brace, and World, 1936), pp. 130-131.

56. Huizinga, *The Waning of the Middle Ages*, p. 270.

57. Robert B. Asprey, *Frederick the Great: The Magnificent Enigma* (New York: Ticknor &Fields, 1986), p. 143.

58. Maurice Keen, *Chivalry* (New Haven: Yale University Press, 1984), pp. 91-92.

59. Keen, p. 142.

60. Keen, pp. 92-93.

61. F.G. Crookshank, "Individual Psychology and Nietzsche," *Individual Psychology Medical Pamphlets*, 1933, 10, p. 57.

Chapter Three

1. Way, p. 311.

2. Oliver Brachfeld, *Inferiority Feelings in the Individual and the Group* (New York: Grunc and Stratton, 1951), p. 51.

3. Adler, *Individual Psychology*, p. 113.

4. Adler, *Individual Psychology*, p.113.

5. Adler, *Individual Psychology*, p. 351.

6. David Jones, *The Dying Gaul*, p. 19.

7. Jones, *The Dying Gaul*, p. 103.

8. Jones, *The Dying Gaul*, p. 103.

9. Ernst Bertram, *Nietzsche Attempt at a Mythology* (Urbana and Chicago: University of Illinois Press, 2009), p. 38.

10. Bertram, *Nietzsche Attempt at a Mythology*, p. 41.

11. Friedrich Nietzsche, *On the Genealogy of Morals and Ecce Homo*, trans. Walter Kaufmann (New York: Vintage Books, 1969), p. 294.

12. Friedrich Nietzsche, *Twilight of the Idols and the Anti-Christ*, trans. R.J. Hollingdale (Harmondsworth: Penguin, 1968), p. 81.

13. Friedrich Nietzsche, *Beyond Good and Evil*, trans. Walter Kaufmann (New York: Vintage Books, 1966), p. 208.

14. Nietzsche, *Genealogy*, p. 33.

15. Nietzsche, *Genealogy*, p. 113.

16. Nietzsche, *Genealogy*, p. 102.

17. Nietzsche, *Genealogy*, p. 40-41.

18. Walter Kaufmann, *Nietzsche: Philosopher, Psychologist, Antichrist* (Princeton: Princeton University Press, 1974), p. 225.

19. Oswald Spengler, *The Decline of the West*, Vol. I, p. 260.

20. Ronald Hayman, *Nietzsche: A Critical Life* (Harmondsworth: Penguin, 1980), p. 1.

21. Hayman, *Nietzsche*, p. 19.

22. Robert Edmund Jones. *The Dramatic Imagination* (New York: Harper and Row, 1962), p. 47.

23. Friedrich Nietzsche, *The Portable Nietzsche*, trans. Walter Kaufmann (New York: Viking, 1975), pp. 138-139.

24. Robert Desoille, *The Directed Daydream*, trans. Frank Haronian (Lexington: Psychosynthesis Press, undated), p. 7.

25. James Hillman, "The Great Mother, Her Son, Her Hero, and the *Puer*," in *Fathers and Mothers* (Zurich: Spring, 1973).

26. de Rougemont, *Love in the Western World*, pp. 69-70.

27. Lou Andreas-Salome, *The Freud Journal of Lou Andreas-Salome*, trans. Stanley A. Leavy (New York: Basic Books, 1964), p. 6.

28. C.S. Lewis, *The Allegory of Love: A Study in Medieval Tradition* (Oxford: Oxford University Press, 1936), pp. 9-10.

29. Huizinga, *The Waning of the Middle Ages*, p. 72.

30. Arthur B. Ferguson, *The Indian Summer of English Chivalry: Studies in the Decline and Transformation of Chivalric Idealism* (Durham: Duke University Press, 1960), p. 87.

31. Ferguson, *English Chivalry*, p. 172.

32. Ferguson, *English Chivalry*, p. 223.

33. Huizinga, *The Waning of the Middle Ages*, pp. 76-77.

34. Huizinga, *The Waning of the Middle Ages*, p. 77.

35. Werner Jaeger, *Paideia: The Ideals of Greek Culture*, trans.

Gilbert Highet (New York: Oxford University Press, 1976), p. 5.

36. Homer, *The Odyssey*, trans. Richmond Lattimore (New York: Harper Torchbooks, 1965), p. 67.

37. Jaeger, p. 7.

38. Jaeger, p. 8.

39. Jaeger, p. 7.

40. Huizinga, *Homo Ludens*, p. 64.

41. Nietzsche, *The Gay Science*, p. 38.

42. Quoted in Kenneth Burke, *A Rhetoric of Motives* (Berkeley: University of California Press, 1969), p. 222.

43. D.H. Lawrence, p. 319.

44. Jose Ortega y Gasset, *The Revolt of the Masses*, (New York: W.W. Norton, 1932), p. 65.

45. Ezra Pound, quoted by Hugh Kenner, *The Pound Era* (Berkeley: University of California Press, 1973), p. 156.

46. James Dickey, *Poems 1957-1967* (Middletown: Wesleyan University Press, 1978), p. 280.

47. Peter Berger, *The Homeless Mind: Modernization and Consciousness* (New York: Vintage Books, 1974), p. 80.

48. Berger, p. 80.

49. Berger, p. 84.

50. Berger, p. 78.

51. Miguel de Unamuno, *Tragic Sense of Life*, p. 301, trans. J.E. Crawford Flitch (New York: Dover, 1954), p. 325.

52. William Faulkner, *The Reivers* (New York: Vintage Books, 1962), pp. 50-51.

53. William Faulkner, *Go Down Moses* (New York: The Modern Library, 1950), pp. 183-184.

54. Isak Dinesen, *Winter's Tales* (New York: Vintage Books, 1961), p. 225.

55. James Dickey, p. 149.

56. Octavio Paz. *The Labyrinth of Solitude*, trans. Lysander Kemp (New York: Grove Press, Inc. 1961), p. 31.

57. Peter Blos, *The Adolescent Passage* (New York: International

Universities Press, 1979), p. 306.

58. Kaufmann, pp. 382-384.

59. William Barrett, *Irrational Man: A Study in Existential Philosophy* (Garden City: Doubleday Anchor Books, 1962), p. 198.

60. Christopher Dawson, *Christianity and the New Age* (Manchester: Sophia Institute Press, 1985), p. 5.

61. Erich Heller, *The Artist's Journey into the Interior* (New York: A Harvest Book, 1959), p. 197.

62. Manes Sperber, p. 81.

63. Nietzsche, *The Portable Nietzsche*, p. 104.

64. Quoted in Huizinga, *The Waning of the Middle Ages*, pp. 77-78.

65. Huizinga, *The Waning of the Middle Ages*, p. 70.

66. Nietzsche, *Ecce Homo*, p. 232.

67. Huizinga, *Homo Ludens*, p. 146.

68. Huizinga, *Homo Ludens*, pp. 146-147.

69. Huizinga, *Homo Ludens*, p. 147.

70. Adler, *Social Interest*, p. 32.

71. Bottome, *Alfred Adler*, p. 79.

72. Bottome, *Alfred Adler*, p. 184.

73. Harold Bloom, *A Map of Misreading* (New York: Oxford University Press, 1975), p. 200.

74. Bloom, p. 29.

75. Sir Walter Scott, *Ivanhoe: A Romance* (New York: The New American Library, 1962), p. 41.

76. Nietzsche, *The Portable Nietzsche*, p. 91.

77. de Rougemont, p. 122.

78. de Rougemont, pp. 78-80.

79. de Rougemont, p. 65.

80. Hans Jonas, *The Gnostic Religion: The Message of the Alien God and the Beginnings of Christianity* (Boston: Beacon Press, 1958), p. 70.

81. Friedlander, p. 76-77.

82. Adler, *The Individual Psychology of Alfred Adler*, p. 268.

83. Alfred Adler, *The Neurotic Constitution: Outline of a Comparative Individualistic Psychology and Psychotherapy* (New York: Moffat Yard, 1916), p. 353.

84. Adler, *The Neurotic Constitution*, p. 96.

85. Way, p. 103.

86. Gaston Bachelard, *On Poetic Imagination and Reverie*, trans. Colette Gaudin (Indianapolis: Bobbs-Merrill, 1971), p. 42.

87. Bachelard, pp. 45-46.

88. Quoted in Edward Whitmont, *The Return of the Goddess* (New York: Crossroad, 1984), pp. 162-163.

89. Whitmont, p. 163.

90. L.R. Farnell, *The Cults of the Greek States*, Vol. 5 (Oxford: Oxford University Press, 1909), pp. 43-44.

91. William Lynch, *Images of Faith: An Exploration of the Ironic Imagination* (Notre Dame: University of Notre Dame Press, 1973), p. 44.

92. Lynch, p. 45.

93. de Rougemont, p. 70.

94. Susan Sontag, *Under the Sign of Saturn* (New York: Vintage Books, 1981), p. 96.

95. Jan Kott, *The Eating of the Gods*, trans. Boleslaw Taborski and Edward J. Czerwinski (New York: Vintage Books, 1974), p. 196.

Chapter Four

1. Way, p. 310.

2. Adler, *The Individual Psychology of Alfred Adler*, p. 142.

3. Brachfeld, pp. 40-52.

4. Adler, *The Individual Psychology of Alfred Adler*, p. 24.

5. Thomas Mann, *Death in Venice*, trans. H.T. Lowe-Porter (New York: Vintage Books, 1930), p. 70.

6. Alfred Adler, *Study of Organ Inferiority and Its Physical Compensation: A Contribution to Clinical Medicine*, trans. S.E. Jelliffe (New York: Nervous and Mental Disease Pub-

lishing Company, 1917), pp. 58-59.

7. Adler, *The Individual Psychology of Alfred Adler*, p. 26.

8. Adler, *The Individual Psychology of Alfred Adler*, p. 23.

9. Stepansky, pp. 259-260.

10. Charles Norris Cochrane, *Christianity and Classical Culture* (London: Oxford University Press, 1957), p. 75.

11. Aeschylus, "The Persians," in *Aeschylus II*, trans. Seth G. Benardete (Chicago: University of Chicago Press, 1956), p. 51.

12. Cochrane, p. 135.

13. M. Owen Lee, *Fathers and Sons in Virgil's Aeneid: Tum Genitor Natum* (Albany: State University of New York Press, 1979), p. 163.

14. Mumford, p. 52.

15. Aeschylus, pp. 58-67.

16. Mumford, p. 151.

17. Cochrane, pp. 77-78.

18. Cochrane, p. 82.

19. Quoted in Kott, p. 27.

20. Alfred Adler, *Cooperation Between the Sexes: Writings on Women, Love and Marriage, Sexuality and Its Disorders*, trans. Heinz and Rowena Ansbacher (Garden City: Anchor Books, 1978), p. 282.

21. Cochrane, p. 277.

22. D.H. Lawrence, *The Collected Letters of D.H. Lawrence*, ed. Harry T. Moore (New York: Viking Press, 1962), Vol. II., p. 789.

23. Adler, *What Life Should Mean to You*, p. 60.

24. Adler, *Social Interest*, p. 125.

25. Adler, *Individual Psychology*, p. 291.

26. Rudolf Allers, *The Psychology of Character* (New York: Sheed and Ward, 1957), p. 184.

27. Kott, pp. 25-26.

28. Elias Canetti, *Crowds and Power*, trans. Carol Stewart (New York: Farrar Straus Giroux, 1962), p. 305.

29. Fyodor Dostoyevsky, *The Possessed*, trans. Constance Garnett (New York: The Modern Library, 1936), p. 42.
30. Philip Hallie, *Cruelty*, (Middletown: Wesleyan University Press, 1982), p. 37.
31. Adler, *Individual Psychology*, p. 268.
32. Adler, *Individual Psychology*, p. 261.
33. Adler, *What Life Should Mean to You*, p. 69.
34. Adler, *Social Interest*, p. 70.
35. Quoted in Elémire Zolla, *Archetypes: The Persistence of Unifying Patterns* (New York: Harcourt Brace Jovanovich, 1981), pp. 84-85.
36. David Jones, *Introducing David Jones* (London: Faber and Faber, 1980), p. 202.
37. John Holland Smith, *The Death of Classical Paganism* (New York: Charles Scribner's Sons, 1976), p. 97.
38. Smith, p. 117.
39. Smith, p. 117.
40. Cochrane, p. 89.
41. Cochrane, pp. 88-89.
42. Smith, p. 98.
43. St. Augustine, *The Confessions of St. Augustine*, trans. Rex Warner (New York and London: New American Library, 1963), pp. 123-124.
44. Hallie, p. 136.
45. Smith, p. 115.
46. Cochrane, p. 500.
47. Cochrane, p. 505.
48. Alfred Adler, *The Problem Child* (New York: Capricorn, 1963), p. 3.
49. Quoted in Ansbacher, "Social Interest," p. 136.
50. William Faulkner, *The Mansion* (New York: Random House, 1959), pp. 435-436.

Conclusion

1. Alfred Adler, *Individual Psychology*, pp. 174-175.
2. Will and Ariel Durant, *The Age of Napoleon*, p. 703.
3. Unamuno, p. 293.
4. William Shakespeare, *The Tempest*, ed. Frank Kermode (Cambridge: Harvard University Press, 198), appendix.
5. Quoted in Ernest Jones, *The Life and Work of Sigmund Freud*, Vol. I. (New York: Basic Books, 1953), p. 348.
6. Jones, Vol. II, p. 152.
7. Jacques Derrida, *Margins of Philosophy*, trans. Alan Bass (Chicago: University of Chicago Press, 1982), p. 213.
8. Jacques Derrida, *Of Giammatology*, trans. Gayatri Chakravorty Spivak (Baltimore: The John Hopkins University Press, 1974), p. 12.
9. Quoted in Elizabeth Sewell, *To Be a True Poem* (Winston-Salem: Hunter Publishing Company, 1979), pp. 69-70.
10. Sewell, p. 70.
11. Sewell, p. 69.
12. Sewell, p. 69.
13. Sewell, p. 71.
14. Sewell, pp. 73-75.
15. Adler, Individual Psychology, p. 48.
16. William Faulkner, *Go Down Moses*, pp. 329-330.

Epilogue

1. Mark Salzman, *Iron & Silk*, (New York: Vintage, 1990), p. 34.

BIBLIOGRAPHY

Adler, Alfred.
  – *Cooperation Between the sexes; Writings on Women, Love and Marriage, Sexuality and Its Disorders.* Translated and edited by Heinz L. Ansbacher and Rowena R. Ansbacher. Garden City, New York: Doubleday & Company, Inc., Anchor Books, 1978.
  – *The Education of Children.* Translated by E. and F. Jensen. New York: Greenberg, 1930.
  – *The Individual Psychology of Alfred Adler: A Systematic Presentation in Selections from his Writings.* Edited by Heinz Ansbacher and Rowena Ansbacher. New York: Harper Torchbooks, 1964.
  – *The Neurotic Constitution: Outline of a Comparative Individualistic Psychology and Psychotherapy.* New York: Moffat, Yard, 1916.
  – *Organ Inferiority and Its Psychical Compensation: A Contribution to Clinical Medicine.* Translated by Smith Ely Jelliffe. New York: The Nervous and Mental disease Publishing Co., 1917.
  – *The Problem Child.* New York: Capricorn, 1963.
  – *Problems of Neurosis: A Book of Case Histories.* Edited by P. Mairet. New York. Harper & Row, 1964.
  – *The Science of Living.* New York: Greenberg, 1929; Anchor books, 1969.
  – *Social Interest: A Challenge to Mankind.* Translated by J. Linton and R. Vaughan New York: Putman, 1939. Reprinted, New York: Putman Capricorn Books, 1964.
  – *What Life Should Mean to you.* Edited by A. Portor. Boston:

Little, Brown, 1931. Reprinted New York: Putman Capricorn Books, 1958.

– *Minutes of the Vienna Psychoanalytic Society*. ed. H. Nunberg and E. Federn. New York: International Universities Press, 1962.

Adler, Kurt A., & Deutish, Damica. *Essays in Individual Psychology*. New York: Grove press, 1959.

Aeschylus. *The Persians. In Aeschylus II, The Complete Greek Tragedies*. Edited by David Green and Richmond Lattimore. Chicago and London: The University of Chicago Press, 1956.

Allers, Rudolf. *The Psychology of Character*. New York: Sheed and Ward, 1957.

Anderson, B.R. O'G. "The Idea of Power in Javanese Culture." In C. Holt (ed.) *Culture and Politics in Indonesia*. Ithaca, New York: Cornell University Press, 1972.

Andreas-Salome, Lou. *The Freud Journal of Lou Andreas-Salome*. Translated by Stanley A. Leavy. New York: Basic Books, 1964.

Ansbacher, Heinz L. "The Concept of Social Interest." In *Journal of Individual Psychology*, 24:1968.

Aristotle.

– *Nichomachean Ethics*. Translated by Martin Ostwald. Indianapolis and New York: The Bobbs-Merrill Company, Inc., 1962.

– *Aristotle's "Poetics."* Translated by S.H. Butcher. Introduction by Francis Fergusson. New York: Hill and Wang, 1961.

Asprey, Robert B. *Frederick the Great: The Magnificent Enigma*. New York: Ticknor & Fields, 1986.

Auden, W.H. *Collected Shorter Poems 1927-1957*. New York: Random House, 1975.

Augustine.

– *The City of God*. Translated by Henry Bettenson. Harmondsworth, Middlesex, England: Penguin Books, 1972.

– *The Confessions of St. Augustine*. Translated by Rex Warner. New York and London: New American Library, 1963.

Bachelard, Gaston. *On Poetic Imagination and Reverie*. Translated by Colette Gaudin. Indianapolis, Indiana: Bobbs-Merrill Co., 1971.

Baldrick, Robert. *The Duel: A History of Dueling.* London: Chapman & Hall, 1965.

Barrett, William. *Irrational Man: A Study in Existential Philosophy.* Garden City, New York: Doubleday Anchor Books, 1962

Berger, Peter, and Berger, Brigitte, and Kellner, Hansfried. *The Homeless Mind, Modernization and Consciousness.* New York: Vintage Books, 1974

Bertram, Ernst. *Nietzsche: Attempt at a Mythology.* Urbana and Chicago: University of Illinois Press, 2009.

Blake, William. *The Portable Blake.* New York: Viking Press, 1974.

Bloom, Harold.

    – *The Anxiety of Influence: A Theory of Poetry.* New York: Oxford University Press, 1973.

    – *A Map of Misreading.* New York: Oxford University Press, 1975.

Bottome, Phyllis. *Alfred Adler, A Biography.* New York: Putman, 1939.

Brachfeld, Oliver. *Inferiority Feelings: In the Individual and the Group.* New York: Grune & Stratton, Inc., 1951.

Brown, Norman O, *Closing Time.* New York: Vintage Books, 1973.

Burckhardt, J. *The Age of Constantine the Great.* London: Routledge and Kegan Paul, 1969.

Burke, Kenneth.

    – *A Grammar of Motives.* New York: Prentice-Hall, 1945.

    – *A Rhetoric of Motives.* Berkeley: University of California Press, 1969.

Canetti, Elias. *Crowds and Power.* Translated by Carol Stewart. New York: Farrar Straus Giroux, 1962.

Carnicelli, D.D. "Beauty's Rose: Shakespeare and Adler on Love and Marriage," in *Alfred Adler: His Influence on Psychology Today.* ed. Harold H. Mosak. Park Ridge, New Jersey: Noyes Press, 1973.

Cicero.

    – *De Oratore*: Loeb Library No. 348-9. Cambridge, Massachusetts: Harvard University Press, undated.

— *On the Commonwealth*. Translated by George Holland Sabine and Stanley Barney Smith. The Library of Liberal Arts. Indianapolis: The Bobbs-Merrill Company, Inc., 1929.

Cochrane, Charles Norris. *Christianity and Classical Culture: A Study of Thought and Action from Augustus to Augustine*. Oxford: Oxford University Press, 1957.

Cossio, Jose Maria de. *Los Toros*. Sexta Edicion, Espasa-Calpe, 1969.

Croll, Morris W. *Style, Rhetoric, and Rhythm*. Edited by J. May Patrick and Robert O. Evans, with John M. Wallace and R.J. Schoeck. Princeton, New Jersey: Princeton University Press, 1966.

Crookshank, F.G. "Individual Psychology and Nietzsche." In Individual Psychology Medical Pamphlets, 10 (1933), 7-76

Culler, Jonathon. *On Deconstruction: Theory and Criticism After Structuralism. Ithaca*, New York: Cornell University Press, 1982.

Dante. *The Divine Comedy*. Translated by H.R. Huse. New York: Holt, Rinehart & Winston, 1954.

Dawson, Christopher. *Christianity and the New Age*. Machester: Sophia Institute Press, 1985.

Derrida, Jacques.
— *Of Giammatology*. Translated by Gayatri Chakravorty Spivak. Baltimore and London: The John Hopkins University Press, 1976.
— *Margins*. Chicago: University of Chicago Press, 1984.
— *Writing and Difference*. Translated by Alan Bass. Chicago: University of Chicago Press, 1978.

Desoille, Robert. *The Directed Daydream*. Translated by Frank Haronian. Lexington: Kentucky Center for Psychosynthesis, undated.

Dickey, James. *Poems 1957-1967*. Middletown, Connecticut: Wesleyan University Press, 1978.

Dinesen, Isak.
— *Out of Africa*. New York: Vintage Books, 1985.
— *Winter Tales*. New York: Vintage Books, 1961.

Dostoyevsky, Fyodor. *The Possessed*. Translated by Constance Garnett. New York: The Modern Library, 1936.

Durant, Will and Ariel.

– *The Age of Faith*. New York: Simon and Schuster, 1950.

– *The Age of Voltaire*. New York: Simon and Schuster, 1965.

– *The Age of Louis XIV*. New York: Simon and Schuster, 1963.

– T*he Age of Napoleon*. New York: Simon and Schuster, 1975.

– *The Age of Reason Begins*. New York: Simon and Schuster, 1961.

Eliade, Mircea. *Shamanism: Archaic Techniques of Ecstasy*. Translated by Willard R. Trask. Bollingen Series LXXVI. Princeton: Princeton University Press, 1964.

Eliot, T.S. *The Complete Poems and Plays: 1909-1950*. New York: Harcourt, Brace & World, Inc., 1971.

Ellenberger, Henri. *The Discovery of the Unconscious*. New York: Basic Books, 1970.

Farau, Alfred. "C.G. Jung: An Adlerian Appreciation," *Journal of Individual Psychology*, 1961.

Farnell, L.R. *Greek Hero Cults and Ideas of Immortality*. Oxford: Clarendon Press, 1921.

Faulkner, William.

– *Go Down Moses*, New York: Random House, 1942.

– *The Reivers*. New York: Random House, 1962.

– *The Mansion*. New York: Random House, 1959.

Ferguson, Arthur B. *The Indian Summer of English Chivalry: Studies in the Decline and Transformation of Chivalric Idealism*. Durham, North Carolina: Duke University Press, 1960.

Fortescue, John. *De Laudibus Legum Anglie*. Edited and translated with introduction and notes by S.B. Chrimes. London: Cambridge, 1949.

Foucault, Michel.

– "Power and Sex: An Interview with Michel Foucault." In *Telos*, 32 (Summer 1977)

– *Discipline and Punish: The Birth of the Prison*. Translated by Alan Sheridan. New York: Vintage Books, 1979.

– *Power/Knowledge: Selected Interviews and Other Writings 1972-1977*. Edited by Colin Gordon, Translated by C. Gordon, et al. New York: Pantheon, 1980.

Freud, Sigmund.

– *The Origins of Psycho-Analysis: Letters to Wilhelm Fliess, Drafts and Notes*, 1887-1902. Edited by Marie Bonaparte, Anna Freud, Ernst Kris. Translated by Eric Mosbacher and James Strachey. New York: Basic Books, 1954.

– *A General Introduction to Psychoanalysis*. Translated by Joan Riviere. New York: Pocket Books, 1953.

– *Collected Papers, III*. London: The Hogarth Press, 1924.

Friedlander, Paul. *Plato: An Introduction*. Translated by Hans Meyerhoff. Ballingen Series LIX. Princeton: Princeton University Press, 1958.

Gracián, Baltasar. *The Art of Worldly Wisdom*. trans. Martin Fischer. Springfield: 1942.

Grassi, Ernesto. *Rhetoric as Philosophy: The Humanist Tradition*. University Park: The Pennsylvania State University Press, 1980.

Greek-English Lexicon. Edited by Henry George Liddell and Robert Scott. 9th edition. 1940.

Guerard, Albert. *The Life and Death of an Ideal: France in the Classical Age*. New York: Scribner, 1928.

Hallie, Philip. *Cruelty*. Middletown: Wesleyan University Press, 1982.

Hayman, Ronald. *Nietzsche: A Critical Life*. Harmondsworth, Middlesex, England: Penguin Books, 1980.

Heller, Erich. *The Artist's Journey into the Interior and Other Essays*. New York and London: A Harvest-Book, Harcourt Brace Jovanovich, 1976.

Highet, Gilbert. *The Art of Teaching*. New York: Vintage Books, 1959.

Hillman, James.

– "The Great Mother, Her Son, Her Hero, and the Puer." In *Fathers and Mothers*. Zurich: Spring Publications, 1973.

– *Animal Presences*. Putman: Spring Publications, 2008.

– "War, Arms, Rams, Mars: On the Love of War", in *Facing Apocalypse*. Dallas, Spring Publications, 1987.

– *The Thought of the Heart*. Dallas: Spring Publications, 1981.

Homer.
  – *Iliad*. Translated by Richmond Lattimore. Chicago: University
    of Chicago Press, 1951.
  – *Odyssey*. Translated by Richmond Lattimore. New York: Harp-
    er Colophon, 1967.
Hopkins, Gerard Manley. *A Gerard Manley Hopkins Reader*. Ed. John
    Dick. New York and London: Oxford University Press, 1953.
Howell, Wilburn Samuel. *Logic and Rhetoric in England, 1500-1700*.
    Princeton, New Jersey: Princeton University Press, 1956.
Huizinga, Johan.
  – *Homo Ludens: A Study of the Play-Element in Culture*. Boston:
    Beacon Press, 1955.
  – *The Waning of the Middle Ages*. New York: Doubleday, Anchor
    Books, 1954.
  – Jaeger, Werner. *Aristotle*. Translated by R. Robinson. Oxford:
    Oxford University Press, 1948.
  – *Paideia: The Ideals of Greek Culture*. Volume I. Translated by
    Gilbert Highet. New York: Oxford University Press, 1945.
Jacoby, Russell. *Social Amnesia: a Critique of Contemporary Psychol-
    ogy*. Boston: Beacon Press, 1975.
Jaeger, Werner. *Paideia: The Ideals of Greek Culture*. Translated by
    Gilbert Highet. New York: Oxford University Press, 1976.
Joachim, H.H. *Aristotle: The Nicomachean Ethics*. Oxford, 1951.
Johnson, Paul. *Modern Times: The World from the Twenties to the
    Eighties*. New York: Harper Colophon Books, 1983.
Jonas, Hans. *The Gnostic Religion: The Message of the Alien God and
    the Beginnings of Christianity*. Boston: Beacon Press, 1958.
Jones, David.
  – *The Anathemata*. London and Boston. Faber and Faber, 1979.
  – *Introducing David Jones*. London: Faber and Faber, 1980.
  – *The Dying Gaul*. London and Boston: Faber and Faber, 1980.
  – *Epoch and Artist*. London: Faber and Faber, 1959.
  – *In Parenthesis*. London and Boston: Faber and Faber, 1937.
  – *The Sleeping Lord and Other Fragments*. London and Boston:
    Faber and Faber, 1974.

Jones, Ernest. *The Life and Work of Sigmund Freud, Vol. I.* New York: Basic Books, 1953.

Jones, Robert Edmund. *The Dramatic Imagination.* New York: Harper and Row, 1962.

Jung, C.G. *Memories, Dreams, Reflections.* Recorded and edited by Aniela Jaffe. Translated by Richard and Clara Winston. New York: Vintage Books, 1963.

Kantorowicz, Ernest H. *The King's Two Bodies: A Study in Medieval Political Theology.* Princeton: Princeton University Press, 1957.

Kaufmann, Walter. *Nietzsche, Philosopher, Psychologist, Antichrist.* 4th Edition. Princeton, New Jersey: Princeton University Press, 1974.

Keats, John. "On First Looking into Chapman's Homer," in *Romantic Poets.* ed. W.H. Auden and Norman Holmes Pearson. New York: The Viking Press, 1950.

Keen, Maurice. *Chivalry.* New Haven and London: Yale University Press, 1984.

Keegan, John. *The Face of Battle.* New York: The Viking Press, 1976.

Kenner, Hugh. *The Pound Era.* Berkeley: University of California Press, 1973.

Kott, Jan. *The Eating of the Gods: An Interpretation of Greek Tragedy.* Translated by Boleslaw Taborski and Edward J. Czerwinski. New York, Vintage Books, 1974.

Kretschmer, E. *Physique and Character.* New York: Harcourt, Brace, and World, 1936.

Lawrence, D.H.

– *Fantasia of the Unconscious.* London: Heinemann, Phoenix, 1961.

– *Movements in European History.* Oxford: Oxford University Press, 1981.

– *The Collected Letters of D.H. Lawrence.* ed. Harry T. Moore. New York: Viking Press, 1962.

Lee, M. Owen. *Fathers and Sons in Virgil's Aeneid: Tum Genitor Natum.* Albany: State University of New York Press, 1979.

Lewis, C.S. *The Allegory of Love: A Study in Medieval Tradition.* Oxford: Oxford University Press, 1936.

Lorca, Federico García. *The Havana Lectures.* trans. Stella Rodriquez. Dallas: Kanathos, 1981.

Lord, James. *Giacometti: A Biography.* New York: Farrar, Straus and Giroux, 1984.

Lynch, William F. *Images of Faith: An Exploration of the Ironic Imagination.* Notre Dame, Indiana: University of Notre Dame Press, 1973.

Mann, Thomas. *Death in Venice.* Translated by H.T. Lowe-Porter. New York: Vintage Books, 1936.

McLuhan, Marshall.

　－ *The Gutenberg Galaxy.* New York: The New American Library, A Mentor Book, 1969.

　－ *The Interior Landscape: The Literary Criticism of Marshall McLuhan.* New York, Toronto: McGraw-Hill, 1971.

Montaigne, Michel de. *Essays.* Translated and with an introduction by J.M. Cohen. Harmondsworth, Middlesex, England: Penguin Books, 1958.

Mosak, Harold H. ed. *Alfred Adler.* Park Ridge, New Jersey: Noyes Press, 1973.

Mumford, Lewis. *The City in History: Its Origins, Its Transformations, and Its Prospects.* New York: Harcourt, Brace & World, Inc. 1961.

Murray, Albert. *The Hero And the Blues.* University of Missouri Press; 1st edition December 1973.

Neuer, Alexander. *Mut and Entmutigung. Die Prinzipien der Psychologie Alfred Adlers.* Munich: Bergmann, 1926.

Nietzsche, Friedrich.

　－ *Beyond Good and Evil: Prelude to a Philosophy of the Future.* Translated by Walter Kaufman. New York: Vintage Books, 1966.

　－ *On the Genealogy of Morals and Ecce Homo.* Translated by Walter Kaufmann. New York: Vintage Books, 1969.

　－ *The Portable Nietzsche.* Translated by Walter Kaufmann. New York, Viking, 1954.

– *Ecce Homo.* Translated by Walter Kaufmann. New York: Vintage Books, 1968. Published with On the Genealogy of Morals.

– *The Gay Science.* Translated by Walter Kaufmann. New York: Vintage Books, 1974.

– *Twilight of the Idols. The Anti-Christ.* Translated by R.J. Hollingdale. Hamondsworth, Middlesex, England: Penguin Books, 1968.

Ong, Walter. *Fighting for the Life: Contest, Sexuality, and Consciousness.* Ithaca and London: Cornell University Press, 1981.

Onians, Richard B. *The Origins of European Thought About the Body, the Mind, the Soul, the World, Time, and Fate.* Cambridge: At the University Press, 1951.

Orgler, Hertha. *Alfred Adler: The Man and His Work.* New York: Capricorn Books, 1965.

Ortega y Gasset, Jose.

– *Meditations on Quixote.* Introduction and notes by Julian Marias. Translated by Evelyn Rugg and Diego Marin. New York: Norton, 1961.

– *What is Philosophy?* Translated by Mildred Adams. New York: W.W. Norton, 1960.

– *The Revolt of the Masses.* New York: W.W. Norton, 1932.

Oxford English Dictionary, 1953 edition.

Patterson, Annabel M. *Hermogenes and the Renaissance: Seven Ideas of Style.* Princeton: Princeton University Press, 1970.

Pausanias, *Description of Greece.* Translated by W.H. S. Jones. Loeb Classical Library.

Paz, Octavio. *The Labyrinth of Solitude.* Translated by Lysander Kemp. New York: Grove Press, Inc. 1961.

Pindar. *Odes.* Translated by J.E. Sandys. Loeb Classical Library.

Plato. *The Collected Dialogues of Plato.* Edited by Edith Hamilton and Huntington Cairns. Bollingen Series 71. Princeton: Princeton University Press, 1936.

Plutarch. *The Lives of the Noble Grecians and Romans.* Translated by John Dryden and revised by Arthur High Clough. New York: The Random House, undated.

Romanyshyn, Robert. *Psychological Life: From Science to Metaphor.* Austin: University of Texas Press, 1982.

Rougemont, Denis de. *Love in the Western World.* Translated by Montgomery Belgion. New York: Random House, 1956.

Salzman, Mark. *Iron & Silk.* New York: Vintage, 1990.

Sardello, Robert.
  – "Beauty and Violence." In *Dragonflies: Studies in Imaginal Psychology,* 1980.
  – "City as Mystery, City as Metaphor." In *Spring: An Annual of Archetypal Psychology and Jungian Thought,* 1985.

Scott, Sir Walter. *Ivanhoe: A Romance.* New York: The New American Library, A signet Classic, 1962.

Selzer, Richard. *Mortal Lessons.* New York and San Francisco: Harper Torchbooks, 1981.

Severson, Randolph and Sardello, Robert.
  – *Money and the Soul of the World.* Dallas: Pegasus Press, 1985.
  – "Peur's Wounded Wing." In *Puer Papers.* Edited by James Hillman. Zurich: Spring Publications, 1979.
  – "Titans Under Glass: A Recipe for the Recovery of Psychological Jargon." In *Dragonflies: Studies in Imaginal Psychology,* 1979.

Severson, Randolph. *A Catholic Soul Psychology.* Benson: Goldenstone Press, 2013.

Sewell, Elizabeth. *To Be a True Poem.* Winston-Salem, North Carolina, 1979.

Shakespeare, William.
  – *The Tempest.* Edited by Frank Kermode. Cambridge: Harvard University Press, 1984.
  – *Troilus and Cressida.* New Haven and London: Yale University Press, 1927.

Smith, John Holland. *The Death of Classicial Paganism.* New York: Charles Scribner's Sons, 1976.

Sontag, Susan. *Under the Sign of Saturn.* New York: Vintage Books, 1981.

Spengler, O. *The Decline of the West.* 2 volumes. New York:

Knopf, 1932.

Sperber, Manes. *Masks of Loneliness: Alfred Adler in Perspective.* Translated by K. Winston. New York: MacMillian, 1974.

Stepansky, Paul E. *In Freud's Shadow: Adler in Context.* Hillsdale, New Jersey: The Analytic Press, 1983.

Stevens, Wallace. *The Palm at the End of the Mind, Selected Poems and a Play.* New York: Random House, 1972.

Unamuno, Miguel de. *Tragic Sense of Life.* Translated by J. E. Crawford Flitch. New York: Dover Publications, 1954.

Vaihinger, Hans. *The Philosophy of "As if."* London: Routledge & Kegan Paul, 1965.

Vico, Giambattista. *The New Science.* 3rd ed. Abridged and translated by Thomas Goddard Bergin and May Harold Fisch. Ithaca: Cornell University Press, 1970.

Way, Lewis. *Adler's Place in Psychology.* New York: MacMillan, 1950.

Whitmont, Edward. *The Return of the Goddess.* New York: Crossroad, 1984.

Wilhelmsen, Frederick D. *Christianity and Political Philosophy.* Athens, GA: University of Georgia Press, 1982.

Wills, Garry. *The Kennedy Imprisonment: A Meditation on Power.* Boston/Toronto: Little Brown and Company, 1981.

Wind, E. *Pagan Mysteries in the Renaissance.* New York: W.W. Norton, 1968.

Yates, Frances. *Giordano Bruno and the Hermetic Tradition.* New York: Vintage Books, 1969.

Yeats, William Butler. *Selected Poems and Two Plays of William Butler Yeats.* New York: Collier, 1966.

Zimmer, Heinrich. *Myth and Symbols in Indian Art and Civilization.* Princeton: Princeton University Press, 1972.

Zolla, Elémire. *Archetypes: The Persistence of Unifying Patterns.* New York: Harcourt Brace Jovanovich, 1981.